I0884486

In 1919, Afghanistan invaded British India and precipitated the short Third Anglo-Afghan War. Although this Anglo-Afghan War was more limited than the first two, it drove defeated Afghanistan toward Revolutionary Russia. The Kingdom of Afghanistan worried about Britain's intentions and so Afghanistan became the first country to recognize the new Bolshevik government. Relations improved to the point that In May 1921, the Kingdom of Afghanistan signed a treaty of friendship with the Soviet Union. The British perceived the recognition and the treaty as a threat to British India. There were fears that Britain would invade Afghanistan and the Workers and Peasants Red Army (RKKA) began preparations to aid Afghanistan. Britain was still actively aiding the hold-out elements of the White Army in the Russian civil war. The Soviet Union needed to finish their civil war and prepare to deal with Britain and the Soviet southern border. The most decisive way was to invade British India through Afghanistan. The second way was to prepare to counterattack a British invasion. The Soviets put their best regional scholar, General Andrei Snesarev, on the job. Snesarev's lectures in 1919 and 1920 were part of this preparation. Students of the Oriental Department of the RKKA Military Academy would lead the Soviet aid effort to Afghanistan. Snesarev's knowledge was critical and so his lectures were taken down by stenographers and then printed as a book. The expected British invasion did not materialize, but the thoroughness of Snesarev's works and his presentation of materials from a military specialist's point of view served the Soviet planners decades later during their invasion of Afghanistan in 1979. Snesarev's work still has relevance today. His book was not available to the Russian public until recently and has not been available in English until this printing.

Snesarev's book presents the geography, terrain, climate, natural resources, ethnic groups, history, languages, government, law, bureaucracy, economy, taxation, military industry, military qualities of the people, organization of its armed forces, armament and equipment and a discussion of the recent Third Anglo-Afghan War. It ends with a detailed look at the strategic points of Afghanistan and its lines of communication. The book presents a good look at the region almost a century ago, yet is strangely current in this war-ravaged land.

Andrei Evgenievich Snesarev was a noted Tsarist general who remained with the Bolsheviks after the Russian Revolution. He was born in 1865. His career as an orientalist began with a lengthy tour of British India. He served throughout Central Asia and traveled throughout Afghanistan, the Pamirs, Tibet and Kashgar (Western China). During World War I, he commanded at regiment, brigade, division and corps level. During the Russian Civil War, Snesarev successfully defended the city of Tsaritsyn against White Army attacks, but ran afoul of the local political commissar-Josef Stalin. Only Lenin's intervention saved Snesarev from Stalin-this time.

Snesarev trained Bolshevik officers for the invasion of British India, through Afghanistan. This book is the basis of that training. In 1924, Snesarev was appointed professor and senior instructor of geography and statistics at the Naval Academy. In 1926, he was appointed professor of oriental studies at the Military-Political Academy. Snesarev spoke 14 languages. In 1930, Snesarev was arrested in the Stalin purges and twice condemned to death by firing squad. In 1934, he was given an early release since he had contracted a serious disease. He died at home in 1937 after a lingering illness.

About the Translators

Lester W. Grau is a retired US Army Infantry Lieutenant Colonel who fought in Vietnam. He speaks Russian and served as a Soviet Foreign Area Officer. He has a Doctorate in Military History from the University of Kansas. His books include *The Bear Went Over the Mountain: Soviet Combat Tactics in Afghanistan*, *The Other Side of the Mountain: Mujahideen Tactics in the Soviet-Afghan War* (co-authored with Ali Jalali) and *The Coils of the Anaconda: America's First Conventional Battle in Afghanistan.* He is the editor of *Passing It On: Fighting the Pushtun on Afghanistan's Frontier.* He works at the Foreign Military Studies Office at Fort Leavenworth, Kansas.

Michael Gress is a native of Siberia who served in the Soviet Army. His books include *The Soviet-Afghan War: How a Superpower Fought and Lost* and *The Red Army Do-It-Yourself Nazi-Bashing Guerrilla Warfare Manual (The Partisan's Companion)* (both co-translated and co-edited with Les Grau).

AFGHANISTAN

PREPARING FOR THE BOLSHEVIK INCURSION INTO AFGHANISTAN AND ATTACK ON INDIA, 1919-20

The 1919-1920s Red Army lectures on Afghanistan by the Russian Empire's and the Soviet Union's foremost Orientalist and Afghanistan expert

Andrei Evgenievich Snesarev

Translated and edited by Lester W. Grau & Michael Gress

Helion & Company

Dedicated to the Memory of Professor-General Andrei Evgenievich Snesarev, 1865-1937

Helion & Company Limited
26 Willow Road
Solihull
West Midlands
B91 1UE
England
Tel. 0121 705 3393
Fax 0121 711 4075
Email: info@helion.co.uk
Website: www.helion.co.uk
Twitter: @helionbooks
Visit our blog http://blog.helion.co.uk/

Published by Helion & Company 2014
Designed and typeset by Bookcraft Limited, Stroud, Gloucestershire
Cover designed by Paul Hewitt, Battlefield Design (www.battlefield-design.co.uk)
Printed by Lightning Source, Milton Keynes, Buckinghamshire

Cover: *The Turkestan Detachment Crosses the Amu Darya River in 1873.*
A fragment of the original by Nikolai N. Karazin (1842-1908); the original hangs in the State Central Artillery Museum in St. Petersburg.

ISBN 978 1 909982 03 1

British Library Cataloguing-in-Publication Data.
A catalogue record for this book is available from the British Library.

For details of other military history titles published by Helion & Company Limited contact the above address, or visit our website: http://www.helion.co.uk.

We always welcome receiving book proposals from prospective authors.

Contents

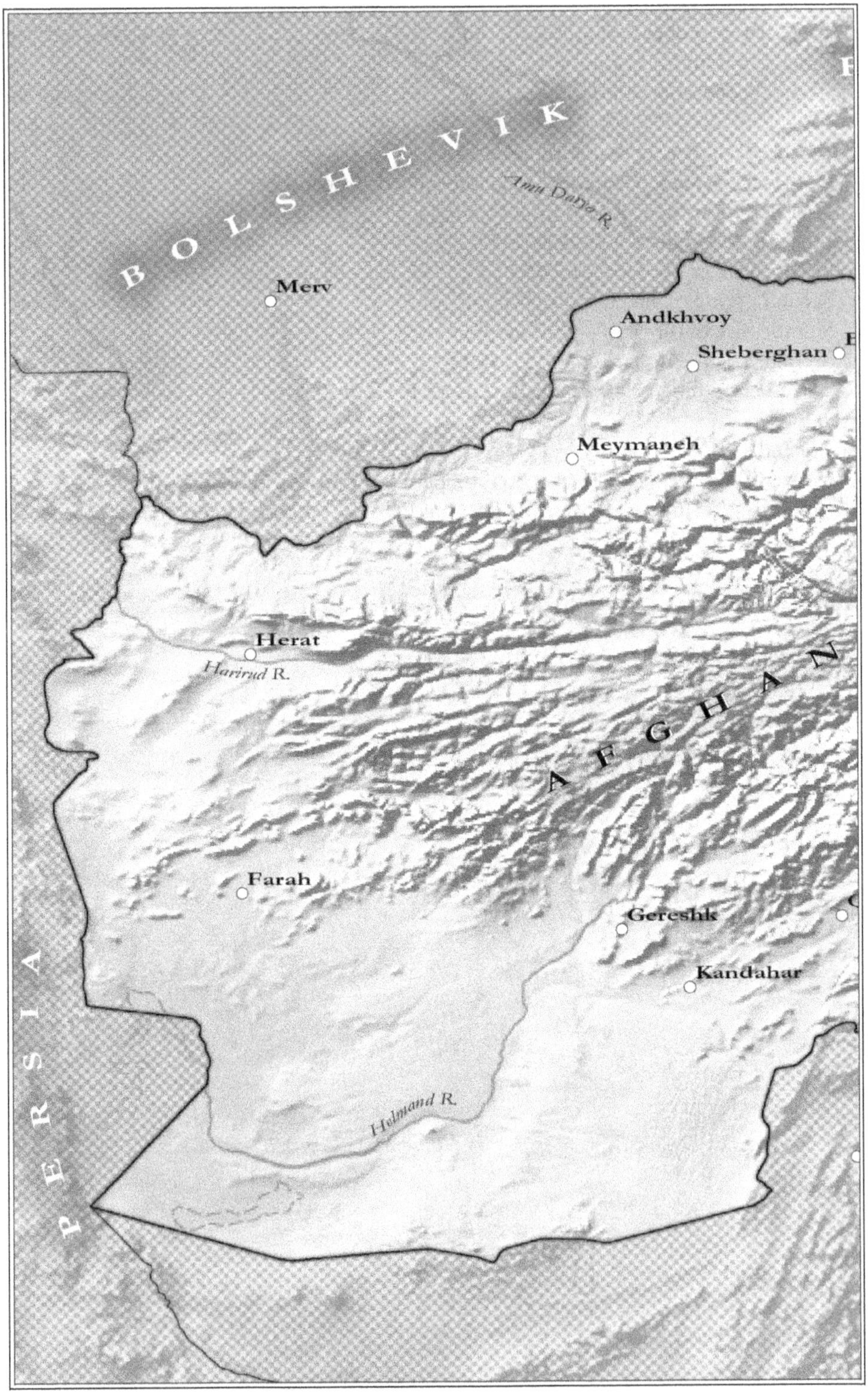

BOLSHEVIK
Amu Darya R.
Merv
Andkhvoy
Sheberghan
Meymaneh
Herat
Harirud R.
AFGHAN
Farah
Gereshk
Kandahar
Helmand R.
PERSIA

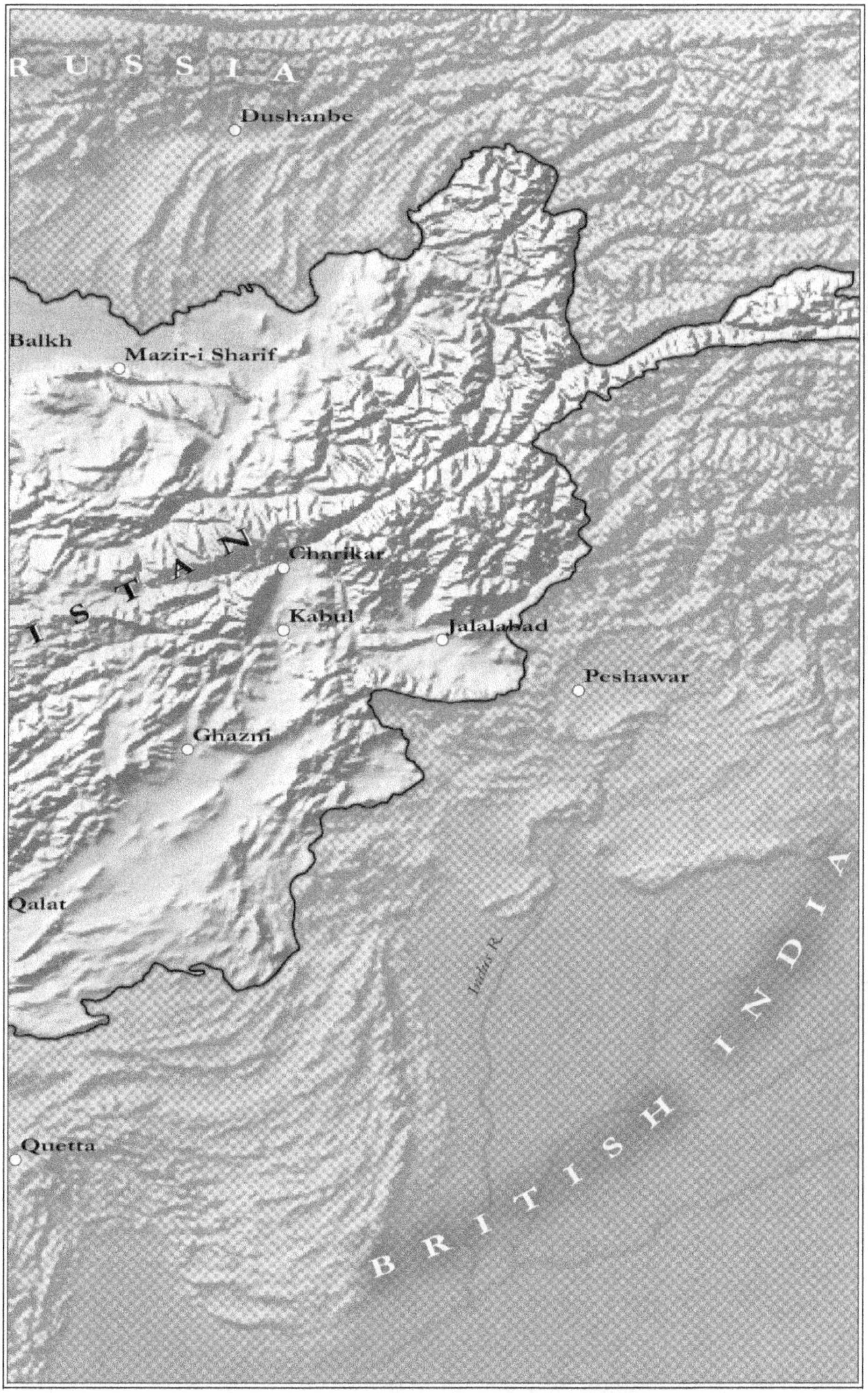

RUSSIA
Dushanbe
Balkh
Mazir-i Sharif
ISTAN
Charikar
Kabul
Jalalabad
Peshawar
Ghazni
Qalat
Indus R.
Quetta
BRITISH INDIA

Acknowledgements

The translators are indebted to the family of General Snesarev and their efforts to preserve the memory and accomplishments of their distinguished ancestor. The translators thank Hommy Rosado and Chuck Bartles for designing and making the map of Afghanistan which appears on pages viii-ix of this book.. The translators also thank Duncan Rogers of Helion & Company, for bringing this book to publication. Finally, the translators thank their long-suffering families for putting up with our projects and shenanigans—and for making life very worthwhile.

Foreword

This work is a stenographic record of my lectures which I delivered in the fall of 1919 and the spring of 1920 at the Oriental section of the General Staff Academy. To avoid delay in the appearance of this work, all additions and details have been moved to the second volume,[1] which will supplement this volume and will include the latest information on Afghanistan which we have obtained from the development of relations with that interesting country.

The lectures were intended for students completely unfamiliar with the world of Asian events. And this is the reason for so many explanatory details and repetitions in the delivery of the subject which are characteristic of any popular presentation, but to a large extent hinder the clarity and conciseness of the overall picture. Unfortunately, the author did not have either the time or opportunity to correct those shortcomings.

Snesarev
Moscow, 22 November 1921

1 A.E. Snesarev's second volume with its additional material was never published. (Translator's note).

Preface

This classic military book is unknown in the West. This work of the famous military leader, geographer and oriental scholar, Professor-General A. E. Snesarev (1865-1937) was first published in Moscow in 1921. It was produced to train the leaders and planners who were selected to conduct a possible incursion into Afghanistan and an invasion of India at the end of the Russian Civil War. The incursion and invasion did not happen, and the work disappeared from view, although copies were available to the General Staff planners for the Soviet incursion into Afghanistan in 1979. Moscow finally republished the book for general consumption in 2002. Unfortunately, the 2002 republication was sloppily done and was printed in a volume along with some salacious political material trying to link this scholarly work with authoritarian ideals. This translation is based on the original work. It is a classic military country analysis done in the thorough style of the Imperial Russian General Staff. Amazingly, it is still of great value and accuracy.

Who was Snesarev?

Andrei Evgenievich Snesarev was a noted Tsarist general who remained with the Bolsheviks after the Russian Revolution. He was born in 1865 in Stariya Kalitva in Voronezh Province. His father was a Russian Orthodox village priest. He received a gymnasium education in the city of Novocherkassk, the center of the Don Cossacks. Snesarev graduated from the Mathematics faculty of Moscow University in 1888. Like all university graduates, he had a half-year military obligation as a privileged volunteer. Andrei chose to pursue his obligation seriously by attaining an officer's commission. He then entered the Alekseyevskiy Junkers Infantry Academy in Moscow and began his uniformed service as a junior officer in an infantry regiment 1890. He decided on a career of uniformed service. He graduated from the three-year Nikolaevskiy General Staff Academy in 1899 and was sent on a lengthy tour of British India. Following this, he did research in the British Museum in London. Snesarev's career as an orientalist was underway.

Snesarev was next assigned as the Chief of Mission [ober-ofitserom dlya porychenniy] to the Turkestan Military District. In 1902, he became the Chief of the Pamir Mountain Detachment. He was actively involved in the study and military mapping of Central and South Asia. He traveled through India, Afghanistan, the Pamirs, Tibet and Kashgar (Western China). In 1904, he was assigned to the Directing Staff as a desk officer and deputy secretary to the Quartermaster General Directorate of the General Staff. This is the same year that he married Evgeniya Vasilevnaya Zaitseva. She was the daughter of the border guard's commander in Osh in modern-day Kyrgyzstan. In 1905, his duties expanded to include teaching military geography at the St. Petersburg military academy. In 1906, he graduated from a course in Oriental studies. In 1910, he became the Chief of Staff of the Second Composite Cossack Division stationed on the Austro-Hungarian Frontier.[1]

When World War I broke out, Colonel Snesarev first commanded a regiment, then a brigade. Then he became the chief of staff of a division and then a division commander. He was promoted to General-Lieutenant in 1917 and became the chief of staff of a corps. He was decorated for bravery and merit with the Orders of Saint George Third and Fourth Degree and the Sword of Saint George.[2] In September 1917, he commanded the Ninth Army Corps. After the Russian Revolution, he became a member of the Central Commission for the Improvement of Scholastic Life. In May 1918, after the Russian Civil War broke out, Lenin appointed Snesarev the Military Commander of the North Caucasus Military District.[3] Snesarev arrived at the city of Tsaritsyn to bedlam. Guerrilla bands, gangs, freebooters and communist party officials had attempted a half-hearted defense. Snesarev took action, organized the various groups into units, imposed military discipline and established a credible defense. This usurpation of authority did not sit well with many of the guerrilla leaders who complained to the local Revolutionary Soviet—Joseph V. Stalin. Stalin played to the masses and detested former Tsarist officers with culture and education. Stalin set out to remove Snesarev in the middle of the war. General Krasnov's White Cossacks attacked Tsaritsyn and were repulsed with some difficulty by Snesarev's force. Still, in July, Stalin's thugs arrested most of Snesarev's staff and imprisoned them on a prison ship in the middle of the Volga River. Stalin then arrested Snesarev and accused him of being a saboteur. Moscow did not believe the charges against Snesarev and sent a special commission to investigate. Stalin ordered the staff officers killed before the commission arrived. The barge was towed to a deep channel in the Volga and sunk. The commission found that Snesarev was blameless and freed him.[4] Lenin quickly moved Snesarev far away from Stalin. This would not be the last time that Stalin and Snesarev clashed.

In September 1918, Snesarev became the Commander of the Western Defensive Region.[5] In November, he became Commander of the Western Army that reoccupied Belorussia and Lithuania from the withdrawing Germans. In July 1919, he returned to academic life as the Chief of the General Staff Academy. In August 1921, Snesarev became the Director of the Oriental Department of the Workers and Peasants Red Army (RKKA) Military Academy and Professor of Military Geography and Statistics.[6]

1 *Voyennaya entsiklopediya* [Military encyclopedia], Volume 7, Moscow: Voyenizdat, 2003, 534 and Military Academy of the General Staff, *Zhizn' I trydi Klauzevitsa* [The Life and Work of Clausewitz] by A. E. Snesarev, Moscow: Kulikovo Pole, 2007, pp.11-32 (a republication of Snesarev's 1924 work directed by Professor-Major General I. S. Danilenko).

2 The Order of Saint George was Imperial Russia's highest military award for officers and generals, granted for special gallantry. The Sword of St. George was a rarely bestowed separate award—a gold saber inscribed "For Gallantry".

3 *Voyennaya entsiklopediya* and General Staff.

4 Vitaly Rapoport and Yuri Alexeev, *High Treason: Essays on the History of the Red Army, 1918-1938*, Durham: Duke University Press, 1985, pp.26-28.

5 A. G. Kavtaradze, *Voennye spetsialisty na sluzhbe Respubliki Sovetov 1917-1920gg* [Military specialists in the service of the Soviet Republics, 1917-1920, Moscow: Nauka, 1988, pp.109, 206.

6 *Voyennaya entsiklopediya*.

Although former Tsarist officers comprised over 30% of the senior commanders and key staff officers in the Soviet RKKA,[7] these old Tsarist officers, particularly the General Staff officers [Genstabisty], were not fully trusted by the members of the RKKA. The Russian Civil War was still on-going, but the major battles were past. The Bolsheviks still needed Snesarev and his special talents. In 1919, the Third Anglo-Afghan War flared up and although it was much-more limited than the first two, it drove the Kingdom of Afghanistan toward the Bolshevik government. The Kingdom of Afghanistan worried about Britain's intentions and so Afghanistan became the first country to recognize the new Bolshevik government. Relations improved to the point that In May 1921, the Kingdom of Afghanistan signed a treaty of friendship with the Soviet Union. The British perceived the recognition and the treaty as a threat to British India. There were fears that Britain would invade Afghanistan and the RKKA began preparations to aid Afghanistan early on. After all, Britain was still actively aiding the hold-out elements of the White Army in the civil war. Snesarev's lectures in 1919 and 1920 were part of this preparation to aid Afghanistan. Students of the Oriental Department of the RKKA Military Academy would lead the Soviet aid effort to Afghanistan. Snesarev's knowledge was critical and so his lectures were taken down by stenographers and then printed as a book. The expected British invasion did not materialize, but the thoroughness of Snesarev's works and his presentation of materials from a military specialist's point of view, makes this work still relevant today.

Professor Snesarev continued his academic career. In 1924, he was appointed professor and senior instructor of geography and statistics at the Naval Academy. In 1926, he was appointed professor of oriental studies at the Military-Political Academy. Snesarev spoke 14 languages! He translated the works of Clausewitz, von Falkenstein and von Schliffen into Russian. In 1930, Stalin caught up with him again. He was arrested in the purges and twice condemned to death by firing squad. But Snesarev was no longer a threat to Stalin. After all, Tsaritsyn was now named Stalingrad after its putative savior, not Snesarevograd as it should have been. Snesarev's death sentence was commuted to ten years hard labor. In 1934, he was given an early release since he had contracted a serious disease. He died at home in 1937 after a lingering illness.[8]

The world in 1920

World War I was over and the world was adjusting to new geographic and political realities. The Austro-Hungarian Empire, the Ottoman Empire and the Russian Empire had collapsed. The Soviet Empire would take decades to regain the Russian Empire's former borders and economic might. Many new and old states emerged and reemerged. Great Britain became the leading world power and the British Empire expanded with the addition of the Kingdom of Iraq, Palestine, Transjordan, Cyprus and Southwest Africa. Still Great Britain was in trouble. The empire was close to bankrupt and had lost over a million military dead. Forty percent of government spending went solely to service its

7 Kavtaradze, p.224.

8 *Voyennaya entsiklopediya.*

debt. Britain lost the Irish Free State. The British balance of power system in Europe was shattered.

British India was restless. During the war, Germany had agents working in British India fomenting rebellion. Further, Germany had tried to convince the Emir of Afghanistan to abandon neutrality and to invade British India during 1915. Many Indian revolutionaries promoted the hope of an invasion from Afghanistan to overthrow the British. Only after the World War, on 6 May 1919, Afghanistan invaded British India. By 8 August 1919, Afghanistan was driven back and brought to the peace table. Abortive revolutionary attempts in British India were effectively suppressed. The British Army, at the start of the war, was in the process of demobilizing and many of the seasoned units which had fought on the Northwest Frontier were absent. Still, the British Army struck back aggressively and, backed by new artillery and the Royal Air Force, rapidly regained their territory. The treaty imposed no real territorial losses or financial punishment on Afghanistan. This was particularly worrying to Afghanistan, since the real result of the war was that Britain ceased to regulate Afghanistan's foreign affairs. Afghanistan was concerned about future British intentions. When and how Britain would punish Afghanistan caused Afghanistan to reach out to the new Bolshevik government. The Treaty of Friendship between Britain and Afghanistan would be signed in Kabul in 1921 and laid many of these concerns to rest.[9]

The nascent Soviet Union was in a state of chaos. The Russian Empire had lost over three million lives during World War I and would lose over five million more during the Civil War. The new Bolshevik government was determined to create a new social order and destroy all vestiges of the old. They waged a vicious class war that attacked institutions, religion, social classes and even other communists. Although there were communist parties and revolutions in Europe, the Soviet Union was short of allies. The governments on the Soviet Union's periphery were hostile as were many overseas governments. Friendly governments, such as the Kingdom of Afghanistan, were rare and welcome. The friendly relationships between the governments would fade but never totally disappear despite a 1930 Soviet incursion into Afghanistan during the Central Asian Bashmachi Rebellion. The Soviet Union provided a convenient counter to the British, so Afghanistan signed friendship treaties with both in 1921. The threat of the Royal Air Force was countered with a fledgling Afghan Air Force stocked with Soviet aircraft and pilots. British artillery was countered with Soviet cannon and tanks provided to the Afghan Army.

The United States had made its debut on the world stage during the war. After the war, the disillusioned country withdrew in isolation. The League of Nations and other schemes to settle the planet fell short of the mark. United States interest in Afghanistan was nonexistent and would not surface until World War II when the allies were looking for an alternate route for Lend Lease supplies to the Soviet Union.

9 Two excellent books that cover this period are Brian Robson, *Crisis on the Frontier: The Third Anglo-Afghan War and the Campaign in Waziristan 1919-1920*, Staplehurst: Spellmount Limited, 2004 and Andrew Roe, *Waging War in Waziristan: The British Army in the Land of Bin Laden, 1849-1947*, Lawrence: University Press of Kansas, 2010.

Reading this book

This book has been a work of discovery for the translators since many of the terms and titles have changed. Things change over time. Language changes, place names change, public knowledge of events changes. Further, there are several alphabets and languages at work here-Cyrillic, Turkic, Arabic, Persian and Pashtu. Consequently, transliteration of place names can be challenging. To the maximum extent possible, the spelling of place names is in accordance with *Afghanistan: Official Standard Names Approved by the United States Board on Geographic Names*[10] *and The Historical and Political Gazeteer of Afghanistan.*[11] Some place names have still evaded identification despite the seven map sets the translators consulted. There was no map included with the original book, but access to a map is essential for a careful reading of the book. The map included in this book is a copy of map 61 of *Steller's Atlas of Modern Geography.* This map provides an example of maps in use at this time. For the reader's convenience, Hommy Rosado and Chuck Bartles designed and produced the map of Afghanistan found inside this book, which has less detail, but is easier to use. The spelling of the names of historic figures is in accordance with Percy Sykes' *A History of Afghanistan.*[12] However, this book uses Timur instead of Tamerlane, since Snesarev considered Tamerlane as a Persian sneer at this central figure. Russian names are transliterated in accordance with the United States Board on Geographic Names for Cyrillic. There are a mix of footnotes in this book, those of the author and those of the translators. The translators' footnotes are included to provide further granularity to the author's statements or to provide information that was common knowledge at the time of the book's publication but is forgotten now. Translator's brief notes are enclosed in [square brackets] within the body of the text.

---

10 Geographic Names Division, U.S. Army Topographic Command, *Afghanistan: Official Standard Names Approved by the United States Board on Geographic Names*, Washington, July 1971.

11 Ludwig W. Adamec, *Historical and Political Gazetteer of Afghanistan*, Four Volumes, Graz: Akademiche Druck-u. Verlagsanalt, 1975. This gazetteer is based on the 1914 secret British Gazetteer of Afghanistan.

12 Brigadier-General Sir Percy Sykes, *A History of Afghanistan*, London: Macmilllan & Co. Ltd., 1940, 2 volumes.

Introduction

Practical study of the Orient. Military geography. Near and Middle East. Near East. Middle East. Political content of these terms. Lecture plan. Order of presentation.

Before I begin, I direct your attention to the main principal which underlies the study of the languages and the countries in the Oriental Section of the Academy.

Practical Study of the Orient

This study could be titled the study of *living* people and *living* languages. The idea of this so-called practical study of Oriental countries is relatively new. Now it has the right to exist, but in the not-so-distant past it had been disputed, and I, among others, was forced to cross swords often to argue that studying Oriental countries, studying the peoples that putter about there, studying their languages which are possibly often coarse and irregular: Represents quite a large interest and Is as scientific as the study that until recently was counted as the only scientific one – namely the theoretical study of the Orient.

I remember that, in 1908, at the International Congress of Orientalists in Copenhagen, when I gave a talk on the practical study of Oriental countries, I got very serious attention. After the talk I was surrounded by correspondents piling questions on me. I think it was not the character of the report itself, which was not that interesting or good, but the topic and especially the interpretation of that topic from the point of the live study of those countries – that aroused the interest of many people.

What is the difference between practical and theoretical study? It is as follows: any theoretical study of a country tends to drift toward its past, into the evolution of its peoples' language, its origin; while studying a country's geography and territory, which are right before one's eyes, it still descends into long-gone times, it searches for the researcher's comprehensive base to support the researcher's required conclusion based on his deep analysis, comparisons and analogies between events past and present – to determine people's language in its general clarified forms. Of course, one cannot reject the significant usefulness and undeniable scientific quality of this method. But it is weak as seen from the viewpoint of the practical necessities of life and that practical *study*, to which many are turning. Practical study considers a country in its current actual state; it looks at live contemporary people with their ways of life and customs; it studies those live languages which live people speak – and not only a privileged minority but the majority, the masses. In a word, it studies a country without a microscope or telescope but with live (if imperfect) eyes, deeply penetrating its dull but actual and active reality. This practical study is criticized as a fleeting thing; that the language study is not conducted in serious general forms but in the ignorant rough reflection given to it by these or those people; that it catches a current moment – quite often without historical interest; that it studies some types that could be just accidental. Also, some would say that the individuals, who study a country practically, quite often are not very well versed in the country language's history and its past; they do not know what kind of blood flows in the people's veins, etc. But that point of view on the practical study has died out and we can remember it now as past history. Nowadays, the practical study has a strong scientific appreciation and sufficient experience in some institutions, such as the Institute of Live Languages in Paris, the Seminary in Berlin, universities' departments in England and in the now-defunct Practical Oriental Academy in Petrograd.

Here, at the Oriental section, we will follow only the practical method of study of the Oriental countries. Why? Because it will lead us to the doorsteps of the countries and languages you are going to study in a quick and sound fashion. Thanks to practical study of the languages and customs of those countries, you will have ability to communicate with the people of Orient; you will be able to understand their way of life and will not scare them with unacceptable questions and manners; you will know how to find ways to their hearts and minds. This method, besides obviously being economical, is also practically expedient – it will lead you directly to the object of your study that has an interest for you without deviations into unnecessary history or theoretical detail....It will lead you to inquiries of life's matters that are dictated by the actual shifting situation via a straight and speedy road.

I will deliver a course of military geography of the Middle East. Then, if there is not another instructor, I will continue with military geography of the Near East connecting my teaching to the principles I have just described to you.

Military Geography

First, a few words about military geography. Military geography is the description of a country, people and the historical moment that the country is living through, which is done from the military-political angle of observation, i.e. the description of general geography with the assumption that a war could crop up on the territory of one country or another one in the neighborhood, regardless of kind of the war – it could be an offensive or defensive war or even a small guerilla war. Those of you who are students of the Academy already have a picture of the general principles and basic methods which are necessary for military-geographical research and I will not dwell on them. I would however, like to ask you a single essential question in relation to that. If I am going to deliver lectures to you – what would be a difference between these and the lectures that I would deliver to the students of the general course of the General Staff Academy? What would the difference be for me and what responsibility would it load on me as of a representative for the practical study of the Orient in the course of achieving the goal I set for myself? I shall tell you that the principal motives of the military-geographical research remains the same; therefore that leaves us with the same geographical objects in either case: the geographical situation, the masses of the people, population movement and distribution, the labor force, etc. All of those should be examined from the military perspective. As an example, if the people are studied, then I am going to look at them as a large labor force which also serves on one side as a general reserve for building military might, and on other side – it is the tool for creating those diverse valuables which are necessary for a war. If I go to another element of geography – terrain – then I would examine it in general first, i.e. to what degree it conforms to strategic requirements by its general relief, character of the mountains, rivers, climate and the people's character.

That would be the review of geographical material from a broad military point of view. I could then go into specifics: studying in detail the direction of the mountain ridges, their folds, continuity; discerning the rivers' character on predetermined scale; examining open or wooded areas – then I could work on tactical questions. Studying the country's communications, I would look at how useful they would be for moving troops and logistics during different seasons, etc. This is going to be the canvas for the military study of any country, including those of the Orient.

What peculiarities am I going to introduce to teaching military geography since I belong to the school that studies countries using the practical method? There will be two of them. First of all, while describing any military-geographical elements – the people, roads, rivers, languages, etc. – I will do that from a closer perspective, in greater detail, and with greater attention to the realities, probably with more day-to-day specifics than I would do if I were delivering lectures at the main course of the General Staff Academy. Here, I probably will omit some statistics and historical references – things that support theory, but I will give greater attention to the people's dull everyday life, their ordinary realities – in a word – on their real life. And this responsibility – to get to the people and the country's real life – I will put first.

The second aspect is related to lecturer's experience. I think that one can become familiar with the military-geographical description after reading several books. After that it is possible to pursue a professorship – and this is acceptable when doing the theoretical study of a country. But if a professor teaches using the methods of the school based upon practical study, then he has an unavoidable responsibility to be practically familiar with the country. He cannot limit himself to things he has heard somewhere, read in a book, even talked to someone who has seen the country personally. That is not enough. The instructor must see the country he describes, its nature, have contacts with the people that live there, talk to them and even share with them small joys and sorrows. Only through a connection with them, living through sunny or rainy days, can the person later say a sure word about the country and its people.

I am going to deliver to you lectures on Middle East military geography. You could ask if I have been there. Yes, I have. The most of what I am going to tell you I have seen personally. The things I have not seen – I will leave out or specify. I have lived in India for seven months, moved through different corners of the Northern India which later I have studied specifically. I have been in remote corners of the Eastern Bukhara, lived in Pamir almost for two years, visited Kashgaria[1], Afghanistan, etc. And due to that – anything I am going to speak about I've lived through; the people I will tell you about I knew personally, had contacts with them and even more: I have many friends among them. If they do not write to me – that is because they cannot write. But any time someone goes to Asia or back – I restore my spiritual contacts with them. In one word – I am going to speak about those countries not as a theorist but a practical person.

1 Contemporary Kashgaria is located in Xinjiang Province in the Uyghur Autonomous Region of the Peoples Republic of China. (Translator's note).

Near and Middle East

Thus, after shedding light on the main idea which is the basis of the study of Oriental countries in our Oriental section, and pointing at what is the essence of the practical method of the military-geographical study and how it differs from the ordinary theoretical method, I will move closer to my topic. First, what is the so-called Near East and Middle East; what countries and peoples do they include and why in literature, especially political literature, do such concepts of "Far East", "Near East" and "Middle East" endure? For example, what countries belong to the Middle East—the first I will begin with? They are our Turkestan, Khiva, Bukhara, Tibet, Kashgaria, Pamir, Afghanistan, Eastern Persia, Baluchistan, and India.[2] After I named those countries you would have a legitimate question: what unites them? What is the reason to lump these countries that are so different in languages and government, under the term "Middle East"? I need to dwell on this matter to justify to you the name that we will use afterwards – and we shall do it consciously.

Near East

The Near East – we need to talk about it at least in passing – has the longest history. Long ago, it was the cradle of the great kingdoms of Assyria, Babylon and Persia. To tell the truth, some of those kingdoms stretched out their tentacles (tails) far beyond their original borders – to Europe and North-Eastern Africa but what they had in common was that they all stayed in the Near East. If you have a chance to familiarize yourselves with the history of the Roman Empire – the period when the Near East was brought into its zone of influence – then you will see that during that time it consisted of a group of peculiar pro-consular or semi-autonomous states, totally unlike the pro-consular states or provinces of Africa, Spain or contemporary Central Europe. The small Asian governing entities had their peculiar faces, lived through their special history and Rome had a different attitude toward them.[3] It is significant that special people were assigned or spontaneously ended up in the region. They usually strengthened their careers with accumulation of huge wealth, but were also infected with the failings and vices of the Orient. The influence of the Orient over Rome was enormous,[4] both in the transfer of its complex spiritual values into the heart of Rome and in the preparation for the major (if indirect) deadly blow at the granite stronghold of the Eternal City.

---

2 Today, this area is commonly called Central and South Asia. The contemporary Middle East includes the countries of the Arabian Peninsula and north to Iraq, Syria, Jordan and Israel and east to Iran and west to Egypt. This region, other than Iran (Persia), was part of the Ottoman Empire, which was disassembled by the victors of World War I. Before World War I, Near East referred to the Balkans and the Ottoman Empire, while the Middle East was as Snesarev described it. Today, the terms Middle East and Near East are synonymous. (Translator's note).

3 The East played a peculiar role in those wars that Rome fought and which built its might. The East was a "gold bag" or a huge cash box used to finance the wars – R.Yu. Vipper, Public lecture "Civil wars in Ancient Rome", June 1920. (Author's note).

4 See the classic works of [Edward] Gibbon (*The History of the Decline and Fall of the Western Roman Empire*) or [Theodor] Mommsen (*History of Rome*). (Author's note). Snesarev added 'Western' to Gibbon's title, presumably to separate it from the Byzantine Empire. (Translator's note).

During the Middle Ages, you can see the fate and face of the Near East changing with the demands of history. In time, the wave of the Arab invasion flooded the Near East in a turbulent torrent. It did not move into Europe, but rolled over Northern Africa and come to a stop in Spain. That wave made the East both Arabic and militaristic and instilled a flourishing if short-lived culture. When the Turkish wave came after the Arab rule, Europe again began turning its attention to the Near East. It was the moment that Europe became vigilant and began to fight off the menacing advance of the Orient; it was the single fight of Byzantine against the Turks with very weak assistance from South-Eastern Europe that attracted the attention of Europe and was closely connected to the issue of the Near East. The founding of the first language schools in Venice and Vienna for studying Turkish, Arabic and Persian belong to that time. During the Crusades, all the attention toward the Near East was concentrated around a completely new idea – the fight for the Holy Land. You could say that there were other forces directing the Crusade – economic forces and the emancipation of peasants…this is absolutely correct. But the region that the Crusade's waves rolled onto represented a collection of territories with a common name – the Near East.

So far, we can see that the interest in the Near East contained a hodge-podge of different ideas which replaced one another randomly and were not known for their durability. But after Turkey moved into Europe, rumors arose about a country of incalculable wealth that was discovered somewhere far away – the extraordinary country we call India became a reality in our minds. At the end of the 18th Century, India inspired hopes and new political ideas in people's imagination. Since then, the political trend, even if not clear to the general public, has always clearly been linked to the issue of who is going to rule India and possess its riches. At the end of the 18th Century, Mirabeau, who always had time for everything and Napoleon, who had the very naïve idea of penetrating all the way to India through Russia, were the first to attach a special value to the Near East and since the beginning of past century[5] the issue became a definitive political factor. The term "Near East", from a political point of view, carried two major issues: one was linked to Turkish governance – an easily understood and clearly visible idea; and another one – murkier and more serious was the matter of countries that had routes leading to India. I have to mention that nowadays, when you study these long-ago issues, you may be astonished by the nervousness which was attached to problems of the Near East and the number of hare-brained attempts to resolve them. It is really difficult to imagine that Napoleon's Egyptian campaign, which ended so brutally at the Syrian coast, may have in fact ended up with the conquest of India. And what about the project of Czar Paul I (whom some historians regard as sick) – is that not a project from a psychopathic mind?[6]

5 19th Century (Translator's note).

6 Napoleon Bonaparte and Czar Paul the First agreed to a joint attack on India in 1801. Russia would contribute an infantry corps of 35,000 plus a large contingent of Cossack cavalry. France's contribution would be similar. General Andre Massena would lead the French contingent from the Danube, across southern Russia to linkup where the Volga enters the Caspian Sea. The force would cross the Caspian Sea to Persia and then advance through Herat and Kandahar toward India. The invasion was cancelled when Czar Paul was assassinated in March 1801. (Translator's note).

In any case, since the beginning of the 19th Century, the Near East has absorbed everyone's attention since the region includes those territories on the approaches to India. Of course, England was the country most interested in the issue, and in the first half of that century it exhibited exceptional nervousness. But after the crown got everything under control in India, the mightiest states of Northern India were conquered, the Sepoy Mutiny of 1857 was suppressed, the First Afghan War (1839-1842) was concluded successfully, our Black Sea Fleet was destroyed and the Suez Canal came under English control – then, the issues of the Near East stopped causing as much nervousness as before. Although India still attracts the world's attention, it is mostly limited to current issues such as the rivalry between England and Germany. All the world attention has moved to a new center of gravity – a new European child – which is called the *Middle East.*

Middle East

The growth of the literature on the Near East and the extent of its influence is demonstrated by the fact that the Near East is part of the studies at children's schools. Not so with the Middle East. My main topic will be the Middle East and we need to clarify the reason for that ambiguity. I've already listed the countries of the Middle East. One can see that these countries are very different in size and political influence. Then what put them in the same group? Why do we unite them under a common name as countries belonging to Middle East? First of all I refer to their history. But I need to point out in advance that obviously the issue of the Middle East was somewhat unclear for a while. Only Curzon, who now is the Foreign Secretary of England, highlighted the essence and significance of the Middle East in his political works with irrefutable certainty.

I am not speaking about his recent political plans such as his idea for a railroad that would cross Aravia [Saudi Arabia], turn north at Kuwait, continue around the Persian Gulf and from Bushehr [Basrah] go across Persia and Afghanistan through Shiraz, Kerman, Nusirabad[7] and Kandahar to connect to the railroad network of India. The latter, in turn, would connect to the Chinese railroad network with access to Shanghai, i.e. a grandiose (but exclusively British) steel ribbon cut across all the Asian continent and connected with the Trans-African line (Cairo – Cape Town).

We can consider this as a politician's quixotic plan. But when Curzon was younger, during the time when he was Viceroy of India, he was less fanatical and more objective as a researcher. He described the content of the Middle East authoritatively and intelligently in his works (*Russia in Central Asia, Persia and the Persian Question, The Pamirs and the Source of the Oxus*). The works of his predecessors – Rawlinson, McGregor[8] and the like – were too nervous and one-sided to reveal clearly the vast issues of the Middle

7 This is one of Snesarev's mysteries. Possibly this is Nasirabad by Jacobabad, Pakistan. If this is the case, the line would run across Baluchistan and linkup would occur at the Jacobabad railyard. The Kandahar connection would actually be an extention of the rail line from Quetta. (Translator's note).

8 [Henry] Rawlinson wrote *England and Russia in the East* and [Charles] McGregor wrote *Defense of India* (Author's note).

East. After Curzon, the idea of the Middle East became widespread among the general public while before that it was only the domain of specialists.

What is the data supporting the association of the forenamed countries into the Middle East entity?

If we look at history, we can see a series of large states within the territory of the contemporary Middle East, states such as Alexander's the Great's Empire. Look at the winding paths that this great military leader followed while moving his forces in his campaigns. He started with a campaign along the Syrian coast toward Egypt, and then pressed toward the heart of ancient Persia, moved along the southern coast of the Caspian Sea; maneuvered some of his forces to Merv[9]; across the Amu-Darya River and infiltrated contemporary Turkestan. Then he tangled himself in eastern Bukhara around Kulyab[10], and after that moved across the Hindu Kush Mountains into India...what was the sense of all those movements and maneuvers?

Strategists of our time (Leer) would like to explain it as an attempt to expand and solidify his invasion base before the Indian campaign.[11] I see that in different light. To me it is the conclusion of establishing power – by presence – over all those regions to form something unified within the inter-relations; the unity that needed to be taken under one ruling hand. And when Alexander moved his residence to Babylon, the territory under his control included the Middle East exactly. He still needed Macedonia[12] as a source of infantry and cavalry commanders, he needed Egypt which was his economic base, but all his power was concentrated precisely in the territory we call the Middle East today.

Moving closer to our time, we can see many new kingdoms form in the Middle East, many kingdoms that filled the territory one by one. I will point out the most notable. Here is the kingdom of Genghis Khan, born in the depth of Asia. European history is very often wrong about and malicious toward the Orient. European history tells you that due to a misunderstanding between Ghenghis Khan and Khorezm (contemporary Khiva),[13] Genghis conquered it, then pursued Jelaludinn and arrived at India. He built a world power – and there were blood, horrors and destroyed kingdoms everywhere! I will not dwell on this European method of the historical depiction. After all, if you would look into one of the many of Genghis' uluses[14] you will see that it reflects all the Orient of our interest.

But this idea appears even more clearly in the next wave – the wave of Timur or Tamerlane – a derisive name given him by Persian historians. He was the son of a Turkish father and an estranged Mongolian mother. He died in the early 15th Century. He

9 Merv is the most ancient city of Central Asia and is located in the South-Eastern part of Turkestan. It was first mentioned in the 3rd Century BC. Its contemporary name is Mary. (Translator's note).

10 Kulyab(now Kulob) is a city in the South-Western part of Contemporary Tajikistan. (Translator. note).

11 General Genrikh Antonovich Leer (1829-1904) was a leading Tsarist military theorist, historian and field commander. (Translator's note).

12 In this, Mahaffy's book, *The Progress of Hellenism in Alexander's Empire*, Chicago, 1905 is interesting. (Author's note).

13 City in Western Uzbekistan. (Translator.note).

14 Ulus – administrative unit of the Mongol Hordes (Translator's note).

reconstructed an empire which once had been under Alexander the Great's rule. Looking at the territory under Timur's power, we can see that it included the following countries: Russian Turkestan, Afghanistan, Eastern Persia; probably all Pamir, Kashgaria. Northern India also temporarily belonged to the empire; though not completely – the Ganges Valley in its lower part was outside of the empire, because it was so primitive it did not attract the interest of anyone. Thus you can see that the cup of Middle East is again filled to the brim. It would lead us to the conclusion that at the epoch of building large states in Near Asia, they for some reason or other concentrated on this select territory. Obviously, there was something in those territories which gave great conquerors the ability to unite them under their power, control them and contain the peoples' masses in them – in the territory we now call the Middle East. Then the time of the great conquerors passed – and everything fell apart – until a new conqueror came.

If this picture did not convince you – I am going to lead you to other side – the issue of national design. While I speak about it, you will see at the first glance, a very complex phenomenon: on the Middle East territory you will find, besides Persians and Turks, Arabs, Jews, Mongols (the Hazara or Kalmyk), even Gypsies. That is a somewhat disconcerting conglomerate. But if you cast aside those ethnographic minorities and look at which major people fill the Middle East, then you will see two primary groups – the Turks and the Persians and you will not be disturbed by finding unexpected guests – the descendants of Mongols or Jews. They probably got into the area from some other nest and their numbers are miniscule. But the general ethnic picture is clear. The Middle East is a container for two major nationalities: Persian and Turkish – the former lying at the bottom and the latter building the upper stratums and that reveals them as a specific ethnographic entity.

There is a third aspect to our question–religion. Someday, should you study the growth of religion, you will note an interesting phenomenon: religion often develops and grows deep roots away from the place it first appeared and was preached. It roams the world, quite often seeking shelter for a long time and finally becomes rooted in a completely different place from where one would expect it. This is one of the most mysterious geographical puzzles. I always regarded the religious factor as one of the most serious factors–even more important in the study of peoples and countries then say language. You will notice that in some countries which are very similar to each other, that groups of people speak two-three different languages. Yet in other countries, the youngsters speak one language, while their mumbling elders another. In the latter case, we can actually observe a most-interesting process where one language is dying and is being replaced by another. Religion though is a fairly stable factor, a strong and constant unifier of large groups of people. Looking at the Middle East, the major religion is Islam. Needless to say, for a specialist this statement is muddled, since there are a vast number of interpretations of what Islam is. There are several branches of Islam just within the Shia. But it is correct to say that the Middle East professes Islam. Layers of Judaism, Christianity, and Buddhism are still present in small batches. Yet Islam rules and puts its definite imprint on all the Middle East. You can confidently say that the Middle East is a collection of countries that are under the dictate of the Prophet's law.

Political Content of the Term

This information will help you understand how the term, the Middle East, came into existence. But there is one more aspect which shows the idea in even more relief and which proves even more that the Middle East is not some fictitious or unnatural term, but that it is definitely linked with the geographical and ethnographical volume [of evidence]. It is new evidence, a new side to the issue – the political component. The political side clearly appeared in the 1870s, but its first outlines emerged earlier. First, in continental Europe, Mirabeau[15] and Napoleon pointed out – one theoretically and the other practically--the value and significance of India, mainly due to its natural resources, and huge population which could be exploited. But as long as the Russians did not move into Central Asia, as long as they stayed far away, the idea was not widespread within the wider political circles of England. We can see this from this fact: only after Napoleon established contacts with Persia, did England send Elphinstone's mission to Afghanistan – the mission which did much for Afghan study and attracted the attention of specialists to the country.[16]

But for the rest of the world, the remote countries of the Middle East took on a clearer focus only during the 1860s when Russia began moving into Central Asia. Russia took Khiva, Tashkent, Kokand and later – Pamir and thus created the appearance of a deliberate, systematic approach toward India. Then the alarm sounded. These conquests and the political and various other obstacles uncovered during the process led to the study of the regional countries and showed us Russians, and later – the rest of the world, the significance of the regions comprising the Middle East. Studies also disclosed the essence of their total value – at that time we understood – first specialists and later wider social circles, that the political value and all political significance of the conquered territories is not in their immediate resources but mainly lies in the fact that they represent areas of approach to the exclusive source of wealth – India, that they border on it. As soon as this became clear, a new depiction of what we meant by the Middle East appeared. From the political point of view, the Middle East is *first* –India; *second* – it is a ring of states – small, weak, poor which surround India (these are Baluchistan, Afghanistan which cups India as a rectangle, Pamir, Kashgaria and then Tibet); and finally *the third* – we need to include Russian Turkestan, which Englishmen consider the base for threatening or invading India.

Thus the multi-faceted and vast wealth of India produces an avid desire in the English to keep it under their rule and safeguard all the approaches to the country; and on the Russian side it creates a natural gravitation toward the countries that surround India: not

15 In the 1786 *Histoire secrete de la Cour de Berlin, Ouvrage posthume*, tome premier, lettre XXIX. (Author's note).

16 Mountstuart Elphinstone was a political agent of the East India Company who was one of the first English visitors to Afghanistan in 1808. Napoleon's envoy to Persia was interpreted as a possible attempt to unify Persia and Afghanistan in an attempt on British India. Elphinstone did not succeed in negotiating a treaty with Shah Shuja, the ruler of Afghanistan, but produced a detailed country study (*An Account of the Kingdom of Cabul and its Dependencies in Persia, Tartary and India* published in 1815). He should not be confused with Major General William George Elphinstone who lost an entire army in Afghanistan in 1842 in the First Anglo-Afghan War. (Translator's note)

for those countries themselves – there is very little good in them, but to have an opportunity to influence India or – if there is a chance – to capture it. England and Russia collided in Central Asia and their century-and-a-half rivalry represents the main knot of Middle East's problems.

To clarify my position even further I am going to repeat that from a political viewpoint, the Middle East is the vast territory which contains India itself as an object to reach, possess or keep, then the group of countries that surround it and are buffer states or states-glacis,[17] and finally huge Russian Turkestan which is viewed as the staging base to invade and capture India. In my work *India as a Major Factor in the Central Asian Question* which some of you are familiar with, I clearly disclosed my point of view. Those of you who will take the time to read it will see on one side that we – the Russians strived to move toward India (we are not talking how successful or unsuccessful this was) and on other side – who opposed it. One chapter of the work is dedicated to the issue of the economic importance of India to England and another chapter speaks about the Englishmen's dominance over the blacks as the master people over the slave people.

Thus, besides the reasons I described earlier to reveal the Middle East as the territory, I had to posit the fourth one – the political. Due to these reasons and issues, the contemporary Middle East is definitively a political-geographic term. The major factor, of course, is the political one. That side of the issue was revealed in innumerable works. When we finish moving the General Staff library from Petrograd you will find a solid mass of political works dedicated to the topic, especially English works, which discuss it from all points of view. In truth, you will find a lot of chewing over of matters, repetitions, nervousness, bias and nationalistic narrow-minded approaches, but also a wealth of serious and profound material.[18] All of it shows India's importance to England and to the rest of the world and how correct is the point of view that combines India and the surrounding countries under one common term – with India as the center of the issue.

Lecture Plan

I think I have sufficiently explained the issue of the Middle East to you, and I now move to its examination. But before that, I need to state what my lecture plan is for our course on the Middle East geography. As I've said before, it has several countries: India, eastern Persia, Afghanistan, Baluchistan, Pamir, Kashgaria, Tibet and Russian Turkestan. Naturally, you are wondering what is the plan, what country will we begin with and at what level will we have our discussion? In order to prevent our stretching out among all these countries we need to establish some starting point which will be the basis of

17 A glacis in military engineering is an artificial slope of earth used in late European fortresses so constructed as to keep any potential assailant under the fire of the defenders until the last possible moment. On natural, level ground, troops attacking any high work have a degree of shelter from its fire when close up to it; the glacis consists of a slope with a low grade inclined towards the top of the wall. This gave defenders a direct line of sight into the assaulting force, allowing them to efficiently sweep the field with fire from the parapet. (Translator's note).

18 The Tsarist General Staff facilities were located in St. Petersburg (Petrograd, later Leningrad). The Bolshevik government moved all central government functions to Moscow. The process took years. (Translator's note).

my course. I am going to proceed on the premise of military-political reasons which are fundamental for my statement that India is the main object in the territory of the Middle East. Countries which adjoin India are called buffers, i.e. the territories that include the immediate approaches to India, and further to the North is the country which is the source of necessary resources for executing military operations against India.

I mean, of course, only the *possibility* or *probability* of war with India. I specify that because, in England, I have a reputation as a person who preaches the idea of Invasion of India at all costs and this requires complete clarity from me while addressing the issue. To build our course one way or another, we will need to stick to some plan; otherwise it will be impossible to expound on so complex an issue. We cannot do that without some main pivot and I will build my course on the basis of a *hypothetical offensive on India* as the main idea – and there is nothing improbable in it.

But moving into the depth of our plan we stumble across two military-operational questions: is it in our interests i.e. in the interest of the republic to attack India or it is more in the interest of the Englishmen to attack our Turkestan? I assert that the latter case is totally improbable, because England cannot set as its goal the very remote objective of seizing Turkestan. First of all – it is impossible for them and they are also up to their eyeballs with problems in India. Thus I conclude that there is no sense to study the Middle East from the aspect of an English invasion of Turkestan, i.e. under the aspect of our defense of Turkestan from the Englishmen. This leaves us with only one point of view – we are going to conduct the study under the aspect of *the possibility of a grand (offensive) operation against India*. I will use this as the basis for the study of the Middle Eastern countries—a possible, if very remote, large military operation against India.

Based on this, I am going to dwell on India as the final objective of those operations, on surrounding countries as areas of approach to India and, finally, on Turkestan as the base for the operations. If I chose this method, you will see that my presentation has some coherence and consistency. This method establishes a certain system to the presentation and simplifies a very complex topic.

The question appears: due to the complexity of the topic where we start? I think that it would be more convenient to begin with the countries surrounding India and this is why: first – India itself is too far away and it would be the last stage of the conquest; second – we cannot step over those countries which surround India before we get into it. And it is the real reason for me to digress from talks about India and begin with one of the buffers. As to Turkestan – it is ours. We know it sufficiently; have our organizations, headquarters, and military units there. Recently representatives of Turkestan University went there and we are not afraid that military actions will begin there. We can put Turkestan aside for the time being. Since India is too far away and Turkestan is familiar enough to us, this gives us the right to start with one of the buffers.

I'll begin with Afghanistan which now commands the most interest, later we will come to Pamir and describe the peculiarities of that small country; then move to Kashgaria, then Tibet which represents a bit more interest in itself and will finish the cycle with the story of the Eastern Persia. After that I will consider the first part of the course concluded and move to the main object of our course – India. But I have to note that my presentation is going to be narrower, because India as a subject of a research is immense and I would be able to give you only the synopsis of the study – but I will try to present you with the necessary information. My thought is not to lead you into the wilderness of

Deccan, not to go to Ceylon which has no interest for you – but mainly to direct your attention to the Indo-Ganges Valley and to the North-Western and Northern borders of India – the borders which have an interest for us as the last barriers before India. And the wondrous and very rich valley is of interest as a vast treasury-house and the constant subject of many conquests. India will constitute the second part of the course. After I am done with India, I will move on to Turkestan.

Order of Presentation

While presenting the course, I am going to stick to the following order: as I start to describe any country I will try to point out sources for study, picking from the literature the most essential, and briefly characterizing those sources. After that, I will move to the military-geographical description of the country, according to the scale of it.

1
Afghanistan

Our knowledge of the Orient – degree of reliability

Finally, I am moving on to Afghanistan. First of all I have to make a general remark that knowledge on Afghanistan – as in general for all Asian and especially Muslim countries--does not give us precise geographical or other data on the terrain surface, climate, population, etc. We shall agree in advance that while studying Asian countries you will generally use much different material then if you were studying countries in Europe. There are many reasons for that. All of the literature that I will point on for you – when you find the time to study it – suffers from all kinds of inaccuracies. Let's take, for example, Captain Yate's book on the Northern Afghanistan.[1] I was very disappointed when I read it. It is the bubbling of an Englishmen who goes over well-traveled routes and writes down anything he sees or hears. In the book you will not find specific information on the people, country's character or communication routes. His journal does mention the roads he traveled and is filled with endless gossip and political tales. Another book –*Afghanistan* by Hamilton – is a number of pictures from political and ethnographical points of view; but there is neither a clear scientifically-based outline of the customs and the ways of life of the people nor the history of the people's origin.[2] The author cribbed a lot and did quite a compilation, but he did not personally see anything or live through anything there.

And this is the reason that I warned you that you cannot find precise and reliable information in literature. And why is this so? Take as an example any Asian country. There is no press, large cities, resorts, trade fairs – with the exception of small bazaars of little importance – there are no sources or centers where one can find some literature or can genuinely talk about the country, study the people, their ways of life, customs, etc. By looking into how people settle down, one can notice that they are attached to a particular area – river basins, mountain pasture regions, but very rarely live in cities or large villages. They communicate, but in a limited way. Take the Hindu Kush Mountains as an example: people there are tied to separate valleys which often do not have any communications between them. Thus, you see that in an Asian country there is no common culture, economic ties or information centers.

1 [Charles Edward] Yate, *Northern Afghanistan [or Letters from the Afghan Boundary Commission* Edinburgh and London: William Blackwood and Sons], 1888. (Author's note). Yate was a Major when he published this book. (Translator's note).

2 Agnus [Angus] Hamilton, *Afghanistan*, [New York: Charles Scribner's Sons,] 1906. (Author's note).

Further, these are people speaking different dialects and sub-dialects with different life styles. If they've settled in valleys or [on high plateaus], then they grow grain.[3] If they live in the mountains or steppes, they breed livestock. These differences in occupation and languages lead to weakness in communications and the separation of the population's groups. You cannot familiarize yourself with one group while studying another. Each and every group must be studied individually.

Further on, are there any written sources which you can use while studying one or another Oriental country? No, there are almost none. Travelers from Europe – Englishmen or Russians – must move along a designated route under the protection of an armed escort, they stay overnight at designated places; their contacts with the locals are severely limited for political reasons, and if they have a chance to meet local people, these are either specially-prepared agents sent on this secret mission or uneducated illiterate persons who cannot say anything useful about the country in general. Of course, you can lure a native for some research or to get information, but the native's main concern would to earn money, so he will try to satisfy your curiosity with loads of lies or fantasies. In a word, the locals will not help you gain understanding.

Finally, there are purely religious and national reasons. In the Asian countries – primarily Islamic – you have to deal with religious edicts, which do not permit you to closely approach the natives' lives. When one studies a people's way of life, one has to begin with the study of a family, its customs, structures, interrelations between family members, and even housing construction; location of windows and the stove's design sometimes speak louder about a people's way of life than other signs. Speaking in general, you cannot bypass that kind of small research if you conduct a strictly scientific study. But in Asia you will run into big obstacles if you are working in an Islamic country. The descendents of Mohammed strictly adhere to his order that a woman covers her face outdoors and does not talk to strange men. This is why quite often you will be at loss and cannot understand one event or another – and only because you will be deprived of an explanation from a woman. The female half of the population, due to the spirit of Islam, cannot help you, even if a woman is most often the best guardian of the family tales and peculiarities which would be of interest to the researcher of the country. Women preserve the more refined language and the best folklore. While men begin to forget a country's language and its customs – women, as more conservative element, remember the old language, customs and lore much longer. And you cannot ask the best authority about ways of life, family or the country's past – it is unacceptable for a woman to talk to a stranger. One needs to be a Muslim or a relative to be able to come into a family and talk to a woman. Thus, without the help of an authoritative woman, one cannot get always determine an explanation of an event, even after seeing it. Much of what happens in an Islamic country remains a mystery.

Because of that, everything that I am going to tell you about the countries' history, terrain topography, climate, trade, industry or mineral resources – all this will be imprecise and based on sources that are not sufficiently definitive and reliable.

3 The original is "high mountains", which was probably a stenographer's or typesetter's mistake. (Translator's note)

Literature on Afghanistan

Now I am going to switch to the issue of books on Afghanistan – which of those deserve your attention – for those of you who would like to learn more about Afghanistan than I will deliver in my lectures. What books you need to read? As to that, almost all major literature on Afghanistan comes to us from England. Anything on Afghanistan in German or French represents a rehash of the extensive English literature. In the latter, I will only mention works which deserve your attention and do not contain too much nonsense. I recommend *The Life of Abdur Rahman Amir of Afghanistan* and *Laws and Constitution of Afghanistan* written by Sultan Mohamed Khan–the secretary of Abdur Rahman.[4] The most recent book on Afghanistan, *Afghanistan* by Agnus [Angus] Hamilton has a Russian translation published by Berezovski. Notably, Hamilton was a young correspondent when the London Royal Geographic Society gave him an assignment to go to the Middle East. He went through Turkestan–I've seen him in Osh–and on the way he saw some things. He very skillfully used information from English and Indian literature, was able to find the most appropriate sources and wrote the book. It combines everything that English literature had on the topic, but Hamilton himself had not seen much because he rushed too fast through Turkestan into India – but even in India his mission was short. The book does not have anything solid or in depth. Anything related to our Turkestan is uninteresting and full of errors; as to Afghanistan–that information is more solid. This book could serve as a good source of Afghan study. But the book, as in any English work related to the matter, is too biased. For example – the narrative about Russia is inappropriately false, while anything about Britain is sheer flattery.

Now I jump into the past and recommend the book *An Account of the Kingdom of Cabul* by Elphinstone[5] published in 1815 (there is a "New and Revised Edition" – London, 1839).

You may ask why so old a book? The fact is that Oriental countries live by very conservative ways and we cannot expect big changes. In his expedition, Elphinstone had some very talented people along such as McCartney, Irvine and Strachey – they did a serious study of the country, studied the languages, ethnography, and architecture of Afghanistan and created a very successful and thorough work. From several points of view: ethnography, geography, ways of life, or people's characteristics – the work is still valuable despite its age.

For general information on the ethnography of Afghanistan, I would recommend Bellew. He has several works. The more interesting of them are *The Races of Afghanistan*, 1880 and *An Inquiry into the Ethnography of Afghanistan*.[6] I need to mention that even

---

4 Sultan Mohamed Khan, *The Life of Abdur Rahman, Amir of Afghanistan*, London: John Murray, 1900, 2 volumes, and Sultan Mohamed Khan, *The Constitution and Laws of Afghanistan*, London: John Murray, 1900. (Translator's note).

5 Mounstuart Elphinstone (*An Account of the Kingdom of Cabul and its Dependencies in Persia, Tartary and India*, London: John Murray, 1815). (Translator's note)

6 Henry Walter Bellew, *The Races of Afghanistan: Being a Brief Account of the Principal Nations Inhabiting that Country*, Calcutta and London: Thacker, Spink and Co, 1890 and H. W. Bellew, *An Inquiry into the Ethnography of Afghanistan*, Woking: The Oriental University Institute, 1891. (Translator's note).

though Bellew is serious enough, he did not possess sufficient material and his books resemble a conglomeration of newspaper articles.

To familiarize ourselves with the country from an ethnographic point of view, we have works written in Russian, by Aristov [7] *Anglo-Indian Caucases*[8] *(1900) and About Afghanistan and its Population*[9] (1898). Aristov's works are very interesting because he exhausted all the necessary literature and he did not miss any small detail, but the works are primarily related to the field of anthropology and represent significant but purely theoretical summations. Unfortunately for us, those works have almost no practical value – if at all.

Next, you must have an interest in Afghanistan's wars. On this topic, I can point to the following works: Kaye, *History of the War in Afghanistan*, 1878; Hensman, *The Afghan War of 1879-80*, London, 1881; Forbes, *The Afghan Wars 1839-42 and 1878-80*, London, 1892.[10] All these works, with the possible exception of Kaye, leave an impression of collections of raw material with unnecessary details, sometimes with a large political appendix as if they were written by civilians–that is correct to a certain degree. The works have neither military-technical analysis nor a definite military criterion. But they present a huge mass of detail, so you can draw necessary conclusions. Next, if you want to familiarize yourself with the history of Afghanistan I may point to Malleson's *History of Afghanistan*.[11] It is a very voluminous but not very serious book; it is occupied with the history of rulers instead of the history of people, but it still can provide some help.

Then, I've mentioned that there are a number of political works which describe the interrelations between England and Russia toward Afghanistan. There is a whole multitude of them.

These are the most serious of them which at the time created quite an impression:

Russo-Indian Question[: Historically, Strategically and Politically Considered] by F. [Frederic Chenevix] Trench. [London: MacMillan], 1869.

England and Russia in the East by H. [Henry] Rawlinson. [London: John Murray,] 1875.

Russian Turkestan, etc. *[Turkistan: Notes of a Journey in Russian Turkistan, Khokand, Bukhara, and Kuldja]* by [Eugene] Schuyler, in two volumes, [London: Sampson Low, Marston, Searle and Rivington,] 1876.

Invasions of India from Central Asia by Anonymous. [London: Bentley and Sons], 1879.

Russian Campaigns against the Akhal Tekke Turkomans, by Charles Marvin. [London: Allen and Co.], 1880.

7 N.A. Aristov (1847-?) – Russian orientalist and ethnographer. (Translator's note).

8 Англо-Индийский Кавказ

9 Об Афганистане и его населении

10 John William Kaye, *History of the War in Afghanistan*, London: Richard Bentley, 1851, 1858, 1874;, 2 volumes Howard Hensman, *The Afghan War of 1879-80*, London: W. H. Allen and Co, 1881; and Archibald Forbes, *The Afghan Wars 1839-42 and 1878-80*, New York: 1892. (Translator's note).

11 George Bruce Malleson, *The History of Afghanistan From the Earliest Period to the Outbreak of the War of 1878*, London: W. H. Allen and Co, 1879. (Translator's note).

Russia in Central Asia by Hugo Stumm. [Translated into English from German by J. W. Ozanne and Captain H Sachs, London: Harrison and Sons], 1885.

Coming Struggle for India by A[rminius] Vambery. [London: Cassell and Company,] 1885.

Russian Central Asia [including Kuldja, Bokhara, Kiva and Merv] by H[enry] Landsell, two volumes, [Boston: Houghton, Mifflin and Company], 1885.

Russia in Central Asia [in 1889 and the Anglo-Russian Question] by G[eorge N.] Curzon. [Longmans, Green & Co.], 1889.

The Rival Powers [in Central Asia] by [Josef] Popowski, [translated from German into English by Arthur Baring Brabant, edited by Charles E. D. Black, Westminster: Archibald Constable and Company], 1893.

Asiatic Neighbors by [Septimus Smett] Thornburn. [Edinburgh and London: William Blackwood and Sons], 1894.

Russia in Asia[, 1558-1899] by Alexis Krause. [London and New York: Henry Holt & Co.], 1899.

The Heart of Asia by F[rancis] H[enry] Skrine and Ed[ward] Den[ison] Ross, [London: Methuen & Co.] 1899.

The Middle Eastern Question [or some Political Problems of Indian Defence] by Val[entine] Chirol. [New York: E. P. Dutton and Company, 1903].

Due to lack of time to provide detailed characteristics of these books, I will limit myself to several remarks. The listed books 2, 7, 9 and 12 are the most fervent and Russophobic; the most moderate (and also most truthful) are numbers 10, 11 and 13. Thornburn's book is of more interest because while he talks about the Central Asian issue, he links it and its different stages to the issue of India and its politics. It is fundamentally correct and is a thorough and deep study. In the work of Skrine and Ross, thanks to Ross--who is a professor of the Persian language—there is a panoramic and well-elucidated historical perspective that many of the other books lack. Curzon's book, besides its sharp content, is also interesting for its bibliographic index.

As I've mentioned, I named only a number of the most prominent works. There are a whole series of minor works such as Malleson's *The Russo-Afghan Question*; Jerningham's *Russia's Warning*; Colonel Hanna's *Can Russia Invade India*; Noyce's *England, India and Afghanistan*, etc.[12] These were actually up to the political moment at the time, but did not have a lasting significance. Finally, there are quite a few interesting articles spread throughout English weekly publications which a specialist cannot bypass, but to name them in our study is impossible.

On North Afghanistan I recommend Yate's *Northern Afghanistan* which I've mentioned already. Further, for someone who is interested in Afghan language I can point to works of Dorns, Leech, Raverty, Trumpp and Darmesteter.[13] These scientists developed Afghan

12 George Bruce Malleson, *The Russo-Afghan Question and the Invasion of India*, London: George Routledge and Sons, 1885; Huburt Edward Henry Jerningham, *Russia's Warnings*, London: Chapman & Hall, 1885; Henry Bathurst Hanna, *Can Russia Invade India?*, Westminster: Archibald Constable and Co., 1895; and Frank Noyce, *England, India and Afghanistan*, London, C. J. Clay and Sons, 1902. (Translator's note).

13 B. A. Dorn, *A Chrestomathy of the Pushtu Language with a Glossary*, St. Petersburg, 1847; Leech,

grammar, its content and established its affiliation with family of Persian languages. But this is the area of theoretical study and what has been said is enough.

Those are the works in English that I recommend to you for study. They deserve some attention.

In Russian I can name Hamilton because as I was told it is in Russian translation right now. Then, there is the Abdur Rahman Khan's Autobiography in Persian, English translation or Russian translation by Grulev, 1910. The work is written by the Emir's secretary Mohamed-Khan. The work is interesting. But we need to emphasize two things: first of all the big lies and boasting of this Asiatic person, which permeate the entire book make difficult to see the real truth behind it; then there is that English flavor we often see in English works and which (voluntarily or involuntarily) Abdur Rahman Khan adopted. Then, I cannot bypass the old work of Gregoriev – *Kabulistan and Kafiristan*.[14] The author was the very-well read secretary of the Russian Geographical Society who had been able to exhaust all the materials related to Afghanistan beginning from time immemorial. Much in the book today is almost laughable, but a lot still of interest. As to the part of the book on Kafiristan –it is better to leave it out. To learn about Kafiristan, one would better take the book *The Kafirs of the Hindu Kush* by Robertson.[15] There is a Russian translation by Polovtsev and myself. To learn about the Afghan war I would recommend reading Sobolev's *Anglo-Russian Quarrel*, volumes 1-4, 1882.

To clarify economical issues related to the Middle East and to Afghanistan in particular, we cannot leave out a book by M.P. Fyodorov *Rivalry of Trade Interests in the East*. A book by P. A. Rittikh published as a manuscript *Afghan Question, 1905* is very useful for a brief familiarization of the country. It has a list of sources for Afghan study that is not too bad. If someone wants the full list of the sources – he can find it in the *Bibliography of Afghanistan* published by the Society of Oriental Studies in Petrograd and edited by myself. A wealth of ordinary life pictures and peculiarities can be found in a book *The Russian Embassy's Travel in Afghanistan 1878-1879* by observant Yavorski who was a doctor with General's Stoletov's mission at the court of Emir Shir Ali Khan.

I need to point out the work of Captain V. Oranovski *Afghanistan*, Ashkhabad, 1895. It was written using general information but also some secret materials. This small work nowadays is obsolete.

Those who would like to do a deeper study of Afghanistan should not limit themselves to the suggested short list of materials, but need to expand it significantly. They cannot bypass periodical issues such as *The Collection of Materials on Asia* which has been

---

R. 1838. "Epitome of the Grammars of the Brahuiky, the Balochky and the Panjabi Languages. With Vocabularies of the Baraky, the Pashi, the Laghmani, the Cashgari, the Teerhai, and the Deer Dialects." Calcutta. *Journal of the Asiatic Society of Bengal* 7: pp.711-32; H. G. Raverty, *A Grammar of the Pukhto, Pushto or Language of the Afghans*, London: Williams and Norgate,1859; Ernst Trump, *Grammar of the Pashto or Language of the Afghans, Compared with the Iranian and North Indian Idioms*, London: Messrs Trübner & Co., 1873; and Darmesteter, James. 1890, *Chants Populaires des Afghans*, Paris: Imprimerie Nationale, E. Leroux. (Translator's note).

14 This is a translation of the corresponding volume of Ritter's *ZEMLEVEDENIE* (Earth Study), but much expanded and corrected with classic additions. Also E.Reclus' *Earth and People* deserves some attention. (Author's note).

15 George Scott Robertson, *The Kafirs of the Hindu Kush*, London: Lawrence and Bullen, Ltd., 1896.

published by the General Staff; *Information on Countries bordering the Turkestan Military District*, published by the district's headquarters and newspapers such as *Turkestan Records*, *Trans-Caspian Review* or Indian newspapers such as *The Pioneer* (Allahabad), *Times of India* (Lahore), *Civil and Military Service Gazette* (Lahore), etc.

Many items of interest, especially from a political point of view, are possible to find on pages of English newspapers such as *The Times*, *Morning Star*, *Standard*, etc.

Geographical position of Afghanistan

And now I move to a description of Afghanistan itself. First of all military essays usually define the country's geographic location, i.e. its position against the geographic grid. On that matter, we have data of English origin (*Statesman's Year Book*, 1910) which positions Afghanistan between 61° and 72° East longitude with a narrow strip going to 75° (the Wakhan Corridor) and between 29° and 38° 20' North latitude.[16] I need to mention that here in the lectures I will not tire you with numbers or details which you could not remember anyhow; but in the printed version of the lectures that I am going to publish, I will make references to various sources, put in exhaustive information, use figures and numbers and develop some aspects of the lectures in detail.

By the just-mentioned English sources, Afghanistan's area is 250 thousand square miles. If we look into Russian sources (*Brockhouse and Efron Encyclopedic Dictionary*, Volume 1 for example), then we would see that our data does not align with the English: the longitude is about same (difference in a few minutes), but the latitude difference is quite significant. Russian sources show the Northern border going to 37° 15', i.e. somewhat lower than the English version; and the Southern border is shown at 28°, i.e. 1° lower than the English. We should remember that these numbers are taken from different sources, which are not coordinated with each other. Some of the information is taken from travelers' data which sometimes is a guess. But we could ask what produces the differences? It is the result of differences of the view angles – usual in the practice toward Oriental countries. One European power presses its way and another – in other direction, depending on what they find necessary based on political considerations.

Looking at that area of 250 thousand square miles, one can see an irregularly shaped quadrangle. By its size, Afghanistan is just short of Hungary's and eight times larger than Belgium. If more detailed information on Afghanistan geographical location is of interest to you, Afghanistan represents an interim step from India to Iran. For those interested, I recommend Grigiriev's work *Kabulistan and Kafiristan.*

Borders of Afghanistan

The next issue that should interest us is the Afghanistan border. Even a passing glance at the Afghan borders reveals the following: the border with Persia in the West is practically a straight line and only has some curves in the South. And the border with Baluchistan

16 We can see how variable these numbers are: in the same book of 1904 which positions Afghanistan between 60° 30' and 74° 30' East longitude and latitude 30° and 38° 20' North latitude. Afghanistan's area was shown as 215 thousand square miiles in the 1904 book. (Author's note).

is also simple. But there is a completely different picture with Afghanistan's border with Russia and India. Those lines are very broken; they change directions depending on rivers, mountain ridges and passes. But this border is shaped not only nature, but also political struggle. You know that borders have great importance in relation to military geography. The border is a line where the forward forces of countries armies' contact each other during peace time. There one nation or the other locates reconnaissance, advance guards of political struggle, customs, etc. It is a line which is taken into an account when fortresses' are built and the future strategic deployment of armed forces is planned. Finally, the border has a small, but often important, everyday facet. Quite often the border area houses a complex sum of political enforcements, old undecided quarrels, badly-divided resources and sediments of temporarily-quelled enmities. Most often that happens in Asiatic countries where borders are established by an agreement between two European powers – too large and busy with their imperial policies to try to grasp the essence of what the border area needs and the misunderstandings of small, unenlightened groups of Asian peoples. I have an example.

The border between Bukhara and Afghanistan in the Western Pamir area runs along the Panj River which has never served as a border through long centuries of Central Asian history. But, in 1895, the river was declared a border on the suggestion of England. On one side sprawled Afghan (English in essence) possessions, on other side – Bukhara's (Russian in essence). How insurmountable that obstacle is we can judge by the following case. Often a Tajik (the local mountaineer) had his hut on the left bank of Panj, but his small patch of arable land was on the right bank: that was the way his ancestors lived for entire centuries. But two European countries entered the area and told him that the right bank is only for Russian citizens or person under the Russian protectorate; the left bank – is only for British citizens or their protectorate.[17] Crossing the river was prohibited under any circumstances. And the owner of that usually miniscule patch across the river is forced to resort to the following method of cultivating it: covertly at night he wades or swims across the river, plows the field and before the dawn sneaks back like a thief. And it continues. He waits until harvest time, covertly crosses the river again, reaps his crop and again returns home like a thief.

Of course, under such circumstances in Asia, where conflicts are common, there could be a provocation. There will be a person whom that kind of the border does not suit and that will produce an argument over land or other quarrels.

Not far from the Amu-Darya River, next to Bosaga kishlak[18] there were continual border disputes that always ended in brawls and beatings. A careful on-site study of the situation revealed the source of discontent – it was improper distribution of irrigation water. A commission with included representatives of the governments of Afghanistan and Bukhara, supervised by one of our General Staff officers, figured it out, organized water redistribution and things quieted down.

17 The right or left bank is judged from the perspective of looking downstream in the direction that the river is flowing. (Translator's note).

18 Kishlak – a small village in Central Asian countries. (Translator's note).

Afghanistan's border with Russia

This and other examples show us that, from a military-geographical point of view, borders have significant importance – especially in Asia – and we need to pay serious attention to them. Let us examine the Russo-Afghan border first. You can see that it starts at the point where Persia, Russia and Afghanistan meet each other. The place, called the Zulfikar Pass – is interesting historically and is a very picturesque mountain corridor squeezing the riverbed.[19] From the pass, the border goes eastward across low mountains, uvals[20], steppe plateaus, and shortly before reaching the Amu-Darya River – through the desert. The border then continues along the Amu-Darya. The border length before it reaches the Amu-Darya is about 615 versts.[21] Out of those 615 versts, the most interesting to us are the first 250. The far spurs of the western part of the Safid Kuh mountain range (*Parapamisus*) reach there. But mountains there are not too high and are passable almost everywhere – the mountain passes practically do not differ from the mountains themselves. Some bordering regions represent the steppes but with a shorter period of grass vegetation than in Europe. The water supply is somewhat more critical there, but if you look carefully at the map, you can notice some names marked with either K or *rod.*[22] These are very important points in the waterless areas. These points are fairly numerous in this area and there are enough of them to support crossing the area with sizable detachments, let alone small expeditions. South from there lies the western Safid Kuh (Parapamisus), but is fairly accessible and has several passes which are open for traffic all year around. Cross the mountains – and you step into the rich Herat valley.

You can see that this 250 versts stretch of the border is accessible and provides a convenient entrance to the Harirud Valley[23] and from there it is an approach to the so-called Kandahar operational direction of advance. There are three such directions of advance for an offensive on India on an operational scale: Kandahar, Kabul and Pamir –I will pay special attention to these later. The border area adjacent to Kushka leads into the first sector – the most important of the three. Out of the three directions, this is the furthest by its length, but it is the most convenient, with no serious obstacles and is even accessible by wheeled conveyance.

For the next 400 versts, the border goes north-east and runs into the Amu-Darya River. There are fewer and fewer wells and movement across that area is much more difficult. Before you reach the Amu-Darya, movement becomes much harder. Studies of the border area show that many people suffered and even died there because they could not

19 Harirud River. (Translator's note).

20 Uval – in Russian, low outstretched heights with a flat, slightly prominent or rolling top. (Translator's note).

21 Versta – a now-obsolete Russian unit of length equal to 1.067 kilometers, 3500 feet or 0.66 miles. (Translator's note).

22 K stands for *колодец* – well; род. – Russian abbreviation for *родник* – spring (water). (Translator's note).

23 The Harirud River is called the Tedzhen River in Turkmenistan and Russia and the Hari Rud in Afghanistan and Iran. The river flows north from Afghanistan to Turkmenistan, then borders Iran and Turkmenistan and finally turns into Turkmenistan where it disappears into the sands of the Kara Kum desert in modern-day Turkmenistan. (Translator's note).

find a well. As if that is not enough, if a detachment crossed that border area and moved southward – it would run into the Band-i Turkestan Mountain Range and even deeper South into the understudied – judging by the blank white spots on the map – and barely accessible part of the Safid Kuh Mountains (Parapamisus) and its spurs. Consequently, this 400-verst stretch has very little interest for us.

I have to mention the official acts which define our border there. We had three demarcation agreements with Afghanistan. They were signed: the first on January 31, 1873; the second in July 1887 and the third in March 1895. The first agreement declared the Amu-Darya River as the northern border of Afghanistan. The second agreement defined the north-western Afghan border up to the Amu-Darya – it mainly settled the issue of the Panjdeh oasis which was the cause of a dispute and the agreement. The third agreement deals with the section of the border adjacent to Pamir.

The Russo-Afghan border meets at the Amu-Darya River near Bosaga kishlak. The Amu-Darya is a huge, natural and historic barrier – a first-class barrier – a serious and unmistakable border. Still, throughout Central Asia's history it has been crossed by small and large forces. Alexander the Great of Macedonia, Genghis-Khan and Babur crossed it in strength. Abdur Rahman Khan crossed it in the upper part when he was leaving inhospitable Russia to ascend the Afghan throne.[24] To give you a chance to know what the river is like even in places suitable for crossing, I am going to tell you my own impression of it. In the summer of 1904 I was doing research of the so-called Chubek crossings leading from East Bukhara to Badakhshan.[25]

Before me the water was turbulent as if it were in a boiling kettle, a muddy yellow water mass about 12 versts wide. The noise of the running water was unbelievable. It was a river-giant, capricious and willful. Looking long at the water produced dizziness and cancelled any thought that a human could dare to cross it. But I understood that it was possible after I was briefed on the specific technical peculiarities of crossing such a river. First – one needs to move by zigzags, not straight – from one shoal to another (using the shoals for rest). One needs to pick a specific time to cross and to find a suitable horse and guide. Smugglers cross the river quite often and they frequently do it at night which is even riskier. It is funny that the smugglers' dogs know how to cross the river, having developed the special skills. While this mighty river could be crossed in its wide places it is hard to imagine crossing it in the narrow places where it runs like a waterfall. But history preserves memories of light cavalry units crossing the river even by swimming in such places.

And so, beginning from the western part and up to its sharp curve near Kalai- Khumb, the Amu-Darya represents a solid border and a very serious barrier; crossing the river in the course of a war would entail huge tactical and technical difficulties.[26]

From the curve past Kalai-Khumb, the Amu-Darya course runs north-south and changes its name to the regional Panj (Five Rivers). The Panj border runs as follows:

24 Abdur Rahman Khan was Emir of Afghanistan from 1880-1901. He spent 1869-1879 in exile in Tsarist Samarkand and Tashkent. (Translator's note).

25 One of the 34 provinces of Afghanistan. It is located in the north-east of the country, between the Hindu Kush and the Amu Darya. (Translator's note).

26 One can find details in V. Grulyov's work *Amu-Darya*. The work though is purely a compilation and is imperfect in many ways. (Author's note).

the first 200+ versts run north-south; near Ishkashim, it turns eastward and changes its name to the Vakhan-Darya River (local name for Amu-Darya) until it joins with its tributary with the Pamir River. Then the border becomes the Pamir River and Lake Zorkul. The eastern bank of the lake marks the end of the water border and after that, the border goes by land for about 250 versts up to the Beik mountain pass, where the borders of Russia, China and Afghanistan meet each other. This last part goes through the world's highest mountains (Beik's altitude is 16,000 feet).

I called Lake Zorkul by its ancient local name, which in Kara-Kirgiz means "Big" (or more precisely – "Strong) lake. I have to mention that I will keep using local names and not European or new Asian rechristenings. There is nothing more laughable than the plagiarism of travelers – European or Asian – who are always trying to glorify their own names or the names their relatives or rulers by replacing the ancient names (always very precise) with new, often dull, names which testifies to human vanity. Zorkul has several other names: Grand, Wood's Lake, Victoria Lake – those are fruits of European ambitions; or Haus-Kalyan, Kol-i-Sikandari, Sir-i-kol – the same, only Asian.

A few words about the Panj River. The Panj constitutes 400 versts of the Russo-Afghan border and only after the Kalai-Khumb curve it becomes the Amu-Darya. The ability to cross the Panj depends on where you are along it. If it is a narrow space, then you will encounter a turbulent water corridor with no chance to cross it on foot. You will not find a boat and crossing it on horseback is dangerous. In such places, people usually cross the Panj by using a *tursuk* – a kind of a raft made of inflated animal skins. At other places, where the currents are not that strong, people can cross, except during the May – August period when the Panj swells up with water from the melted snow of the mountains. In wintertime, one can cross the Panj anywhere. In a word, the Panj is not really difficult to cross, but that fact does not have serious practical significance, since there are no major routes in the North-South direction, so the river has nothing to block.

Now I will talk about political origin of the border. As I've already mentioned, the border was established in March of 1895. It was caused by actions of the Afghan emir, Abdur Rahman Khan, who misused the vagueness of articles in the agreement between England and Afghanistan and declared all Wakhan, Shugnan and Rushan as part of Afghanistan's Badakshan. He exploited the locals' ignorance as well as the ignorance of some of our old time diplomats. He first accused the Russians of wrongly taking Shugan and Rushan from him, and later occupied these areas with troops. In 1893, there was a sensational clash near Somatashi where Colonel Ionov destroyed the Afghan post. When the investigation of the incident began, it turned out that Abdur Rahman Khan was wrong, that Shugnan and Rushan did not belong to Badakhshan and all that business ended up with the 1895 agreement. By the agreement, Bukhara got the right bank's Wakhan, Shugnan and Rushan. Afghanistan received Darvaz from Bukhara's left bank. As a result, the Panj became a political border. Of course, if you look deeper into the matter you will realize that was pure hypocrisy – two European powers disposed of poor mountaineers as was advantageous for them without consulting the people or history. As the result, there were tears and injustice. Seven year later I was there as the commander of the Pamir detachment and saw with my own eyes, the fate of natives' pushed into evil yoke of Bukhara in Rushan and Shugnan. It was a painful picture. I fought as I could. I acquired a brutal enemy in the person of the local bek[27] who even tried to poison me; but I hardly could do anything to repair the damage done by Russia. And do not doubt those pictures of people's hardship and suffering: they are taken from life and in back countries of Central Asia and those scenes will not be overcome anytime soon, believe me.

Looking at our border with Afghanistan you will see that in the area closest to India – in the south of our Pamir – there is a small tongue of the mini-country Wakhan inserted between the borders. It was ceded to Afghanistan by England. Politically and historically, England could keep Wakhan or give it to Russia – which would be fair for many reasons, but did not do it. What sense does that little tongue riveted between Russian and English borders make?

The little patch of land is a modest buffer between Russia and India, an interesting addition to the long belt of buffers surrounding India – to make sure that the buffer system is not broken even in that inaccessible place. Establishing such buffers around India is an axiom for England. Little Wakhan obviously must carry out the same political and strategic mission as Afghanistan, Eastern Persia, Tibet, etc. You can be sure that there are no Afghans [Pashtuns] in Wakhan and it is a foreign country for them. There is only one mini-fortress, Kala Bar Panj, with some "general" commanding a hundred or so people. The country is completely Tajik, mountainous and poor; the real masters are Englishmen and the [local authorities] are probably only sentries manning guard posts. And the masters achieve everything [in Wakhan] that is required from a buffer – organizing reconnaissance, providing a command and control system, building roads, undertaking political machinations of all sorts. [The British] use it as a reliable vista to cover their actions under the guise of Afghanistan's despotic decisions.

Now, after [my earlier] brief description of the Kandahar operational direction, I need to say a few words about the Kabul operational direction, which has a road network running from the Amu-Darya crossing to the Hindu Kush and then across it through one of several mountain passes to Kabul. From there it goes by mountain passes across the Suleiman Mountain Range into the Indus River valley. As you see, on this relatively short distance there is the first barrier – the Amu-Darya River. The second one is the Hindu Kush Mountain chain with its passes. And, finally, there are the Suleiman Mountains which, if not very difficult topographically, there is a lack of food, fuel and water; the local economic conditions are severe. You noticed that even though the distance is relatively short, it has first-rate obstacles across it. Even taking Kabul – the center of the country's life – would involve difficulties. And if this is done – do not think that something really big has been accomplished. One has to remember that in Afghanistan, the people live in proud and freedom-loving communities and the ties which hold them together as one entity are tentative and artificial. Even if you capture the center of such a country – as is Kabul – that means nothing. The Anglo-Afghan wars showed us that the English capturing Kabul did not mark the subjugation of the country or its pacification. Contrary to that, it gave rise to a nation-wide popular upspring. In a word, the Kabul sector has many obstacles. Nonetheless, history shows us that military leaders usually moved to India using this way, despite the need to overcome great obstacles. Thus, in 1221, Genghis-Khan pursued Jalaluddin – Khan of Khorezm; Babur used

27 Local ruler in Central Asian countries. (Translator's note).

this direction several times. One should note that in history, things happen that do not conform to contemporary scientific conclusions. History disproves geography and must be heard.

And finally I will talk about the Pamir operational direction which is extremely difficult due to its conditions. When using that direction starting from the Fergana Valley, you would have to overcome the Alai Mountain Range, then move through Alai Valley which is free of snow drifts only four-five months a year and after that – to cross the even-higher Zaalaiski Mountain Range. Your route continues into the Pamir mountains– easier to cross but still, poor, severe and without any food resources. Suppose you overcome all these problems, crossed the chain of mountain passes, survived the hardship of 12,000 feet altitude – it is still far from over. Before you rises the white wall of the Hindu Kush – accessible in a few places but not year around. From its snowy peaks you move down into godforsaken Dardistan. Reading my translation of Durand,[28] you will get a full impression about all the horrors of that road and it will shock you. Imagine wild rock and cliffs and people crawling on them with loads on their back. Horses cannot go on these paths. Once I traveled these trails. My friend's translator – a fit and vigorous man – became an old man on the trip; people become gray-haired and begin to feel a fear of open space. I stayed behind once and when I caught up with the detachment – I found two our translators crying. They were saying: "We are afraid to go there – we will die."

This small vignette suggests to you how difficult the sector is. Continue your trek and you will descend into the Kashmir Valley – the most beautiful valley in the world, but your ordeal is not over yet. After the valley, there are more mountains before you, if not as difficult as before. In essence, all that direction is horror incarnate. Neither artillery nor cavalry can move that way. The most you can do – is to move infantry and it is still questionable what would remain of it. But history tells us that there were cases when some detachments went through that operational direction. It is prudent to note that Englishmen spent a lot of money fortifying their northern frontier and building fortresses; their political literature is laced with fears that the Russian army can come through this sector. They say that it would be enough for such a cutthroat as Skobelev to get though the Hindu Kush Mountains with a crack detachment – even if it were not too big – and appear in the Kashmir…the consequences of it would be far reaching.[29] If this is so, and the Englishmen are right – then the choice of the Pamir operational direction could justify all the efforts required to cross it. It is very difficult, but if you prepare yourself to push across it, the result will be huge. Surprise will play a big role. There is a story – to tell the truth more like a legend – about one of India's conquerors – Uguz-Khan. That conqueror went by the places where a pack horse could not move. He went on the southern spurs of the Eastern Hindu Kush Mountains, traversed the Karakorum Mountain Range, then moved through the southern part of Tibet and across the Himalayas and, like a bolt from the blue, appeared in the Kashmir Valley. Legend says that he had about 40,000 horsemen. He stunned India and took

28 [Colonel Algernon] Durand, *The Making of a Frontier*, [London: Thomas Nelson & Sons, 1899]. (Author's note).

29 General Mikhail Dmitrevich Skobelev (1843-1882) is remembered for his conquest of Central Asia and his dynamic role in the Russo-Turkish War of 1877-1878. He was a bogeyman for the British in India. (Translator's note).

it by assault. Contemporary scholars doubt this account, but in Central Asia's lore the legend stubbornly survives. And if it is true – it proves that the Asian mountains are not an insurmountable obstacle to the brave and tenacious heart.

Afghanistan's border with India

Such are the Russo-Afghan border and operational directions in brief. We will talk about them in more detail at the appropriate time. Now we come to the border of Afghanistan with India, i.e. essentially with England. If I choose to familiarize you with the Russo-Afghan border in still more detail, I cannot do the same with the Indo-Afghan border because many things about it are unclear and there is so much political guile which conceals the essence and purpose of the border. Some small mountain range, pass or tunnel will stir up a lot of trouble. The Englishmen are masters of the situation there and they wage a systematic struggle to establish the border that they want. The border generally goes from Borogill Pass through Chitral, Peshawar and further toward Kuh-Malik-Siyakh where the borders of Afghanistan, Baluchistan and Persia meet each other. The border was established by Mortimer Durand's agreements in Kabul in 1893. If you discern the main articles of the agreements (we are not talking about details), you will see that the Englishmen gave Wakhan, Kafiristan, the Asmara Valley, Lal-Pur and a part of Waziristan to Emir Abdur Rahman Khan. But they got New-Chaman station, Chagekh, the rest of Waziristan, Bulun-Kel, Kuram, Bajaur, Swat, Dir, Chitral and the Afridi's country.[30] Now, the question is why? After all, some of those territories, such as the Suleiman Mountains, are populated primarily by native Afghan people. How could the emir reject his own people?

Scholars of Afghanistan – Kene and Aristov – conclude that Abdur Rahman Khan did the right thing because the population of the Suleiman Mountains was always volatile – it helped invade India, but was always hard to handle. So Abdur Rahman Khan unloaded them onto the Englishmen's shoulders.[31] The experience of wars on the north-western Indian border seems to support this assumption. In the course of the last 50 years, the Englishmen spent more than 700 million rupees just on wars and expeditions to secure the north-western border with Afghanistan. So thinks Aristov, a civilian, who draws a parallel between our operation in the Caucasus and those of England on the north-western border. I think the civilian scholar is mistaken. Englishmen know the history of conquests of India very well and they are good at applying their political experience from the historical past. And the past tells us that the Hindu Kush [barrier] would not that difficult for a future conqueror. But he will stop short of the Suleiman Mountains – and sometimes for a long time – selecting a base on the Kabul – Ghazni – Kandahar line for future actions. He would then go to work on the Suleiman Mountains: luring inhabitants to his side, setting up his intelligence network, securing his communications, constituting advance guards, etc. And only after completing the complicated task of working on the Afghans, the future victor will move into India. This clearly shows

30 Afridi – Pushtun tribe. (Translator's note).

31 If we to believe Hamilton, Abdur Rahman Khan did that under pressure and tried to keep the tribes in his country. Agnus [Angus] Hamilton, *Afghanistan*, [New York: Charles Scribner's Sons,] 1906, p.409. (Author's note).

that the eastern Afghans always played a major role in the conquests of India. And the Englishmen have studied this thoroughly; no matter how difficult it is for them or how expensive, they have retained the probable launch site for a future advance guard for the invasion of India – its territory, positions and passes. No doubt the Englishmen are right and not Aristov.

As to the northern region, i.e. Bajaur, Swat, Dir or Chitral, this is a different story. There the Russian and English borders are close together. England cannot afford to give these mountain territories into the weak hands of an [Afghan] emir. These mountain territories are ruled by tyrannical kinglets (always demigods) – who are too evil and treacherous to leave without political supervision. Thus, in the late 1880s through the 1890s, England carried out considerable political and organizational work in Dardistan. And again – England is right. The Pamir sector is difficult as we just discussed, but surprises are possible and England tries to mitigate their scale and bitterness.

As to the Afghan borders with Baluchistan and Persia, these are pretty simple because they squeeze against desolate and undesirable regions. There, technical considerations and convenience rather than politics rule the process of creating the borders. That is why we see either a straight line such as the Afghan-Persian border; or zigzags – as at the border with Baluchistan. Only in the south-western corner of Afghanistan – in the Seistan region – the border plays – or should we say "unscrupulously plays". That tasty piece leaves Englishmen sleepless. Once, the Englishman McMahon came to the region under the pretense of establishing the border and regulating Seistan's water, but he stayed in the region much longer than good manners dictate.[32] The business of the border is still unfinished there today.

32 For details about this, see Hamilton, pp.211-222. (Author's note). Colonel Sir Henry MacMahon was involved in trying to settle the border between Persia and Afghanistan in 1903-1905. Seistan is fed by the waters of the Helmand River as well as the Khash Rud and the Farah Rud. It is a marsh land valued for its water and agriculture. (Translator's note).

2

Terrain of Afghanistan

I come to the issue of Afghanistan's terrain. I remind you that our study's scope is going to be more practical than theoretical.

What is Afghanistan? In the sense of terrain, it is a country in which four-fifths of the territory is mountains – wooded or without vegetation at all. Between the mountains lay areas where cereals are grown – they are the major source of food for the population. But such areas are infrequent. Most of the terrain in mountain valleys is either plateaus or mountain slopes; these are open to cold winds, their soil is unsuitable or the slopes cannot hold water because they are too steep and the soil dries quickly.

In a word, for one reason or another, those areas are mostly infertile. Generally Afghan soil is infertile; natural resources are meager and this excludes the possibility of serious agricultural development in the future. One does not have to be a prophet to predict that Afghanistan will never be a wealthy country.

If we look at a general orographic[1] map of Afghanistan, we can see that the basis of the whole system – its skeleton – is the Hindu Kush.[2] It begins in the north-eastern part of the country and goes in a south-south-western direction gradually becoming lower, and disappearing in the western and southern region of Afghanistan. Mountains spread from the backbone to the north, south and south-west like a fan. Somewhere in the south-eastern part of the country is the lowest point of its surface. The average height difference is about 6,000 feet in the north-east, but it is only 2,000 feet in the south-west. It would be proper for us to begin our study of Afghanistan's terrain with the Hindu Kush.

But while studying a country, we have first to define at which angle we look at its terrain. When we study European terrain, we never forget that travel and communication is conducted there by railroads or highways using trains, automobiles, carriages or wagons. Only occasionally we might mention traveling on horseback and even less often – traveling on foot. But when you study an Oriental country, the picture is different. There you can travel either by foot or horseback and methods of human communication are limited to those two primordial means. With such simple ways of communication, the attitude toward terrain is also simple. There we might be less demanding than in

1 Orography -The study of the physical geography of mountains and mountain ranges. (Translator's note).

2 The Hindu Kush's role in Afghan history is very significant. "The Hindu Kush, with its branches and spurs, is the dominant geographical entity of Afghanistan. It is a watershed of the Amu-Darya, Indus and Helmand. It also represents a rampart which separates the Turkish and Afghan peoples. It preserves remains of independent peoples such as the Hazara and Kafirs, among its mountains. It speaks about its natural resistance power." [Septimus Smett] Thorburn, *Asiatic Neighbors*, [[Edinburgh and London: William Blackwood and Sons, 1894], pp.95-96. (Author's note).

Europe. A person here can go almost everywhere and an Oriental horse can do it as well – if it is of mountain breed. Here people are not afraid of mountains and do not expect a special guide like they do in Switzerland. Only those cliffs where just the chamois can jump are considered inaccessible for people. In Europe, we are accustomed to different methods of travel and the terrain is studied from a sophisticated and demanding point of view – we have to remember the wheels.

Hindu Kush

And here is the Hindu Kush before you. If anyone wants to find out the name's origin then you can find some information in Humboldt's[3] and Ritter's works. There are several versions of it. But one of those you may want to remember since it is commonly known. Literally it means "Death of a Hindu". When the conquerors of India returned to the North after their victorious campaigns, they took dark-skinned male and female captives with them. These people, who had grown under the hot southern sun, felt great discomfort even at the approaches to Kabul. And they died from the cold on the snowy ridges of the Hindu Kush. Thus the name: "Death of a Hindu".

By Hindu Kush, we mean that first-rate mountain ridge which serves as the watershed of the Amu-Darya and Indus and continues for 650 versts as a huge arc slightly bent toward the south. At its eastern part, the Hindu Kush joins the Himalayan system (Mustag-Karakorum) which comes almost at a right angle to it and creates a unique folds' cluster (Indian Cluster) with a multitude of mountain peaks above 25,000 feet tall.

I cannot resist the urge to share my memory with you about that majestic area. If you get lucky, after learning some Oriental language or mountain dialect, you may go to these countries. A picture will unfold before your eyes that you have never seen elsewhere and which you will never forget throughout your life. On the horizon before you stand dozens of giant mountains, each at least 25,000 feet high. You will not find such a family of giants anywhere else. They are striking in their size, majestic quietness and white cover. You will talk to the locals about religion, the old ways of life, etc. – the things they like to discuss the most. And one of those giants will be virtually present at that talk standing some dozen versts away. You go on with your talk and the mountain silently watches you, impassive and persistent. No wonder that the local people constantly mention it in their legends and fairy tales.

Lately, the Hindu Kush has been divided into Eastern and Western parts. The former is a southern outskirt of the Pamir mountains with the average height about 19-20,000 feet; the latter – somewhat less. Our subject is the Eastern Hindu Kush. It begins approximately at 74° East latitude. That part of the Hindu Kush consists of two mountain ranges. The northern range represents a watershed; the southern range runs 10-20 versts from the northern and is somewhat lower.

At latitude 69½°, the East Hindu Kush creates a huge knot in the depths in which the Khavak mountain pass lies. Alexander the Great, Timur and others had moved through that pass. From the Khavak pass, mountain spurs run in various directions. West from the knot, the Hindu Kush narrows and keeps this shape up to the Iraqi passes, where it

3 [Baron Alexander von Humboldt]. *L'Asie Centrale.* [three volumes, 1843]. (Author's note).

widens significantly and turns into very tangled system. The snow line of Hindu Kush probably lies around 14-16,000 feet. The height of the passes reaches 12-14,000 feet and higher.

I turn your attention to an entity that has a low priority in European geography. There is so little interest in mountain passes that people do not even try to understand what they are. People just cross the mountains from one country into another and that is that. Even in the works of good geographers, you will find the explanation: a mountain pass is the lowest point of the mountain range where crossing the mountains is the most convenient. This is an error. We will use the term "mountain pass" for the area where people generally cross mountains. It could be the lowest, middle or even highest point – that depends on a number of attendant circumstances. As an example, the Odudi mountain pass lies in the high and rocky Yazgulemski mountain range. It lies at the highest point of the ridge. The rest of the ridge, although lower, is a vertical wall which is totally impassable. If you observe the pass from afar, you will see a small dot projected against the highest point...If you are lucky you may see a caravan crossing the range. And so that high solitary dot is the crossing point.

How can one explain this? It can be explained by the fact that in other places the mountains are covered with snow, in most cases so deep that there is no possibility to walk through it – and so people found a point (regardless of its height) where the snow is cleared away by the wind acting as a broom and a horse has an opportunity to clamber up the rocks. Thus, I repeat, using the term "mountain pass", we imply any point on the range line where the act of crossing from one side of the mountain to the other one occurs regardless of its height. While talking about mountain passes in Asia, we shall examine it from several points of view. First, is it passable for pack animals or a person on foot (here it would be prudent to take into account whether it is a common traveler or a local mountaineer – we need to make this distinction – the reason will become clear later).

Second, is the pass "summer" or "winter"--during what season it is more passable or only passable? And third, what is the duration of time when it is passable? It could be "open year round", or "open such and such months" or "open one month in the year".

Mountain passes are the most important thing in Asian geography and require study. Now the question is what determines the practical importance of the passes?

The regions we are studying are *mountainous.* As long as human groups limit themselves to the resources provided by the valleys they live in, the issue of mountain passes is less important. But when the matter of the wider distribution of the population arises, when the population's activity in a particular region becomes the activity of a state, then the country interests us enough for study (some small band of people lost in a lone valley would not be of interest to us); when the spiritual and economic ties in the country expand – then the importance of mountain passes expands. In the Caucasus as well as in the Hindu Kush, one can find the situation at every turn where there are two valleys separated by a mountain range without a pass. There are two different communities, two peoples, often speaking completely different languages. If there is no passes – peoples live in separate universes. You understand the importance of the passes in such cases. Remember, we are not talking about communication lines, mail or telegraph – we are looking at the issue to determine if there is any kind basic line of communication between two states, i.e. if there are some points that ensure traffic throughout most of the year – and how that would influence their fate. No wonder that the mountain passes in Asia often represent knots holding keys to historical puzzles.

We intellectuals can clearly see that the pass is one of the essential geographical factors, but my observations show me that the ordinary people understand that – if they are living in the mountain countries. When I lived and worked in the Pamir Mountains, I asked myself a question: what primary geographical topics would interest such primitive people as the Kara-Kirgiz? And I concluded that they are interested in water, pastures and *mountain passes* – they give names to these objects first. What is striking that while traveling with a Kirgiz and talking with him about the countryside, if you ask him about the names of mountain ridges, mountains or other things of interest, he may not be able to tell you because he probably do not know them. He would describe a mountain as "white" or "tall" but without its name. But ask him about the pass – and he will name it immediately. Each and every pass has its name, but why? Because it is very valuable: it leads to neighbors, pasture or water. The concept of "pass" itself is described in the Kirgiz language with three or four words. Note that this is in a primitive, poor and undeveloped language as Kara-Kirgiz. A Kirgiz will attach the names of descriptive body parts or adopt a descriptive word from Persian to the pass just to describe it more exactly.

The issue of passes must be highlighted in Asian countries' geography. It would be great to find some special work on the passes with the addition of valuable historical references, but unfortunately such a book does not exist and I cannot recommend anything related to the issue. You can find examples and a description of the methods of research on a series of passes (in the eastern Hindu Kush) in my work *North India Theater*, Volume One.

I now turn to the western Hindu Kush. In its first part, it is higher than the mountains of Switzerland but lower than the eastern Hindu Kush. The average height difference there is 15-18,000 feet and there are more than 20 passes. They all will be listed in my published lectures, but for now I believe it will be sufficient if you memorize some of them.

First of all is the Khavak Pass (11,640 feet); not far away from it is the Tal' or Tul' Pass (12,300 feet), then further – the Kaushan or Kushan Pass (14,340 feet), the Khabardar (Chakhardar or Chardara) Pass (13,900 feet) and the Shibrski Pass (9,800 feet). Among them, the most famous historically is the Khavak Pass through which, according to lore, crossed Alexander the Great, Tamerlane and Genghis-Khan (although another version has Genghis-Khan crossing further to the west). As to their practicability, there is no reliable information. Almost all of them support pack-animal traffic although the Khavak and Khabardar (Chakhardar) passes will handle wheeled traffic. At that time, there was information in the Turkestan Military District headquarters which said that a well-maintained road goes through the Khavak Pass and it would even handle a carriage. It was also said that the road was swept clean of snow during wintertime to keep it passable year around.

It looks like a fairy tale, that in such a backward country as Afghanistan they would clean snow from the road. It is similar to the information that appeared lately in the press that the Englishmen want to build a railroad from Kabul to Mazar-i Sharif. It is highly improbable. And we may ask a question – why clean the snow from the road? To let carts or wagons through? But how many carts or wagons are in Afghanistan? In the

Afghan part of Turkestan you can find *arba* but not to the south of it.[4] One may find a carriage or two in towns and in Kabul – even automobiles. But to clean the road in the passes for them?! It would be an idea of the privileged classes and holds no interest for us. Light cleaning of the snow from the road to let pack animals through – we can grant that. As to the Kabul – Mazar-i Sharif railroad, the Englishmen first need to build one to Kabul and only then run it further. What kind of advantage – political, economical or military – would justify a very difficult endeavor which would have to cross this first rate mountain ridge and then go through a poor, desolate, hostile territory and stop abruptly at the Amu-Darya River?

It is impossible to say for sure during which months the passes of the west Hindu Kush are open for traffic; information in literature is conflicting and there is no systematic surveillance. In any case almost all of the western Hindu Kush passes are open for two-three months – June, July and August. As to the Khavak Pass, it is much more accessible than the others and one can cross it in the wintertime, especially if the snow blanket is light and some road maintenance is provided.

Let's move further. A little bit west of Ghazni, from Khadjikak Pass, there is a lower and less robust mountain ridge. The Kuh-e Baba serves as the continuation of Hindu Kush. Its length is 120 versts with some peaks reaching up to 18,000 feet; the passes' height there is 9-12,000 feet. The western end of the Hindu Kush and Kuh-e Baba flow in a southern and south-western direction in terrace-like heights cut by valleys of the upper reaches of the Helmand River, to create the vast Ghazni Plateau. The plateau serves as a link between the Hindu Kush system and the Suleiman Mountains. The plateau's spurs flow south-west to link to the south spurs of the Siyak-Kuh and fill the space up to the line Farah – Gereshk – Kandahar with low ridges and high hills.

The Kuh-e Baba serves as kind of link that ties the Hindu Kush to the mountain ridges in western Afghanistan. From it three mountain chains fan out: the northern – Band-e Turkestan which goes along the right bank of Murgab River and occupies all the space up to the Russian border with its spurs; the central – Sefid-Kuh (White Mountains) goes along the left bank of the Harirud River – the mightiest out of the three; and the southern – Seyak-Kuh (Black Mountains) goes along the Harirud's right bank. The Sefid-Kuh was called the Parapamisus by the ancient geographers and the name has been preserved somehow up to our time. The Sefid-Kuh and Siyah-Kuh create a significant number of secondary ridges and hills in the southern and northern direction. Those fill Herat province and make the province terrain mountainous or hilly in many places. These mountains' height is significantly lower than those of the eastern Hindu Kush. Though some peaks reach 12-14,000 feet, the passes' height does not exceed 7,500 feet and sometimes as low as three-four thousand feet. It increases the accessibility of these mountains substantially compared to the eastern Hindu Kush. Among the passes across the western Hindu Kush – there are more than 10 of them – I would mention the most important and accessible: Zarmast (7,744 feet), Ardevan (5,250 feet), Cheshme-Sebs (4,810 feet) and Humboy (3,100 feet). The western spurs of Sefid-Kuh and Siyah-Kuh go beyond the Afghan border into Persia as lower and easy-to-cross hills. They connect to mountain systems of Northern Iran (primarily Elbrus) and through it – to the Caucasus.

4 Arba – kind of a cart used in Central Asia and Caucasus. (Translator's note).

This is the picture of the Hindu Kush and its branches. Its mineral composition is primarily granite, sandstone, slate and limestone. As to the vegetation covering the surface of the Hindu Kush, it is has various types of forest – most often we see pines, cedar, fir, spruce, oak and pistachios.

If the Hindu Kush represents an obstacle to troops moving across it, it will be a very difficult barrier when we organize a serious offensive operation across it. When crossing it, one would have to deal with the singular point of the mountain passes – which are well known and defined – and there is no other way to cross it. It is the first problem. Without any doubt, we can expect some [opposing] defensive measures at the accessible passes. Besides, roads to the passes go through narrow valleys formed by rivers which run into the Amu-Darya. Movement through these valleys will be quite difficult. Then, besides the main pass we would have to cross a series of secondary passes. In a word you will have a significant number of physical obstacles which will hamper your movement.

As to the information about the supply of water, forage, fuel, etc, – the available information sources will not give any answers, but you may find some clues in history. Undoubtedly, when Tamerlane, Genghis-Khan and others crossed the Hindu Kush in their time, they did find water and forage. And because nature has not changed much over time, you can find them now as well. Then there is another question – what is the availability of food such as meat? Because the majority of the valleys are populated and there are pastures, one can conclude that it is possible to find meat everywhere. Do not delude yourself. The mountain regions have a many secluded corners – and if you do not rely on the friendly attitude of the locals – than you may get nothing.

Mountaineers are secretive and closely knit people. They can keep collective secrets well. And they hide their possessions, wives with children and livestock in some hole during wartime – a stranger will never find them, and to get to the place without guides – the same mountaineers – would be impossible.

In any case, a military researcher of the Hindu Kush needs to be careful in his assessments. Even if history supports the possibility of crossing the ridge and finding all the necessary supplies, nevertheless the Hindu Kush is such a serious barrier that some would prefer a roundabout way through Herat, Sebsavar [Shindand], Gereshk, Kandahar over the Kabul sector. As to small expeditions and reconnaissance parties which travel with pack animals – for such light organizations there is a vast field. They can go anywhere anytime. Strictly speaking, there is no a pass which cannot be crossed. While in Pamir, I had a subordinate officer who, having been thrown into that hole, was depressed and he drank heavily. I tried to cure him and gave him an assignment to research a pass which even the Kirgiz considered inaccessible that time of the year. Ten days later, my man returned exhausted, gaunt but cheerful; he lost several yaks, barely survived himself but he fulfill the assignment. As you see, even if the Kirgiz say that such and such passes are not accessible – in reality it does not necessarily mean the situation is so dire.

During war, we should always take into account the possibility of crossing the passes at anytime to prevent being surprised. In Central Asia, combat success has been founded on these premises on quite a few occasions. Let's look how Babur moved from Herat by the Harirud Valley. He pushed across the Hindu Kush through snow-covered passes which were considered "absolutely impassable" that time of the year. The future founder of the Mughal Empire overcame unprecedented difficulties, sometimes moving ahead of his host up to his chest in snow, but he emerged completely unexpected and took Kabul.

As to other mountains that branch from the Hindu Kush, they are not of any importance to us. All of them are only possibly interesting in a theoretical sense.

And the map will show you that those branches never stirred any interest. You will find plenty of white spots, dotted lines showing where a river presumably runs, etc. The main reason for this lack of interest is that those areas always have been outside of the historical places and lines of communications, far away from sounds of Central Asian historical life.

Suleiman Mountains

But there is one branch of the Hindu Kush which we need to be concerned with. I mean the Suleiman Mountains which run in a general south-western direction.[5] The mountain country of the Suleiman Mountains spans more than 700 versts (from Nushka to Swat) and has three separate parts: the Quetta-Pishin upland (average height six-nine thousand feet) containing the famous Bolan Pass; the Suleiman Mountain Range (average height 9-11,000 feet) which runs parallel to the Indus River with passageways through the valleys of the rivers Hamala, Tochi and Kurama; and finally the Tira mountain area (Sefid-Kuh, average height 9-12,000 feet) containing the Khyber Pass. The mountain range initially runs as two parallel ranges, then forks, near the Sura River, into 12 prongs. The western part of the mountains is significantly higher than the eastern.

Despite serious interest in the Suleiman Mountains, we cannot find authoritative related information in literature, even though we would expect exhaustive results in the many English works. What is the peculiarity of the Suleiman Mountains? Despite the fact that the mountains are not really high, they have few transverse passes. Life usually forces local people to move across the mountains and this makes the Suleiman Mountains marginally accessible. The main difficulty in crossing the mountains is not their orography, but the lack or absence of forest, water and pasture. That, in fact, is a factor in the life of the people who shelter in the mountains: the hardship of the natural conditions forged a spiritually robust, proud and freedom-loving people. In any case, the fact that the mountain ridge direction does not coincide with human groups' routes, absence of water, fuel and food turned the Suleiman Mountains into a serious barrier on the last leg of the move to India in the past. It is still so today.

I will now name the most important passes in the Suleiman Mountains, beginning in the North.[6] First of all is the Khyber Pass – a narrow gorge more than 30 versts long. Then there is the Kuram Pass leading from Kabul to the Kuram River valley and to Bannu through the Shuturgurdan Mountain Pass (11,500 feet). On the northern side of Takhta-Suleiman are the Gomal and Ghulam Pass which goes from Ghazni to Dera-Ismail-Khan; its length is 200 versts. It is an important trade route between India and Afghanistan. And finally there is a large pass between Quetta and Jacobabad, the so-called Bolan Pass. All these passes are well known to Englishmen due to the Anglo-Afghan Wars: the First (1839-1842) and Second (1878-1882) when their units were

5 In geography textbook, they are sometimes called the "Soliman". (Author's note).

6 Find details in Polozov's *North-Western Frontier of India*. (Author's note).

forced to roam across the country and suffer defeats – in part due to their own mistakes, but in part because of specifics of the operational theater.

Scholars say that there are no less than 300 passes in the Suleiman Mountains. It is hard to say if it is true, but knowing names of the passes does not mean finding or using them. In any case, for a person who studies the issue of conquering India practically, the study of the Suleiman Mountains is one of the paramount topics which cannot be bypassed; learning the mountain passes and their features seems to be unavoidable.

The point is that quite often the completion of a mountain operation depends on crossing mountains in one area or another which are considered unknown or inaccessible. I refer to the Nilt-Mayun position in the Hunza-Nagar operation in 1892 [1891]. The position was believed to by unassailable. All attempts to take it by frontal attack or outflank it on the right were foiled. Everything pointed to a failure. But one night a little sepoy-dogra[7] named Nagdu scaled the almost vertical cliff (I saw it from the fort Nilt side) 1,200 feet high and found an accessible trail. Further the reconnaissance went underway. A small group followed the brave sepoy and the enemy's position had been outflanked from the left. A human found a previously unknown trail and lead the Englishmen to victory on it.

That is why it is so important to know all the passes, roundabout routes and even small trails in the mountains, especially in the Suleiman Mountains – the very strong locking bar of India's gate.

I dwelt on Afghanistan's relief, primarily on its mountains and I must explain why I considered it necessary to highlight this part of the general relief of Afghanistan.

In people's economic life, the mountains provide the major reserve of water which gives life to the people and the animals which work for them. The mountains provide the differences in height that can be a source of mechanical energy useful in an undeveloped country (irrigation) and mountains give shelter to forests as well. But I have to mention that in Afghanistan, mountains do not play a main role in the economy; the major role belongs to the valleys and plateaus that are dispersed all over the country's mountain massifs.

Valleys and plateaus

The valleys and plateaus are of different depths or widths and are the basis of a person's welfare – they feed him and his animals – thus they are a historical and a political factor. You have the right to ask how to determine the characteristics and value of the valleys and how find out their size, fertility, etc. As a geographer, I would tell you sincerely – and I realize clearly it myself – that it is a monumentally difficult task (even literature does not point to it) to find it out the details. It is so because those fertile oases represent state secrets. The following is an example. You are traveling along some route and talk to your Kirgiz guide. Watch him. In some places he glances with his slanting eyes at the mountains like he is looking for something. He is deciding where to move his livestock in the near future. Suddenly, he asks you to stop your horses and begins to observe

7 The Dogras are an Indo-Aryan ethnic group in South Asia. A sepoy is a local native infantry private serving in the British Army of India. (Translator's note).

some remote dark spot in the mountains. You look at the spot but cannot see anything significant. You use binoculars and can see a tiny green patch between the mountains or on the slopes. You ask "Is it possible to graze your livestock there?" "Yes, Tyurya (boss), it is enough for two and a half weeks." But he has more than 2,000 sheep, two camels and two-three horses. I give this example (which happened to me fairly often) to illustrate how enigmatic and hard it is to discover that small, lost patch in the mountains which feeds a local person year after year. The native detects the pasture, by some elusive sign and, with only his naked eyes, and can figure out the size, character of the pasture and the duration for grazing his livestock. This example shows how difficult it is for us to understand a valley, and the native, who possess the information of interest for us, cannot explain it to us. That is why we have to satisfy ourselves with purely theoretical studies when we determine why this or that valley should be of economic interest. The factors we should take into account to determine the fertility of the valley are: the presence of irrigation or natural fresh water which is used by the locals; a reasonably clement weather due to the relative altitude and the presence of a large snow mass since extreme heat kills everything; do the mountains' slopes provide an opportunity to create an irrigation system; and is the valleys' soil fertile (it usually is, though quite often stony). These are the factors which determine the economic importance of the valleys.

We need to make a distinction between the valleys suitable for growing grain and those which provide only grass pastures for nomads. There is some kind of a demarcation line between the grain growing zone and the grass area, but it is impossible to define the line. All attempts by geographers to substantiate this line of separation should be considered unreliable because it is a function of too many variables, such as altitude, distance from snow mass, prevailing wind direction, surface colors, level of moisture, etc.

I encountered the situation in Northern India when, after moving on snow-covered mountains, we descended into a valley which is located at an altitude about 11-12,000 feet, i.e. at an altitude that will not grow even barley or Himalayan grain. And suddenly, a delegation of the locals – if they knew about our arrival – would appear to welcome us and bring us grapes on a plate. It turns out that the grapes are grown in the valley. If a geographer would study the phenomena, he would soon find the explanation: in most cases he will see that the valley's shape represents a concave mirror with the focus located not far from the growing fields. This artificially concentrated heat, along with the moisture, warm and soften the climate to the degree that growing grapes is possible.

Again, defining the demarcation line is impossible for science and we can only say that it is somewhere between 10-12,000 feet. It is enough for you to know about it. I conclude that we must not bypass the study of the valleys and plateaus between the mountains while studying Afghanistan's orography. The valleys and plateaus are the orographic type that are of interest to us. And later when I speak about people's activities, you will see that they live primarily in the valleys and hollows and that they go up into the mountains with their animals only for a period of a few months. And again, they are looking for another valley only higher. The mountains themselves are mostly obstacles to them.

Finally, the third orographic type besides mountains and high valleys is the plain – lowland or low laying areas, such as the steppes adjacent to the Amu-Darya, all the south-western corner of Afghanistan or the so-called Seistan Depression. We should mention that when those lowlands are located away from water sources, they represent pitiful areas, covered with red (yellow) sand or pebbles, dry and without grass. They are without life and sustenance. Those plains did not have any significance in the life of the people and they still do not. But in those places where mountain slopes come close to those areas and can be used for irrigation – there a person, who would exert some effort, could turn the former desert into paradise. And history tells us that some of the current deserts were paradises some time ago. Take the Afghanistan part of the Seistan Depression. It is now a mostly poor, desolate and dry place without population and only a camel can find some sustenance there. But a long time ago, this large area was a thriving wealthy place. When Timur conducted his early operations, one of his objectives was Seistan. The operation initially did not turn out well. Timur was wounded by an arrow in the leg during the siege of a town his which resulted in his life-long lameness. This is the origin of his derisive nickname which was given him by Persians --Tamerlane – "Lame Timur". The legend says that the enraged Timur promised to destroy Seistan forever. When he captured the Helmand Dam – the wonder of its time – he ordered it torn down. The water left, the irrigation canals dried up and soon only dust covered the recent paradise. And up to today, this desert is unsuitable for living.

Again, those lowlands which are not covered with sand and stones represent potentially rich oases which can reward people greatly if they divert water there. There are not many such areas in Afghanistan.

Do not forget to visit these areas during your future journeys in order to connect some concrete images to those places of desolation and sorrow. If any of you are interested in the historical side of research – i.e. the fate of these Asian deserts or riches of the past – you will encounter some interesting prospects. In the Central Asian deserts, where Tsar Sand reigns, after striping layer after layer of this sand, you can uncover the remains of a former palace or a temple stairway. Central Asia is not rich with marble and you will not find it. The building material was humble but the architectural forms were high. You can see traces of Greek or Arabian influence. And where have the buildings, the cities gone? Where did the descendants of the former inhabitants move? Reading history you have a right to make a guess that there was a kingdom where some people lived who had a literature, a language – i.e. they lived as we live today. But a horrible misfortune happened, everything disappeared and now there is only sand. If you want to find out why the kingdom vanished – read history more deeply and carefully – and you will see that the water at the place disappeared for some reason and with it life disappeared. Where did the river go? It may be that the water filtered away through the sand into the Caspian Sea, soaked into the soil or the water source just dried up. It is complicated, but it has many interesting moments for the person who would like to take on the issue.

The waters of Afghanistan

Thus, totaling up the issues of Afghanistan's orography, I should say that there are three types: mountains, plains or plateaus between mountains and at the end – lowlands. The major role, in all respects, belongs to the plateaus and valleys between mountains. The mountains are somewhat significant but less than the valleys and plateaus. And the lowlands are of conditional interest.

Now I will move to a description of Afghanistan's waters. I am going to point to the difference, which you should understand clearly, while dealing with water in Central Asia and water in Europe. In Europe we have stable rivers, defined river beds with a constant volume of water and little change during spring high water. A river in Europe is chiefly a communication route – it carries steamboats and loads of cargo; people use it for moving from one place to another. The river is a technical factor there: it is used for moving, drinking and a very little for irrigation. Looking at the rivers of Central Asia, you see that the human use of water is completely different. First of all you should set aside your notion that goods can be moved by river. There are almost no rivers like that. But as I have already mentioned, water is a substantial factor in people's life – only in a different sense than in Europe. Water is that significant element without which the people of Afghanistan would cease to exist. I already described to you how people quarrel over water. Another confirmation of the issue is Timur's story – when he destroyed the dam and turned the fertile valley into a desert. There are enough similar stories to clarify the major role water plays in Central Asia. There a person cannot manage without artificial irrigation unless the place is located near the mountain snow line, but even in the high places he has to help himself with irrigation. So we need to first consider moisture as the source of field irrigation; then it is needed for humans and animals subsistence; and only after that we can talk about arteries which people use for travel by boats or steamboats, moving cargo, etc. Thus, from a practical point of view, we must approach Asian rivers with a completely different approach than we have toward European rivers. As to the military importance of the rivers – we cannot totally discount it, but it is not so distinctly pronounced as in Europe.

The Amu-Darya River

Afghanistan is a primarily mountainous country with plenty of snowy ridges and is rich with running waters which collect into a significant number of rivers, some of them of substantial size. The major rivers are the Amu-Darya and Indus whose basins cover a vast portion of the country (only the south-western corner is excluded). The Amu-Darya's basin lies north of the West Hindu Kush and Indus' basin – south-east of the ridge. Besides these two basins (one internal and one external), there are two internal ones – the Seistan basin and the small one of Lake Ab-i Istada.

Let's now consider the Amu-Darya with its tributaries. Again I want to repeat that I will look into the essence, the principal facts and not into the small details and numbers which you can find in textbooks. You cannot find the principal facts in the textbooks and that creates a danger for you of overlooking the essence and with it – the practical understanding of Oriental countries.

The Amu-Darya is a "human" river – which stoked the imagination of the Greeks, Arabs, Chinese and Turks to the same extent. It figured in the literature of Sanskrit Puranas[8], the historians of Alexandria and Arab geographers. Even from just the historical perspective, the river represents one of the most attractive geographical problems. For example, did the Amu-Darya flow into the Caspian Sea in the past and if so – why and when did it change its way to the Aral Sea? What is the source of the Amu Darya?

---

8 The Puranas (Sanskrit: purāṇa, "of ancient times") are a group of Indian Hindu religious texts providing narratives of the history of the Universe from creation to destruction, genealogies of the kings, heroes, sages, and demigods, and descriptions of Hindu cosmology, philosophy, and geography. (Translator's note).

The middle and lower parts of the Amu-Darya have been studied relatively well in the 1870s by the expeditions of Zubov, Kaulbars, Obruchev, Ivanov, Stebnitski and Rear-Admiral Baturin (1894). The upper part of the river (called the Panj) was studied later – in the 1890s and early in this century by the Pamir explorers – mainly Russian but some English as well.

The Amu-Darya (Oxus – to the classicists, Jaikhun – to the Arabs, Potsu – to the Chinese) has its source in the Pamir Mountains where it is called the Panj (at the beginning of Wakhan-Darya). It first goes around the Pamirs to the west and south. Then the river makes a sharp turn west and flows in that direction up to kishlak Bosag; from there it turns north-west and leaves Afghan territory. Its length from its source to Bosag is 1,150 versts; its most important segment is adjacent to Afghan-Turkestan and is about 500 versts (from Bosag to Kulyab). Now, let's talk about the Amu-Darya's source.

Since the river had the misfortune to get into the politics of Russo-English relations, the past information defining its source is muddled. Where it is? According to the literature – of course more political than scientific – it has three sources. I will examine the issue in more detail because you will encounter traces of the political struggle between England and Russia in Central Asia and it does make sense to learn its colors, contents and methods since it is far from over. The point is that by the Granville Treaty of 1873,[9] the Oxus River (the Panj primarily) up to the confluence with the river Kokchi constituted the border between Russia and Badakhshan (and its "protectorate" territory of Wakhan district – a purely temporary arrangement). According to Wood,[10] the source of the Amu-Darya was the Pamir River and the Zorkul Lake – it was the first (and incorrect) version of the source. But a member of the Forsyth[11] expedition, Gordon spotted an opportunity to grab some more Russian territory – if he declared that the river Aksu-Murghab-Bartang was the Amu-Darya's source. He put that idea into reality and Rawlinson[12] joined it with pleasure (in one of his works). That created the second version – which was totally absurd. Actually, the river Wakhan-Darya is the source of the Amu-Darya. It is the southern-most version. And now you have before you a typical example of how politics bends science toward its interests. It was advantageous for Englishmen that the northern-most source is the real one; but as it was disadvantageous for Russia – your humble servant maintained that the southern- most source is the true one. The polemics flared, the useless history of the issue had been created (Curzon,

9 Lord Granville Leveson-Gower was the British Foreign Secretary in 1873 The Treaty is probably the treaty of 1871 that established a neutral zone between Russia and Afghanistan. Russia violated the treaty by occupying the Khanate of Kiva in 1873. (Translator's note).

10 John Wood (1812-1871) was a Scottish Naval officer, surveyor and explorer of Central Asia. He is the author of *A Journey to the Source of the River Oxus*, London: John Murray. 1872. (Translator's note).

11 Sir Douglas Forsyth – British diplomat and explorer who explored the Pamirs and Chinese Turkestan. He is author of *Report of a Mission to Yarkand in 1873, 1875*. Gordon is the celebrated "China Gordon", the British Major General killed during the siege of Khartoum. He was part of a Forsyth Expedition of 1857 as a Lieutenant and surveyor. (Translator's note).

12 Major General Sir Henry Creswicke Rawlinson (1810-1895) – British scientist, explorer and author of *England and Russia in the East: A Series of Papers on the Political and Geographical Condition of Central Asia*, London: Murray, 1875. (Translator's note).

Bonvalot).[13] But even now, when there is no need for me to be a hypocrite before you, I still maintain my former view and my understanding of the Amu-Darya's source is as follows.

The Amu-Darya begins at the northern slopes of the Hindu Kush at the altitude of 14,700 feet from a glacier which has no name in English-language literature, but in the Russian sources it is named after the Baron Vrevski.[14] It is a huge glacier which has three branches. The river runs out from icy caverns in two rapid streams. The source itself is concealed from human sight. From under that glacier a small stream named the Vakhjira flows 30-35 versts to Basai-Gumbez and from there it flows west under the name Wakhan-Darya until its confluence with Pamir River – there the river receives another name – the Panj.[15] The name means – "Five Rivers". It flows through the Pamir area for 400-425 versts. The river in its upper part is not of that much interest. The only matter is if you could find a Tadjik who knows where to cross the river. The Panj is a mountain river. If it flows through a narrow gap between mountains and you cannot throw a Caucasus bridge across it – it is impassable.[16] It is the first type of river. The second type is a river which flows through a valley of gradual inclination covered with pebbles; the river divides into several branches and it is easily crossed by foot or horse. The third type of river collects itself into one bed 150-200 paces wide and is a typical European river. All that is lacking is a boat to sail across the quiet waters. During summer (June-August), the water level is very deep and it is very turbulent because it receives uninterrupted and plentiful runoff from the surrounding mountains. First, the Panj feeds from thawing snow from the low mountains, then, in early summer it feeds from medium-altitude mountains and in August from the high peaks. Crossing the river at that time is very difficult. During the winter time, the river shrinks and one can cross it at any place.

In the area of Kala-i Khumb, the main city of the Darvaz province, the Panj makes a huge bend, breaking through canyons toward the west and there it gets its name – the Amu-Darya. On the map you see a great bend. You realize that the river is subjected to a great pressure from the side of the mountain masses which surround it from the North. There are a number of ridges, ledges and the mountain massif which were first too short and too soft to change the direction of the river's flow; and only under pressure of the next mountain ridge (the Peter the Great ridge), the Panj makes the turn and flows in a new direction. In the bend area, the river flows inside of a deep, practically-inaccessible

---

13 *Russia in Central Asia [in 1889 and the Anglo-Russian Question]* by George N. Curzon. Longmans, Green & Co., 1889 cited earlier. Pierre Gabriel Édouard Bonvalot (1853-1933) was a French explorer, author, and legislator who authored *Du Caucase aux Indes à travers le Pamir* in 1889. (Translator's note).

14 Baron Alexandr Borisovich Vrevski (1805-1888) was a Russian General. He was the commander of the Turkestan Military District and was the Turkestan Governor-General in 1889-1898. (Translator's note).

15 More details about the Panj can be found in A.K. Razgonov's work *Through East Bukhara and Pamir*, Tashkent, 1910, pp.117-165. (Author's note).

16 The Caucasus bridge is a type of temporary pontoon (floating) bridge that uses sturdy scows and planking. It was first used to bridge the wide, fast-moving mountain Sulak River in Dagestan during the Caucasian War against Imam Shamil. Engineer General Eduard Fedorovich Kesseler is credited with its introduction in 1846. (Translator's note).

canyon and represents an uninterrupted cascade of waterfalls with water flow speed up to 15 versts per hour. Finally, it comes to the valley and there one can find five crossings.

In this area you can cross the Amu-Darya by wading. And this particular circumstance attaches a major political and military importance to the area and it even creates a special operational direction toward India – named the Badakhshan direction. Out of the five crossings, three allow the use of boats or *tursuks*,[17] and two others let you cross the river on foot: those are Bish-Kapinsk and Parkhar crossings. They go by the Urta-Tyugai Island which is created by separate branches of the Amu-Darya and takes up a large area--25 versts long and 15 versts wide. Due to low accessibility and thick vegetation, Urta-Tugai Island is a kind of a natural zoo where until recently one could find tigers and deer. If anyone would like to study these interesting crossings in detail, I would suggest my work *Eastern Bukhara*.

From Sarai kishlak, somewhat down river of Urta-Tugai Island, the Amu-Darya becomes navigable. First it carries larger boats, then, from Termez – even steamboats. The most interesting part of the Amu-Darya is the part that is adjacent to Afghan Turkestan. It is impossible to determine the river's width exactly. For example, in the segment of the river from its tributary Wakhsh to Keleif, its width varies between 200-300 sazhen'[18] but in four areas it reaches two-three versts. The navigation channel's minimal depth is five feet, but in this sector it is between three feet and 14 feet. The current is very strong. The high water is in the summer with the water level cresting in August. The waterway changes its direction frequently, especially during high water. There are absolutely no bridges across the river. River crossings are done by ferries, natives' boats or *tursuks*. Boats navigate the river and there is steamboat service between Chardzhev [in Turkmenistan] and Termez.

But speaking about the Amu-Darya steamboat service, one has to get a clear image of what kind of communication it is. In Europe the service means that the steamboats go day and night by the defined waterway; the river has navigation signs and everything is measured and defined. But with the Amu-Darya, it is different picture. Before you is an Asian river which seethes and races with murky water. The river is terribly capricious; it changes its navigation channel constantly. Where today the waterway is 7-14 feet deep, tomorrow it may be an island or a shoal and there is no way to move. The steamboats usually stop overnight. The upstream movement is not dangerous and usually goes quite auspiciously. But moving downstream is dangerous because, besides the mechanical propulsion, the steamboat receives the [propelling] force of the water current's pressure. Sometimes a steamboat moves over sand, but the pilot may not notice it if he does not calculate the current force. And when he finally realizes the situation – it is too late. The steamboat slams into the sand and it is very difficult to get out of the predicament.

Essentially, the Amu-Darya, despite its unusual size, remains a mountain river in its middle segment. The middle segment of the Amu-Darya from Vakhsh's confluence to kishlak Bosaga has 12 known crossings, as well as some other insignificant or inconvenient sites. The crossings do not permit wading. For crossing these places, use barges,

17 A tursuk is a leather bag which the locals use to store *kumys*, a drink made out of fermented mare's milk. The bag doubles as a one-man raft. (Translator's note).

18 Sazhen' (Russian САЖЕНЬ) is an obsolete Russian measure of the length equal to seven English feet (84 inches), i.e. 2.1336 meters. (Translator's note).

cargo-kayaks, *tursuks* and even steamboats (Patta-Hissar). The crossings are named after towns or kishlaks located nearby,[19] It would be enough to remember the following four as the most important: Kabiadin (river width – 1.5 versts, channel depth – 5-7 feet); Patta-Hissar or Termez (river width – 1.5 versts; it is inconvenient for kayaks but does well for steamboats and barges); Huzar (river width – one verst; the channel goes between shoals; it is inconvenient but quite lively); Kelif (river width 200 sagen'; has four kayak crossing stations; it is the most convenient crossing). Termez crossing is of historical interest, because Alexander the Great, Genghis-Khan and Timur used it. The major trade route between Bukhara and Afghanistan goes through the Kelif crossing.

As to the use of the Amu-Darya's water for irrigation there are some technical difficulties because water is too turbid. If you use a channel to take out river water, it will bring along so much silt that you will need to clean the channel quite often. The silt removed from the channel builds up its side walls to such a height that cleaning it is too laborious to justify doing it. And for that reason, the Amu-Darya's water is used very rarely and in small quantities for irrigation. In general, one has to consider water turbidity when using irrigation. There is a limit to the turbidity of water beyond which the water looses almost all its value as a source of irrigation.

Tributaries of the Amu-Darya

Out of all of the Amu-Darya's tributaries, our interest should be directed toward its left bank tributaries, which begin near the northern slopes of the Hindu Kush or Kuh-i-Baba. There are many tributaries, but I will describe the following to you: the Kokcha, Kunduz, Khulm, Balkh, Nari and Andkhoi; plus two western rivers – the Murghab and Harirud which are scientifically counted as Amu-Darya's tributaries. At some time in the past, they probably emptied into the Amu-Darya but today they do not reach it.

A word about the appearance of these rivers – they have some interesting details. Looking at the map one can see that a river begins in the high mountains. Soon after leaving the mountains, it acquires maximum water volume, then it descends into a valley and loses its volume; finally it splits into a multitude of channels (they look like threads on the map) and in the end it disappears completely.

Now that you have gotten yourself into the structure of Asian countries, get accustomed to their peculiarities and it will make easier for you to follow my narrative. What contributes to the river's disappearance? There are two reasons: humans and nature. The sun dries the river by evaporating water or water is absorbed by the soil. Humans reduce the river through usage for their own needs. Because the mountain, rivers running from the Hindu Kush have significantly clean water which is devoid of silt, people use this waters for full-scale irrigation. All these rivers are significant (and primary) sources of irrigation for all the terrain of Afghan Turkestan – thus they are the source of all its life activities. But those rivers also have serious military interest. They all move along meridians and coincide with the operational routes that go from the Amu-Darya toward Afghanistan's depth.

19 See Appendix II. (Author's note). The appendix had not been published. (Translator's note).

If we keep in mind that between the rivers are watersheds and it is practically impossible to move along these watersheds or across them and that the high water time is short on those rivers, then it is clear that the only passable routes in Afghan Turkestan are these river valleys. With this I will end the examination of these river tributaries.

As to the rivers Harirud and Murgab, they have a somewhat different significance. Both have their sources in the western part of the Kuh-i Baba flowing west, then encounter mountain ridges in the south and turn north-west. After flowing some distance in that direction through the plains, they disappear. In the beginning these rivers are true mountain rivers, but after flowing into the hilly area, their natures vary depending on the consistency of the rocks and soil in their beds. Not a single geographer in the world will be able to answer your questions about the rivers' size and depth. An Asian river is pure caprice. Their widths and depths vary extremely and cannot be relied on. English travelers studied the issue and in one work of 1873 you can find a note that near Herat the river is six sagen' wide and 1 foot deep. But what does that mean? It is only one particular case. At different times, these numbers will be different and will not repeat themselves next year.[20] If one would measure the river a little upstream or downstream, the picture will be totally different and the width and depth will be different. In a word, the Central Asian River is difficult to frame with numbers. It is possible to make some conclusions about the Murgab's average numbers, but that is an exception. Nothing will be relevant to other rivers. The Murgab's width fluctuates from 10 to 30 sagen'; in its lower part the width will be different than in the mountain segment. As to the depth – it fluctuates from three feet to 10-12 feet. But these marks do not paint the real picture; they are just attempts to theorize the matter at any cost.

Speaking about the possibility of crossing these rivers, the Murgab has several crossings. They are near Meruchak, Takhta-Bazar, Band-i Nadir, Kala-Izmail and Bala-Murgab. But it would be prudent to view this information with some skepticism. Strictly speaking, these rivers have a lot of crossings. But a caravan or a person moves by a specific route from a well to the next well and they cross the river at a particular point. If one goes by a different route, he can find another crossing. As it is today, in the past people went by specific routes and crossed rivers at particular points. There someone usually built a small fortress with a bazaar nearby. Thus the crossing was created and geographers marked it as the *only* place one *can cross* the river. In reality, though, this is completely incorrect. It only meant that people crossed the river at this point more frequently and did not mean that one cannot cross the river at other points. If people can cross the Amu-Darya at quite horrible crossings, then there are no problems with other, relatively small rivers. In Asia people in general are very brave at the crossings. Here is an example, they put one arba atop of another, tie them to each other and tie these to three horses.[21] The horses are hitched ahead of the arbas with sizable distances between them. If one horse stumbles, loses its footing or temporarily goes under water – the two others will

20 [Dr. J. A.] Owen, for example, discusses " the significantly greater depth of the Murgab during their year of visit (December 1885) than it was other years." See [Charles Edward] Yate, *Northern Afghanistan [or Letters from the Afghan Boundary Commission* Edinburgh and London: William Blackwood and Sons], 1888, p. 97. (Author's note).

21 An arba is a bullock cart found in Central Asia. (Translator's note).

continue to pull. I, myself, crossed the Kara-Darya that way during the Chinese War.[22] I was sure that we were drowning: one horse stumbled, choked and sometimes disappeared under water. But the two other horses continued to pull. The arba stopped and almost overturned. My head was spinning from the roaring water, but we survived and crossed the river.

All I have said should tell you that you must not take map crossing marks as finite values and loose the hope of finding other crossings at different places. This is dangerous thinking, especially from a military point of view. Crossing is possible in most places, but it does not exclude the necessity of thorough reconnaissance in advance.

What is the military importance of these two rivers?

I think that as the Murgab and Harirud can be crossed almost everywhere, excluding the highest reaches of the Harirud where, in some places, the soil is so clayish and swampy that it would prevent crossing. What is the tactical importance of these rivers? They cannot serve as obstacles – they are not large and impassable. They do not coincide with operational routes – and that means their valleys cannot serve as roads. The importance of these rivers is not tactical but economic. These rivers give water to the population. The Harirud feeds the huge valley which is one of the richest places of Afghanistan and which Englishmen named the "Afghan Breadbasket". For our discussion, it has a very significant meaning. Now you understand why the Englishmen call Herat "The Key of India". This assertion is supported by history. I will tell you an instructive, even if somewhat legendary, story.

When Genghis-Khan pursued the Khan of Khorezm, he sent one of his grandsons to capture Herat. He said that Herat has great importance and it was imperative, in his expression, "to make our back safe". He insisted that his grandson be decisive, persistent and severe. The grandson arrived at Herat, laid siege and finally, with the weaponry available, captured the city. When he entered Herat, a procession of citizens came to him completely submissive. The legend says that the crying of the women and children walking in front of the procession softened the young victor's resolve. He thought: "What can the little children do?" and he decided to spare the women, children and elderly. He ordered the slaughter of all men capable of bearing weapons and granted mercy to the rest. He was sure that he did the right thing and returned to his grandfather. But news traveled faster than he. When he arrived, Genghis-Khan already knew about his decision and that an uprising had broken out in Herat. The city had revived. And when his grandson reported to Genghis-Khan, the grandfather chastised him. He showed him the dispatch and said: "You have been willful and the result is dismal. Go back and correct your transgression." But this time Genghis-Khan did not let the youngster go alone. He gave him one of the experienced military commanders as an adviser. And when Herat was taken again, all the inhabitants – from the youngest to the oldest – were slaughtered, the walls were pulled down and the city was plowed under. Central Asia remembers the death of the "two-million inhabitant city" to today.

I told you the legend for two reasons. First of all, I believe that is a necessity to introduce you to the peculiarities of Asian countries, which European historians would describe to you completely differently. They will monotonously tell you that Genghis

22 The Boxer Rebellion of 1900-1901. (Translator's note).

Khan slaughtered all the Persian population, and that Genghis-Khan was the scourge of God, that he enjoyed cruelty for the sake of cruelty, etc. I gave you the facts from another– say Asian – viewpoint. Genghis-Khan gave his grandson a cruel directive. But it was caused by the fact that his entire Indian campaign would be hanging by a hair if well-populated Herat, located in the fertile valley, was not secure behind his back. Genghis-Khan was on the southern slopes of the Hindu Kush mountain passes. Herat was on his flank and in the rear. In this case, any sentimentality was unacceptable – and Genghis-Khan understood it. Herat played a grand strategic role in the past as well as it does today. This role is determined by its location and the wealth of natural resources in the valley. Those two aspects – the strategic and economic – justify the nickname of Herat as "The Key to India". To appreciate the valley's wealth, one should remember that the waters of the Harirud irrigate 90,000 desyatina[23] of land, with the rate of usage of about 25 cubic sagen per desyatina per day.[24]

Thus, the Mughab and Harirud do not play any tactical role. But they have an exceptional economic role. And as to the Harirud, it has a very strategic role as well.

Rivers of Seistan

The southwestern corner of Afghanistan is watered by several rivers which belong to the inner Seistan basin. These are the Helmand, Khash Rud, Farah Rud, Kharr Rud [Yazavan] and Lora. The River Helmand has its source in the Paghman Mountains (west of Kabul); it flows generally in a south-western direction for about 1,000 versts and empties into Lake Hamun (eastern). In the lower segment it changes its direction first to the west and then to the north. The river has a mountainous character up to the city of Geresk and from there, after receiving waters from its tributary, the Arghandab (flowing from the Ghazni plateau), it becomes a calm high water river. The river's width near Geresk extends up to a half verst; the river flows through several branches. The widest of the branches is about 70 sagen. The river's depth in the middle and lower segments is no more than three-and-a-half feet with the strong currents. High water is in the summertime when the river overflows its banks. There are four known crossings – all of them in the Geresk area: near the city; up on the river near Sangin and Hyderabad; and down on the river near Qal-i Bisgha (at the confluence of the Arghandab). Everything I said about crossings of the river Murghab applies to the crossings of the Helmand. The Helmand can be crossed on foot in many places even during high water.

The rivers Khash Rud, Farah Rud and Kharr Rud have their sources in the southern slopes of the Siyah Kuh Mountains and flow in the south-western direction. They empty themselves: the first – into the eastern Lake Hamun (near the confluence with the Helmand); the two other empty into the western Lake Hamun. The length of those rivers is almost identical: Khash Rud and Kharr Rud – about 360 versts and Farah Rud – about 400 versts. Initially they are mountain rivers, but from the points of Vasir, Farah and Sabzevar they become common Asian rivers of the plains – used for irrigation. They

23 Desyatina – obsolete Russian unit of area equal to 2.7 acres. (Translator's note).

24 It would make about 8,578 cubic feet per day (one cubic sagen is equal to 343 cubic feet) per desyatina or 23,161 cubic feet per acre per day. (Translator's note).

overflow their banks during short period of high water in the summertime but for the rest of the year they have little water and sometimes dry up completely.

The military importance of these rivers in the southwestern part of Afghanistan is quite insignificant. They flow in directions which do not coincide with the operational sectors across Afghanistan and cannot be used as routes of communications and supply. Carrying little water, they cannot be obstacles for an offensive. Thus, they deserve attention only as the means of irrigation and cultivation in that part of the country due to water that they carry from the mountains.

In theory, because of the difference in altitude and water quality, these rivers have the makings of good sources for building large irrigated farming areas. We can find such areas in the valleys of Harirud and Murghab; even in the Amu-Darya's valley we can find well-developed irrigated farms. Such farms could be established here as well, but unfortunately for a long time everything here has been neglected. The rivers ran loose and are chocked with pebbles. But the fate of the country, which was at one time plundered by Timur, is entirely dependent on creating such farms. Englishmen understand that, with the creation of such farms, the area would be converted into a major source of wealth and the country will come to life. Right now there is desert. And the rivers' significance is as insignificant obstacles.

Indus tributaries

Now I will speak about the tributaries that flow into the Indus River. A word about the general character of those rivers: all of them represent a distinctive mountain type. They possess the following peculiarities. First of all – their bottoms are mostly firm because fast currents and a significant drop of altitude washes the bottoms down to hard rock. You may be fairly sure that there are no muddy bottoms. Second – all these rivers flow swiftly due to the large drop in altitude. In most cases, the water concentrates in a narrow channel and creates a close and constrained river course. Sometimes that creates waterfalls. If you judge the river as an obstacle, you need to take into account the character of adjoining mountain ridges. If the ridges come immediately to the river, then there will be nearly a waterfall. If you cannot throw a Caucasus bridge across it, the river will be impassable. If a river flows through a valley with a small drop of altitude – it widens and becomes a typical European body of water which flows smoothly and can carry boats. Moving by a mountain river's valley is difficult and you are going get exhausted. But the river will gladden and refresh you with a variety of colors and endless change of scenery. In one place you will go by a so-called cornice – i.e. a narrow trail hanging above a bottomless chasm and below you will be an abyss looking like Dante's inferno. No wild beast can get into it. Only birds can build their nests there and your intrusion will alarm their peaceful existence; they will cry nervously. But after moving two-three versts, you will descend from the cornice into a widening valley. It is covered with a mighty forest and you will go by a natural tree-lined walk in the park-like setting. It is warm and cozy; the birds are singing and insects are chirping. Later some other unexpected scene comes before your eyes....In a word – there is a fantastic diversity of nature which can barely be described with a human's tongue.

Out of all Indus' tributaries we can take interest in the large one – Kabul River. Its source is in the Paghman Mountains near the Ownay mountain pass west of the city of

Kabul at 11,300 feet altitude. Near the city, it has a confluence with Logar River which flows from the Ghazni plateau. Then on the left side it accepts three large tributaries – the Charikar, Kunar and Swat and flows in a generally eastern direction. It empties itself into the Indus River near Attok. The total length of the Kabul River is 480 versts or 370 versts if measured as the crow flies. From its source to the eastern part of the Khyber Pass, the river flows through mountains and it is not navigable; but it is passable for land traffic and presents a very convenient route of communication between Kabul and the Peshawar plains.

There is a postal route that uses messengers and runs between Peshawar and Kabul. The rest of the way, the river flows through plains and has multiple bends that sometimes divides into branches until its confluence with the Indus near Attok. Crossing the river in its mountainous segment is possible on foot – though it is a difficult task. There are no permanent crossings. The plain segment has a bridge near Nowshera (on the road to Khoti-Mardan and Malakand) and ferries near Nowshera, Nikot and Michni. The river's width near Michi is about 60 sagen. Near Jalalabad (where there is a very good ford) the river becomes capable of handling rafts and small craft and from Peshawar – the river is navigable.

The Charikar River begins on the southern slopes of the central Hindu Kush. Its sources are two streams flowing toward each other along the base of the mountain ridge. Those streams are starting lines for climbing toward multiple mountain passes which lead to the northern slopes of the ridge. Thus lays the essential military significance of the river. Other rivers – the Kunar and Swat (Panjkora) begin on the south slopes of the eastern Hindu Kush – on the Chitral Upland and flow south-west until emptying into the Kabul River as winding mountain streams. Their currents are very fast and strong and in many places these rivers are impassable. But taking into account the difficulties of crossing that mountain country, those rivers can be used in some places as routes of communication for the areas which lay between Kabul and Peshawar toward Chitral. Lower segment of the Kunar River can be used for floating; the river's valley is covered with forest.

The River Kuram has its source south of Kabul near the Shutergarden mountain pass and flows in a general south-eastern direction. It flows in the mountains up to the city of Tal and further – by a valley to the River Indus. It empties into the Indus 35 versts south of Khalabag. Its length is about 250 versts that includes about 130 versts in the mountains. The river and its right tributaries –the Kaitu and Tochi – have a high military interest because their valleys are routes connecting the Indus' valley with Kabul and Ghazni.

The Gumal River begins on the southern border area of the mountain ridges of the Ghazni plateau. It flows in a winding line first north-east, then east and then south-east. When it exits the mountains, it joins the Zhob River which flows from then south-west. After flowing 100 versts through the plains, it empties itself into the Indus River south of Dera-Ismail-Khan. The river's length is about 300 versts; its longest tributary's length is 250 versts (the Zhob River). The Gumal River's importance is determined by its valley, which is the famous Gumal pass providing passage through the Suleiman Mountains on the Ghazni to Dera-Ismail-Khan direction.

Here I will end the description of the Afghan waters. This is a picture that is different from European geography. An Asian river almost always is mountainous and almost never is used for floating. It is a strategic route or simply a road. Sometimes you will have to consider it as an obstacle – small or big; but the major importance of it lays in its irrigation capabilities. And from this point of view, we will have to evaluate the rivers of Afghanistan.

3

Climate of Afghanistan

The next part of our journey is dedicated to the climate of Afghanistan. We again approach a difficult topic – such as any topic related to Oriental countries – but the matter of climate will probably be even more difficult. You clearly understand that the topic of climate in geography can only be clarified with select numerical data. The numbers should be true, accurate in sufficient quantity to enable you to make a correct conclusion out of their aggregation and combination. Climatic research in India, for example, is organized brilliantly and permits the fairly reliable forecast of some large climatic events. But look at how many meteorological stations there are, the mass of workers involved and the strict and complex records of the events that are needed. Could one hope to have this in Afghanistan? Where are you going to get those numbers? In the Kabul Valley, in large centers of the country, you can find some meteorological stations; as to Afghan part of Turkestan – you can use data from the stations in Termez or Kerka. That is it. What materials are there which would allow you to characterize the climate of Afghanistan accurately? There are no such materials. You may find some clues from travelers. The voyager usually will enter in his diary that in one place one day it was cold or it was warm; he might check his thermometer, and might mention the humidity. But he often would not say at what altitude, in which mountains and what time of the day it happened. This means that the materials from travelers are characterized by imprecision and incoherence. One can make some judgment about climate based on vegetation and to some degree – animals. There is some form of climate in the area where grain is growing and some animals are living, but the despotic and cultivated hand of man has significantly altered the climate. Finally, some considerations of the altitude can give you some clues. And that is a small amount of data which can give you a chance to say something about the climate. Certainly, it is very little and there is no wonder that the Oriental scholars' climate definition is so subjective. Most often you will find in those narratives the word "continental"; it does not matter if they speak about Afghanistan, Northern India, Eastern Bukhara, Ust-Yurt – it is all the same. And it certainly is a mistake.

In science, the term "continental climate" means a dry climate with sharp changes of temperature during the day and night periods as well as during the year. But those two major requirements – dryness and sharp changes in temperature are hardly uniform from the Pamirs to Eastern Bukara; as a whole the regions' climate can hardly be named "continental". I give you an interesting example of a description of Afghanistan's climate. It is out of a small brochure "Military-Geographical Research of Afghanistan" by A. Andogski.[1]

1 Alexandr Ivanovich Andogski (1876-1931) was a Major-General in the Imperial Army and served as Chief of the Nikolaev Military Academy. During the Russian Civil war, he served with the Bolsheviks and later with the Whites of Admiral Kolchak . (Translator's note).

Here is the picture – completely intact. "The *climate of Afghanistan is extremely diverse* – which is determined primarily by differences of altitude in different areas of the country – and is *generally continental*. The fluctuations of temperature extremes are large and fast – not just between summer and winter but between day and night. In particular: *At the top of the peaks of the Hindu Kush*, Kuh-i-Baba and Sefid-Kuh Mountains, winter reigns eternal; *the high mountain plateaus* of the Central Afghanistan have cool summers and long cold winters with deep snow blankets; *mountain valleys* are characterized by a mild climate, but in the lower areas, the summer is very hot; *the northern part of the plains* has very hot summers and winter has very little snow; the climate of *the southwestern plains* is very hot.

Spring takes the period from February to the end of April, but it continues up to the middle of May on the mountain slopes and plateaus. During this time, water and pasturage are abundant and the rivers overflow their banks making crossing difficult. The nights are cold and the days are almost summer-like. The difference between day and night temperatures is initially significant and quite minor later on at the end of March. This time is favorable for quartering troops in bivouac sites.

Summer begins variously from the end of April to the end of May. The hottest time is during June – August. There is always a cloudless sky. The summer heat quickly destroys pasturage and dries rivers out. In the valleys, where the country's population is concentrated due to the shortage and unevenness of irrigation – the days are suffocating with heat and night brings devastating malarial miasmas. The mass of irrigation canals that cut the valleys in various directions contribute to the development of these extremely harmful climatic conditions. Myriads of flies and gnats increase the torture done by the summer heat. Nights in September are cool and the difference between day and night temperatures reaches 20° Centigrade. *We have to acknowledge that summer is an extremely unfavorable time of the year in all regards.* Its length is four-five months. It is an unfavorable time to bivouac troops; spreading diseases in the valley require moving bivouacs to the mountain slopes and this moves the troops away from water sources.

Fall begins at the end of September and is characterized by cold nights in the northern part of the country with occasional rains. At that time, mountains and valleys cover themselves with new green vegetation and the rivers become full of water. Sickness in the valleys declines significantly. The average length of the fall is about three to three-and-a-half months long. Stationing troops in bivouacs meets no obstacles in the areas of the mountain triangle and on the plains of the southern part of the country.

Winter continues for two months on average. It is extremely severe in the mountains; most of the passes are closed because of strong blizzards and deep snowdrifts. In the valleys the winter is mild, snow stays sometimes for just several days. There is no snow in the southern part of Afghanistan and the winter is regarded as the most pleasant time of the year. Only during the winter time, is it comfortable to bivouac troops there."[2]

Do not you feel completely how the author makes conjectures and fantasies? And this is the reason why one cannot make any concrete image of the topic out of the general phrases and supple word tricks. Such a description – which is provided by A.I. Andogski

2 All italics in the quotation were placed by the author. (Translator's note).

– could be applied (by replacing the names) to a great extent to western Pamir, eastern Bukhara, the mountains of Tien Shan, and Dardistan (Northern India). Other authors' descriptions of the Afghan climate are even stranger with the general idea that the Hindu Kush has a cold climate which becomes more moderate on the slopes and it is hot in the lowlands....It is a formula that could be easily applied to the climates of mountainous countries around the world and even could include Mars, Venus, etc.

Typically, as soon as authors come to a concrete issue related to the climate – they sharply disagree on the matter. For example, while discussing the issue of what time of year is best for conducting military operations in Afghanistan, they all give different answers. V.F. Novitski says that "we shall consider the period of time from the end of summer to the beginning of winter (August – October) as the best time for troops' offensive and military operations". P.A. Rittikh decides the issue differently: "The best time for our troops' offensive is the spring – from the middle of February to the end of April; in the mountains of Central Afghanistan, a better time for moving is the summer". And, finally, A.I. Andogski comes with yet another version. In his opinion "the best time of the year for conducting military operations is – in the northern and central (mountainous) parts of Afghanistan – the spring (March, April and the first half of May); in the southern area – the late fall and the winter (November, December, January and February)". The differences among the essential conclusions of the works about climate show all the flimsiness and relativism of the scale that the authors have used. In A.I Andogski's assessment of the climate, we also have to point out actual error. It would be very hard to move through the deep snow blankets still remaining in the mountainous parts during the first two months [March and April-Translator].[3] (This was the problem during one of Babur's marches from Herat to Kabul on the Hazara road – i.e. through the Harirud Valley; and during Timur's march against Kafiristan in March and April of 1398 before his campaign in India). But in May the snow will be too loose and pack animals will get stuck in it. Also, movement across the southern part of Afghanistan is not convenient in all places. For example, on the route Khandahar – Ghazni – Kabul, the traveler will meet with terrible cold, strong winds and in some areas (south of Ghazni) – with deep snow, which could be a death threat to people and animals.[4]

I repeat that clarifying the issue of Afghanistan's climate is a difficult task, especially if one is trying to keep necessary scientific precision and at the same time to comprehend a lifelike and vivid picture of it. On this issue, I am with the explorers of Northern India who used different methods while approaching the matter and named that kind of climate *mountainous*, i.e. they broadly apply the idea of evaluation of the climate in relation to its altitude. And if we evaluate the climate of Afghanistan from this point of view, then we notice some distinctive features of it – if not in general then at least in some areas. In my small work, Eastern Bukhara, I have already used that method. I divided all of eastern Bukhara's territory into four sectors by their altitude and tried to determine

3 I will also point also the strong blizzards which are mentioned by travelers. "These mountains are liable to sudden and severe storms at this time of the year" – says Dr. Owen about the Hindu Kush. He was referring to October, but the storms happen in the spring also. *Northern Afghanistan*, p.325. (Author's note)

4 See A. Martin's *Under the Absolute Amir* 1907 or its Russian translation by A.B. Omel'yanovich, pp.24-27. (Author's note).

the climate for each of them. I think that we can use that method for Afghanistan as well – and use the four sectors.

I call the climate of Afghanistan *mountainous* because the essential factor influencing its climate is the presence of mountains. They create highly-raised relief, which in some places are covered with everlasting snow and with *long- lasting* snow in others. Thus the climate is subject to the influence of high altitude and rarefied and mobile air; quickly warming but quickly cooling as well. But the same mountains have a decisive influence over adjoining highlands and valleys. Other factors influencing the climate of Afghanistan are very diverse, but they are also less significant. Among these are geographical latitude, distance from a place to snow masses, openness of a valley to a warm side or the opposite; the direction of prevailing cold winds from glaciers and the topographic character of the valley – i.e. is it concave, accumulating sun rays or convex dispersing them into space. There are some cases when one of these factors becomes a decisive one; for example – the valley is a corridor through which a cold air stream from glaciers passes...then the valley will always be cold and unhealthy.

Speaking about the mountainous climate of Afghanistan, I divide it into four types. The first type is the areas and plateaus located above 8,000 feet (8,000-11,000 feet on average). We can describe this climate as severe continental, but healthy. Its features are: a usually long and severe winter, snow staying for seven-eight months; a warmer time of three to four months (in lower and protected areas – up to four-five months). Note that the soil will need to dry out and to warm up for about two-three weeks after the snow thaws to let the grass sprout, This makes the pastures in those areas and plateaus available for the nomads for just three to three-and-one-half months per year. Another peculiarity of this type of climate is the large snowfall. In these areas, only undersized though good and nutritious grass grows. It is very filling – *strong* as the nomads say. The most exhausted horse can recover and put on weight in just two-three weeks. The only grain we can find on those plateaus is Himalayan zhito[5] or naked barley[6] and it is possible only if the plateau is located in the presence of warm winds. Such is that type of climate which I would suggest the name of the *Climate of high mountain plateaus.*

The next altitude climate is that of the valleys located at 4,000-8,000 feet. This type of climate needs special attention because this altitude is very typical of Afghanistan's plains. These plains are the source of Afghanistan's wealth. Their climate can be compared to the climate of our Central Russia with the difference that their summer is much hotter than ours. This increase in summer temperature is explained since Afghanistan is closer to the equator and the sun rises higher at its zenith. Further, the heat in the mountain valleys is reflected toward them from the mountain cliffs and rocks; and, finally, there is little movement of air through valleys during clement weather. These factors are the reason why the summers are hotter in the Afghanistan's valleys then in Central Russia. The length of the winters in the valleys is about same as ours but there is more snow. In some valleys, the snow blanket is very deep – it sometimes completely covers up kishlaks (the general name for a village) and stored forage. If hay is stored far away from home, it

5 Zhito – in ancient Slavic countries, this is a generic term for cereal grains. Ukrainians still use it today to describe wheat. (Translator's note).

6 Hulless or "naked" barley (*Hordeum vulgare* L. var. *nudum Hook.*) is a form of domesticated barley with an easier-to-remove hull. Naked barley is an ancient food crop. (Translator's note).

is very difficult to get to it and livestock could perish. As to the spring and fall, the spring there is rainy and it rains up to five-ten days continuously. The fall is very mild and even and is considered the best season of the year. It is healthy for humans. It is fairly warm, the soil does not produce noxious fumes, the change between warm and cold weather is not abrupt and it prevents frequent feverish diseases. The areas have plenty of water and it is of high quality. As to cereals and grasses in those valleys, the abundance of water and good soil let them grow wonderfully. The warmer temperatures, compared to Central Russia, permits them to grow much more southern varieties of cereal grains and grasses beside those that we grow in Russia. Let us name this second type of climate by analogy to the first one the *Climate of elevated plateaus and valleys located at the altitude of 4,000-8,000 feet.*

Next comes the *Climate of steppes and hills* which is located at the altitude of 2,000-4,000 feet. This climate of the steppes and hills can be compared to the climate of our southern Russia with the difference of Afghanistan's generally higher temperature due to its location closer to the equator. That is why we see some peculiarities of the regions' climate which distinguish it from the climate of the Black Sea steppes. First of all, we have a long hot summer which continues for six to seven and even eight months; on the contrary the spring and fall practically do not exist. Anyone who has lived in Southern Russia could sometimes miss the spring: just as soon as the melted snow waters are gone – the dry, hot weather comes. It is the opposite in the fall, just as soon as the ground dries after the autumn rains, the snow covers everything. But these examples are exceptions and one can almost always notice the spring and the fall. But in the hill country of Afghanistan, you may not notice spring or fall: the water runs down from the mountains, the snow is gone – and after two-three weeks the summer heat arrives. You would expect a long and even fall, but one or two weeks after summer's intense heat, everything is covered with snow and blizzards take over. Thus in the area you have a long and hot summer, an extremely short spring and fall and a short but quite severe winter with strong blizzards which are causes of human death from freezing and cold wind. The snow is not normally proceeded by a frost and It happens that migrating nomads who are careless, ill dressed (especially poor people and shepherds of horses, sheep and cattle) can be caught unprepared, get lost and freeze to death – the victim of his own nomadic frivolity and the climate's caprices.

This climate is not unhealthy but there are some cases of fever-like diseases. It is difficult to say if those diseases are endemic in the area or they are transferred from the lower areas. In any case, there are some feverish illnesses though they are not extremely severe.

The fourth type of the climate is the *Climate of the lowland valleys* – below 1,500 and 2,000 feet. This climate is hot and very unwholesome. The summer is unbearably hot and humid – it is difficult to live in these areas during June, July and part of August, not to mention the gnats and mosquitoes which bite mercilessly, especially at nighttime. Sweltering heat does not let you get any rest, even at night. Those of you who have had a chance to spend a night while traveling through Eastern Bukhara near the Amu-Darya River know how hot and humid the nights are there. You know how fervently you want some breeze to cool you a little with its light touch. You spend all night from sunset to sunrise sweating and breathing heavily, unable to fall asleep. As to the climate's impact on the health – it is very detrimental. Especially bad are all kinds of feverish diseases that flourish in the area. I can tell you how nasty and various these illnesses are from my trip through Eastern Bukhara in 1904 when a small group of the Cossacks who traveled with me all came down with fever. One of them almost died. Another one safely got to Skobelev [a town] but there he had another horrible paroxysm of the disease. It turned out that the Cossack had caught a particular kind of fever which had repeat paroxysms exactly two weeks later. On the thirteen day, the person would be okay but on the fourteenth day – gravely ill. That form of the disease happened to be very persistent and I've heard that when the Cossack left for his stanitsa, he was still sick.[7]

While traveling to those [Oriental] countries, you have to keep in mind what you need to be wary of. First and foremost is the water. No matter how clean and clear it appears – be careful drinking it – it often can be poison. I kept a very severe regimen with the Cossacks on that matter. I ordered that one of them be beaten with a lash, if he was caught drinking water straight from a brook and he refused to stop drinking immediately. That severe method saved his life. But a human being is still a human being and no matter how often I would tell him that the water in the area is dangerous to drink, he kept saying that it is clear as crystal and comes from a spring – deep inside he did not believe me and could not restrain himself. In any case, it is necessary to carry boiled water on the trip. And now here is the second issue. The most dangerous time of the day is the sunset when the heat of the day subsides and the night miasmas condense with the sharp cooling of the temperature. At that time it is best to stay inside if possible, but if you are on the road – do not undress and stay wrapped up tightly. And the third issue. While traveling through a mountain region, remember that in one day you may go from one climate zone to another – which normally would take a long period of time. In the mountains, you will often go through a pass – and that means changing the climatic environment in two-three hours; you may go from a warm place into one which has a perpetual snow blanket and then again, once you begin to descend you return into a warmer area. It is as if you are making a trip from the polar region to the equator and return. The human body does not take it lightly. You must try to keep your body temperature even and that means dressing appropriately. You start wearing light white clothing because of the sweltering heat and sharp sunrays; but as you begin to ascend into the mountains, you need to cover yourself with something warm and on the top you even may need a fur coat. It is the same process in reverse as you descend the mountains. Do not forget my words and pay them proper attention because if you will not follow these simple rules – especially in regard of drinking un-boiled water – nothing will save you from diseases in these unwholesome areas.

Thus, speaking about the climate of Afghanistan, I call it mountainous and divide it into four types. First is the *Climate of high mountain plateaus* at the elevation of 8,000-11,000 feet; second – the *Climate of elevated plateaus and valleys* located at the altitude of 4,000-8,000 feet; third – the *Climate of steppes and hills* which is located at the altitude of 2,000-4,000 feet; and finally – the *Climate of the lowland valleys* – below 1,500-2,000 feet. The first type is cold and severe but healthy; the second type – moderate, resembling the climate of Central Russia but with hotter summers and a larger variety of vegetation;

7 The Russian is станица. The stanitsa was a large Cossack village which fielded a company or battalion as part of a larger Cossack host. Cossacks provided part-time military service and were part of the defense structure, normally manning the southern boundaries of the empire. Cossack units were primarily cavalry and infantry.

the third type – similar to our Black Sea steppes but with a hotter summer, with almost no spring or fall and the presence of some feverish diseases; and finally the fourth type – the climate of lowland valleys – which is hot and unwholesome. If we apply this to individual areas of Afghanistan, we will be able approximate what kind of climate we will find there – as long as we know the area's altitude. If you are going to travel there or will be carefully monitoring the movements of an explorer – and do not forget the issue of climate – you will find that the picture is fairly close to my description. I will remind to those who read narratives by Burnes, Vambery, Doctor Yavorski, Yate, Robertson, Martin[8] and others that their narratives speak about the large snowdrifts on the Kabul Terrace slopes (the second type of the climate), the feverish diseases of Afghan Turkestan (the fourth type), the nice and nutritious grasses of the Hindu Kush (the first type), etc. Those individual narratives support the correctness of my climatic outline. On other hand, if you want to use my method to make a conclusion about a chosen area– first you will need to find out the area's altitude as the starting and major factor. Besides that, you must take into an account some other data – geographical latitude, area's distance from snow masses, presence of rivers, soil character, etc. – and then use the described method. Let's test it on a map. Areas of Afghan Turkestan adjoining to the Amu-Darya River or deserts such as the Registan or the Dasht-i-Margo are lowlands and their climate should be considered as of the fourth type. And it is true. The difference between them is determined by the differences in geographical latitude and the quantity of moisture. This explains the hotter climate of the Seistan Valley compared to the Amu-Darya River's left bank area. The areas of the middle segments of the Balkh, Kholm, Konduz Rivers and the southern branches of the Siyah-Kuh mountain ridge are steppe hills. These areas, according to Russian reconnaissance and data in the works of Yates and Vambery, are the *Climate of steppes and hills* as I described.

I believe that my outline of the climate deserve some attention – from a scientific point of view as well as a practical one. It is time to throw away tales of a continental climate and to begin to work trying to prove, broaden and develop this theory or a similar one. If, while traveling, you find some faults and shortcomings in it – I would be greatly interested in receiving the necessary corrections. As for now it is sufficient enough to give a general picture of the Afghan climate.

8 Alexander Burnes (1805-1841) was a British (Scottish) explorer of Central Asia. He wrote *Travels into Bokhara. Being an account of a Journey from India to Cabool, Tartary and Persia.* Also, *A Narrative of a Voyage on the Indus from the Sea to Lahore* (London: John Murray, 1834). He was the British political agent to Kabul when he was assassinated there in 1841, a precursor to the First Anglo-Afghan War. Arminius Vambery (1832-1913) was a Hungarian explorer of Central Asia and prolific author. Dr. J. L. Yavorsky authored *Puteshestvie Russkogo Possolstva po Affganistanu I Bukharskomu Khanstvu v 1878-9* [Journey of the Russian Embassy through Afghanistan and the Khanate of Bokhara], St. Petersburg, 1882. Charles Edward Yate, *Northern Afghanistan or Letters from the Afghan Boundary Commission*, Edinburgh and London: William Blackwood and Sons, 1888. George Scott Robertson, *The Kafirs of the Hindu Kush*, London: Lawrence and Bullen, Ltd., 1896. F. A. Martin, *Under the Absolute Emir*, New York, 1907.

Resources of Afghanistan

Now I should move to the topic of Afghanistan's population, but first I am going to speak about the resources and activities of the population of the country. The fact is that it has such a sizable territory, but such a small population which the Englishmen estimate at four million people (British explorer A.G. Kene estimated it at six million in 1880). Whatever the population, it is modest and of primary importance, the country is not wealthy. Whatever the Englishmen say, whichever statements you hear about the country being a bread basket and how interesting it would be to elevate its standard of living – do not be deluded by them. There is a clear picture before us – this country is poor – and alas! We have the historical evidences that it was poor and unattractive before. We can say that the country will stay the same in the future. The major resources of Afghanistan are divided into two components: farming and nomadic livestock-raising. But I have to point out in advance that I would examine the issue from a somewhat different angle. Using the annual trade volume of the foreign trade as a criterion of its resources is useless because this component of economic activity is underdeveloped, constricted by political circumstances and does not have the necessary widespread skills. Englishmen are afraid to let Russians in; the Afghans do not like commerce and cannot do it efficiently. Their commerce is primarily conducted by the Indians, Persians and some of the Tajiks. The routes of communications are in poor condition. And all this hampers trade development in the country terribly. One cannot compile data on the country's resources by direct observation and counting and there is not any statistic data at all....In a word, in order to study the issue of the resources of Afghanistan one would need some other ways and to do these with great circumspection.

As I have already said and want to emphasize, as large as Afghanistan's territory is, it can feed only five-six million of its population. This immediately catches the eye and provides a clue that this is a country with limited resources. Looking back into history we can see that the country has not been densely populated before. Some areas stayed empty and the country had just certain populated spots such as the Herat and Kabul Valleys and some mountainous regions in the western branches of the Hindu Kush – in a word there were some pockets of sizable population. But history tells us those pockets were fairly small and represented by temporary gangs which controlled everyone by fear and threat of the use of force. They got rich through force and exploited the people driven into these places from all corners of Central Asia. And that created a mistaken picture of a large state.

This is the first factor which I want to turn your attention to.

The following is another factor. If you look into English publications on trade – for example trade in 1910 (according to the Statesman's Yearbook) the conclusion is that the trade activity is small and not diverse. The total financial turnover – i.e. the sum of export and import of Indo-Afghan trade in 1909 was 1,314,733 pounds – just a little below 13 million rubles. Englishmen sell cotton fabrics, sugar, tea and paint. They buy Afghan fruit, vegetables, horses, foods and in small quantities – grains and legumes. Our trade with Afghanistan for many years stayed around four million rubles in export and import. Afghanistan buys cotton textiles, sugar, dishes, iron ware, etc. from us. We buy their livestock products, fruit, woven rugs....This unimpressive picture of the trade shows us that Afghanistan is not a wealthy country.

And history gives us some clues in that direction in the accounts of military expeditions concerning logistics, availability of bivouac areas or the possibilities of building strong long-term bases in some areas – such as the Kabul Valley or Kandahar-Ghazni area. We know that some military leaders stayed there for several years. These facts show the picture of the country's resources – and it is still fairly modest.

The so-called Anglo-Afghan wars also support the idea that Afghanistan is a poor country. Roberts was able to get some provisions from different corners of the country – but very little and the price of it was an uprising by the population.[9] All that information leads us to the conclusion we pointed out several time already – that the Afghanistan is a poor country – a conclusion that has been made by most serious Englishmen as well.

The population's work falls into two major branches – farming and nomadic livestock-raising. Other kinds of work are totally insignificant in size compared to them.

Speaking about farm crops, I have to mention the primary ones: wheat, barley (common or naked), millet, corn, jughara (sorghum) and rice. Peas and beans are supplementary crops. I need to point out that in the south there are two harvest seasons a year – of the winter and spring crops. The winter crop includes wheat, barley, beans and peas; the spring – rice, millet, sorghum and others. For the winter crop, planting is done in the fall and harvest in the summer. For the spring crop, planting is done in the late spring and harvest in the fall. Besides these crops, they grow marena (rubia),[10] tobacco, cotton, opium (poppy), hemp, clover and alfalfa. Clover and alfalfa are used for forage, hemp is used to make intoxicating products; rubia, tobacco, cotton and opium are exported. Wheat is the main source of nutrition for the population; barley and jughara (sorghum) are used to feed the horses; arzan (proso millet) and corn are used for culinary purposes.

Besides grain farming, Afghanistan has a well-developed fruit and vegetable industry. Fruit is grown in orchards that are combined with vegetable gardens and also in the open fields (bakhcha).[11] In the orchards, they grow apples, pears, almonds, peaches, apricots, plums, cherries, grapes, figs, quinces, mulberries, walnuts, pistachios, and pineapples; there also is rhubarb which grows wild on the mountain slopes of the northern and eastern mountains. These vegetables play a major role in their export trade. Industrial crops such as castor beans, mustard, sesame and smelly gum[12] are present in abundance.

9 Field Marshal Frederick Sleigh Roberts, 1st Earl Roberts, (30 September 1832-14 November 1914) commanded the relief force that lifted the siege of Kandahar in 1880 during the Second Anglo-Afghan War. Robert's victory revived British fortunes after their disastrous rout at Maiwand. General Roberts forces paid the Afghans for their supplies and the local Afghans were delighted with the opportunity. General Robert's actions brought the Second Anglo-Afghan War to a close and the rebellion did not break out until after the departure of the British force. It was directed against the Afghan government in Kabul and failed. Snesarev seems to be overselling his point here. (Translator's note).

10 *Rubia* is a plant whose roots are used to produce a dye known as rose madder. (Translator's note).

11 In Central Asia, Southern Russia, Ukraine and Caucasus – the open field (often irrigated) is used to grow melons, watermelons, pumpkins, squash, cucumbers and other ground vine produce. (Translator's note).

12 Ferula Acafoetida – a plant whose root produces an aromatic sap used in Oriental medicine. (Translator's note).

Melons of all kind grow on bakhchas (especially praised is the Kandahar variety); they also grow watermelons, cucumbers and tomatoes on bakhchas.

I have already mentioned earlier that the major type of relief suitable for agricultural purposes is the mountain valleys located at the altitude below 9,000 feet and that they are the major places of the people's employment. The wealthiest regions in the country where we can expect some extra production are the Herat and Kabul Valleys, the area surrounding Kandahar and some parts of Afghan Turkestan.

Because of the military orientation of our talk, we need to first direct our attention toward the Herat Valley. With some reconnaissance, we were able to determine that the grain supply there is quite significant and in terms of wheat it would be around 700,000 puds[13] after satisfying the needs of the population and animals. So says British and our intelligence reports. But I would like to point out the suspicious precision of that number and to a no-less suspicious scientific finesse of the conclusion. I have to say that in Central Asia, the control of agricultural productivity is very careful and systematic – because the control comes from the power wielders – those who live by the results of the people's work. Every sheaf [of wheat]and every newborn lamb are counted. But that information is top secret and to obtain it is much more difficult than to get a plan of any European fortress. The ordinary people see a spy for a khan, bek, aksakal[14] and so on in every observer or inquirer and they try to hide the results of their labor to protect it from the government's encroachment. So, how did the figure of 700,000 puds pop up?

We must note that the primary source for those conclusions about the Herat Valley's wealth is the book *Herat Province* by Artamonov.[15] The author at that time was notorious for his shameless attitude toward geographic discoveries. He quite often stated something he had not seen and checked and he described routes he did not see personally, etc. To trust his numbers is as dangerous as trusting the crocodile that he stated he used successfully to cross the Nile River while seated on its back (sometime after his Asian explorations).

Because of that, I suppose that the 700,000 number is hypothetical and most probably exaggerated. But taking into account that the irrigated area of Herat Valley is up to 90,000 desyatinas and calculating the productivity rate of irrigated desyatina we can estimate the surplus as fairly big in any case; maybe even not too far from the 700,000 puds.

As to the Kabul and Kandahar Valleys, there is some information that the usual fertility of those regions has been shaken up. Several years of famine, drought and other problems, as well as the need to maintain a disproportionally large (for Afghanistan) armed force, all this reduced the overall harvest; on other side – it also resulted in excessive taxation which in turn reduced the population's interest in farming. There has been some information that the valleys now are not able to sustain their populations. In any case if we exclude the Herat Valley – and the Kabul Valley to some degree – where we may be able to find some surplus of food, then we have the rest of the country which can,

13 The pud is an obsolete Russian measure of weight. One pud = 40 pounds = 16.380kilograms. (Translator's note).

14 An Aksakal is an elder in a Central Asian village. (Translator's note).

15 Leonid Konstantinovich Artamonov (1859-1932) was a Russian general and explorer. The referenced work is *Across Afghanistan. Herat Province.* Ashkhabad, 1889. (Translator's note).

with God's help, barely feed its own population. For support of this conclusion we can refer to the Second Afghan War data: Lord Roberts was forced to turn to requisitioning to replenish food and forage; and even those were done within reasonable limits – it did not help the Englishmen and provoked riots among the population. It means there was nothing extra to take.

I want to highlight one more point which should lower our estimates of the farming resources of Afghanistan.

In European countries, the record of the food inventory is computed using a method that is based on a specific coefficient of consumption per capita; this is impossible in Asian countries and there one has to take into account specifics of the environment. The nomads, for example, get along almost without bread consumption and keep their flour-use rate to a minimum. The Kara-Kirgiz began bread consumption only with the arrival of Russians– before that it was mostly for the wealthy (*bai*)[16] while the ordinary Kirgiz population lived primarily on dairy and mutton. The regions in Afghanistan that have nomads are many and probably the picture of people's nourishment there is much the same. If they migrate to the areas which do not grow grain, they probably buy some bread from other areas and in very limited quantities. And when we find, in English sources, information on the trade between India and Afghanistan, grain represents part of it (but not that significant – around the small sum of 140,000 rubles). This is not the sale of surplus grain, but the throwing out of the country the very food that is much needed for its own population's nutrition. But that food is lost for the country as a result of poverty or not being used to it. The same Kirgiz in the Pamir got along without salt, although they suffered from its deficiency even as they were accustomed to its shortage. And thus in our suppositions that there is some surplus of food resources, it is not the result of the standard record of normal nutrition but it is a result of the population's undernourishment.

As to other components of the population's sustainment such as the products of nomadic way of life there is a different picture.

Because of the abundance of mountains and valleys, complex relief, great diversity of climate and plentiful moisture in the mountainous and hilly areas, Afghanistan represents a large grassy terrain and is home to a multitude of animals. Afghanistan is rich in animals and these are of high quality and represent the country's large economic resource. In Afghanistan there are wonderful horses, good quality camels, and an abundance of cattle, sheep and goats. History tells us that Afghanistan was always rich with animals. Genghis-Khan's and Timur's cavalry both used these Northern Afghanistan resources for reinforcements and refitting. Guided by this information we are going to conclude that Afghanistan has a large surplus of animals which could serve as a food source on the one hand and transport on the other, because our supply train, despite our desire, will be certainly depend on pack animals. The horses of Afghan Turkestan are especially high quality and they deserve a special note. These are horses of the Kattahan and Badakhshan breeds.[17] The former are present in very large numbers. As to Badakhshan horses – it is a very interesting mountain horse. If in the future you would need horses for travel – get

16 *Bai* is a historic term for a rich landowner in Central Asia. (Translator's note).

17 The Kattahan and Badakshan breeds are not listed in current breed references, but the Kattahan probably is the Akhal-Teke and the Badakhshan may be the Tatar . (Translator's note).

the Badakhshan – and you will have peace of mind. He will be your reliable companion in the mountains and will never betray you. This horse has very strong hooves which are not damaged by stones; during long descents the horse is not afraid of dangerous spaces but remains calm. And when it has to move down a very steep slope, it sits on its hind legs and slides down on its hindquarters while moving the front legs up and down. It has a great sense of orientation and can find forage anywhere. True, lately these horses have become expensive but are worth the money. As to the Kattahan breed – it is an excellent cavalry horse. It is fast, strong and is a good source for cavalry remounts.

In western Afghanistan, one-humped camels stand out – they are strong and posses high endurance. While organizing your expeditions, you should take these qualities into account and consider using camels.

Thus I would conclude that the animals of Afghanistan represent a rich source of meat and beasts of burden, but since you will be in mountain areas, you will need to remember that the populace is very suspicious and deeply secretive. This will seriously hamper your work when you need to find some supplies. This means that you will need to conduct serious reconnaissance and attract the local population to your side using all means.

Also I have to mention firewood.

We need to study this small necessity especially carefully because its importance in military operations as well as in everyday life. Looking at the country's map, one can readily see that north of the Hindu Kush Mountains stretch vast expanses of steppes and hills practically devoid of forest. The same treeless spaces fill the area south-west of the Chaman – Kandahar – Farakh road. Finally, the same type of treeless space is south-east of the road Kandahar – Ghazni – Kabul… And that in particular is the essence of Suleiman Mountains' severity and inaccessibility – they are devoid of vegetation and inhabitants are forced to cook and warm themselves with kizyak[18].

One can find significant wooded areas: 1) In the Harirud Valley especially in its hilly and mountainous parts; 2) On the northern slopes of the Band-i-Turkestan, Sefid-Kuh and Siyakh-Kuh Mountain ridges; 3) on the Hindu Kush slopes; 4) in the Upper Kabul Valley; 5) In the valleys of the Adraskan and Helmand rivers; and 6) in the Ghazni Valley. We should note that the forests in the western part consist of large deciduous trees (oaks, walnuts); pine trees are prevalent in the mountains of the eastern part; and in the rivers' valleys (after they leave the mountainous areas), the forests are diverse and often have a tropical character.

Thus, supply of timber will be the start point for heating and cooking in military units and for building various wooden structures such as barracks and bridges. Obviously there will be some regions where stocking up and storing firewood or creating a firewood transport system will become a serious issue.

Now I will touch upon the issue of collecting wagons and carts in the event of organizing an expedition. I've already mentioned that the country is notable for usage of a specific kind of transport – pack animals. The mountain passes restrict the use of wagons and you understand that when we are talking about the country's transportation system

18 Kizyak is dried manure (primarily cattle) used in Central Asia and some other areas as fuel. (Translator's note).

in general – wheeled transport is out of question. Although some regions of the country permit usage of wagons and carts, it is an exception. For example, in Badakhshan they have a special kind of wagon; Afghan Turkestan has arbas – two-wheeled carts with very large wheels. There are some unique carts in the Kabul Valley and in the areas adjoining the Indus River which were developed under the influence of India. But in general, you can count on pack animal transport only – no more. And even if you were able to climb up the Hindu Kush Mountains in a cart, you would be forced to abandon it there due to the dry air which dries out and cracks the cart's wheels. For example, during my Pamir expedition, we had a large number of wagons but were forced to abandon them after passing Ghulcha – the wheels dried up and cracked.

One of Ghenghis-Khan's expeditions provides an interesting historical confirmation of the fact that wagons and carts cannot be used as transport. In the summer of 1221, during the Ghazni campaign, he left behind all his wheeled transport in what is now Afghan Turkestan where it was attacked and looted by Emir Mohammed Moragani.[19]

Thus the impassability of the terrain, the snow blankets on the mountain passes and the dryness of the climate requires one to reject wheeled transport and consider pack animals as the common transportation. For individual reconnaissance and trips, it is all the more so – one needs to leave wheels behind and get a saddle horse.

Finally we need to touch upon the other resources of Afghanistan – namely its mineral wealth. You will hear various tales about copper ore, precious stones, iron ore, and so on. For example, Martin, who belonged to the emir's court for eight years, speaks about these treasures frequently.[20] He particularly mentions coal, but he discusses it somewhat ambiguously and you cannot understand if he is hiding something or if something has been hidden from him and he is only making things up. And the author himself feels it and that explains his frequent attempts to prevent the natural perplexity which the readers feel at all the vagueness. So, many times he says that the emirs deliberately hide the mineral wealth of Afghanistan to prevent the unwanted attention of those who would try to conquer the "God Given Country". He also gives some other reasons for the ambiguity. We need to note that as to [the mineral wealth], it is unlikely that anyone has definite knowledge since the people of Afghanistan hide the information about their riches from all for a variety of reasons. To do more detailed research ......[*typographic error – lost text line*] undoubtedly nevertheless. Iron ore is common throughout Afghanistan and the so-called *Afghan iron* is highly praised in India. There are many salt deposits – for example in Darvaz and Northern Badakhshan. I've seen them myself and I have no doubt that Afghanistan has large deposits of mineral salt. The mountains of Badakhshan should have deposits of precious stones – I've heard about them while working in the Pamir. Some rivers have a high content of gold during the summer high water. The Hindu Kush Mountains must have deposits of metals and minerals, especially in its southern slopes....That is all one can say with certainty on the matter. I will say it again – the people keep their mineral resources a deep secret. It is difficult to explain what causes that, but a traveler meets this stubborn secrecy everywhere. It is highly probable that the people fear that

19 V. Bartold, *Turkestan During the Mongol Invasion*, Saint-Petersburg 1900, vol. 2, page 491. (Author's note).

20 F. A. Martin, *Under the Absolute Emir*, New York and London, 1907. (Translator's note).

if a valley or a region becomes known for deposits of valuable minerals, other people will then come, the "strangers with envious eyes". They would drive away the locals from the pastures and rob them of everything. The inhabitants themselves quietly find gold, pan it and keep it in small bags. They mine some coal for heating. But all that happens on a small scale and is not worth discussion.

4

Population of Afghanistan

Now I will move to the issue of population of Afghanistan. I must say that the issue of population is the cornerstone of any military-geographical research and population research requires a broad approach on a complex scale. First of all it is necessary to make sure that the research answers the question of the size of the population because that number is the starting point in calculating the size of the armed forces the country can field during wartime. Before the calculation was based on 10% of the population for the full war effort, but nowadays it would be probably 15% or even 20%. The second question of the research is related to the general moral and spiritual customs of the people, i.e. their origin, religion, peculiar national traits – the *people's character* in general. You will see that all of these considerations are of interest in the event of war as their relation to the political struggle, various connections, trade interests, proselytizing one teaching or another, etc. The answer to these major questions – about the size and character of the population – is a necessity for everyone: the military, politicians, reformer, merchant, etc. More specific questions are embedded in the general issue of the people's character: their way of life; their domestic animals; their working tools; where the people reside (in groups of three-four houses or in large towns); the kinds and peculiarities of their housing; how residents treat foreigners – friendly or with hostility; how a local treats you when you are in his saklya;[1] can you talk to his wife and will she be present with the men; how you need to greet him and how to leave; have you a right to dine with him or is having a meal with a stranger considered discourteous; and a multitude of other questions. In Europe, for example, eating just a little while being visiting is considered to be the rule of etiquette but the Kirgiz will not be satisfied until you get – excuse me – nausea from overeating. All these details play a significant role in everyday life and only they complete the picture of the life and particular features of the people which give you the ability to answer consciously the question *what kind of people are they in general*?

That is why I consider the issue of people important – I think they are the kernel of truth in military-geographical research.

One more word about the method of research. Due to the fact that military-geographical research attaches such importance to the issue of population, the scale of the matter should be extended significantly. We have to step aside from our practical method of study and expand it with necessary theoretical substantiation. It is understandable. When we come to the people's character, temperament – to the complexity of the nation's soul – we quite often feel that we have no ability to get this understanding from observing the contemporary environment. We are forced to look back into the people's past, their origin, religion, etc. There we need to search for the definitive characteristics that the

1 A saklya is a house in the Caucasus and some other mountainous areas. (Translator's note).

people inherited from their ancestors. We also are pressed to answer the questions – is the nation homogeneous or mixed; and if it is mixed – with which other nations? And only a detailed anthropological and ethnographic account may give us the ability to answer these numerous questions.

Thus, obviously, we cannot confine our research to the practical method.

The population of Afghanistan consists of three major groups: the *Afghan* group, the *Iranian* (or Tajik) group and the *Turkic* group. The Afghan group is predominant – numerically as well as politically. Let's start with it. Researchers have different approaches to this group.

The point is that the Afghan group is not only locked inside of Afghanistan. Parts of the group live in British India and some of them are British citizens while others remain part of independent frontier tribes. Looking into the territorial distribution of the population, we find a large group of the Afghan people are in the Suleiman Mountains area, a smaller one (Yusufzi) are in Dardistan in the basin of the Swat and Panjkora Rivers. And here is the question: shall we study the only the Afghan group which lives inside of Afghanistan or study the group in its entirety?

In his work, our academy's professor, V.F. Novitski[2] considers all Afghans as a single entity. So does Rittikh, [3] but Andogski, for example, limits himself to the study of only those tribes which live inside Afghanistan. I think it would be more correct and expedient to study the entire Afghan nation without regard to their location or citizenship. We will consider all issues mainly from the point of view of military concerns and thus we shall consider all the people en masse which could appear in wartime. The divided people may, during time of war, find solidarity and common political goals – and I mean during a large war, not a minor one. There is no doubt that no matter what preventive measures the Englishmen are taking or how much gold they spread – at the decisive minute of the big war, the Afghan groups will merge into one great family – not move in separate directions. There are family relations, mutual history and national interests, common hatred of Englishmen – and many more things which will push Afghans to operate with concerted efforts. I repeat – because our scale of measurement is primarily military we should not be troubled by the fact that Afghans are spread across separate territories and we need to consider them as an entire group.

As to other nationalities – Iranian and Turkish – though their number is up to three million – we can say that by historical circumstances and the contemporary situation, these people occupy the second stage.

So let's first consider Afghans and look into their past. The information about them can be found in works of different historians – but it is vague and murky.

2 Vasiliy Fyodorovich Novitski (1869-1929) was a Russian military leader, general and military geographer who studied Mongolia, Afghanistan and India. He worked as a professor at the RKKA Academy (1919-1929). (Translator's note).

3 Pyotr Alexandrovich Rittikh (1874- after 1920) was a Russian Colonel and Orientalist who studied Persia, India, and Afghanistan. (Translator's note).

The Afghan's Past

Historically, the first mention of Afghans was by Herodotus who, while speaking about the tribes that lived in Eastern Iran, referred to the mountain tribes residing next to India who called themselves *Pactiens*. Afghans call themselves *Pukhtun* or *Pushtun*; the Hindus call them *Pathans*. That makes it fairly easy to recognize the contemporary Afghans in the *Pactiens* of Herodotus. The more so since the Afghan's own legends and tales link their ancient location to the same mountains where they were placed by Herodotus and which are still populated only by them. Herodotus gave us few details about the *Pactiens*, calling them "barbarians dressed in animal skins". There is a historic register of nations ruled by Darius Histasp[4] written on the stones of Persepolis.[5] The register names, among others, the Us-Hangi who lived "lawlessly" (i.e. not practicing the religion of Zarathustra and not following civic laws). Ritter postulated that the Afghans came from the Us-Hangis as well as from the *Assacan,* which Alexander the Great had to fight during his campaign across eastern Kabulistan. Then weighty evidence was presented against that supposition. This forces us to move from Herodotus directly to the Chinese chronicles which, while describing the history of conquest of Kabulistan by various Turkish tribes (the Sak, Ut and Hun) mentioned in passing the people *Pudun* which lived in the Mountains south of Kabulistan (Suleiman Mountains) and who fought the Ut (Yuetchzhee) fiercely. Some Afghan scholars want to recognize these people as the Afghans from this one mention in the Chinese sources. They tie this in with the kingdom of *Falana*, near Ghazni which was mentioned by Tsuan-zan[6] (7th Century A.D.). But the transcription of Patan into Falana does not look appropriate to our Orientalists.

Thus, before the Arab invasion, we find only two more or less reliable mentions of Afghans: by Herodotus (5th Century B.C.) and the Chinese chronicles (early A.D.). They both point out the savagery and bellicosity of the Afghans and place them in the same Suleiman Mountains which the Afghans themselves consider as their ancestral motherland (where they were found later by the Arabs and Turks) and where some of them are still living today. Then, until the 11th Century A.D., we cannot find any information about Afghans (if we do not count the above-mentioned Tsuan-zan). The first mention of Afghans by Muslim sources came from a historian named Abu-Nasr-Mohammed who wrote in the 11th Century and compiled the Ghaznevids dynasty's history. He wrote that they "live on the top of high mountains and make their living by robberies in the surrounding valleys". *Khanykov* commented on this: "The portrait is so accurately drawn from the original that it is impossible not to recognize the contemporary Afghans".[7] The mountains of the Ghazni area where Abu-Nasr places Afghans are the same Suleiman Mountains which were mentioned by Herodotus and the Chinese.

---

4 Darius Histasp (550 B.C. – 486 B.C.) was an ancient Persian ruler known for his military expeditions and reforms. (Translator's note).

5 The Greek name for the ancient Persian city of Pars. (Translator's note).

6 A Buddhist monk who visited the Pamir region as a pilgrim in the summer of 642 A.D. (Translator's note).

7 Nikoli Vladimirovich Khanykov (1817-1898) was a Russian explorer and the author of *Bokhara: It's Amir and People,* London, 1845. (Translator's note).

According to Abu-Nasr, the Afghans at the time occupied the same area where they had lived for fifteen centuries and still had the same way of life. And they stayed as savage as they were during Herodotus' lifetime and during Xerxes' campaigns against Greece when they appeared in the army of the great Persian Shah.

Abu-Nasr did not say if they were Muslims at the time. The Afghan's own legends place their conversion to Islam in the 9th Century, but there are some other sources which place it to the 13th Century. Both versions could be correct because the Afghans are divided into a multitude of tribes and clans which probably turned to the Arab Prophet's teaching at different times. The Mahmud of Ghazni (11th Century) used Afghans in his campaigns, assembling them into detachments which assailed India along with his forces. As a reward for this service, Mahmud (according to the Afghan chroniclers) bestowed on them the lands around Ghazni, Kabul and Peshawar. Those were the first Afghan settlements in the valleys among the Iranian and Hindu majorities. Soon, the invasions of Turks and Mongols opened a way to the wider settlement of the regions by the Afghans. Information about these turbulent times is scarce. We know more details about Genghis-Khan's devastations, but about what was going on later in the subjugated countries, who lived there and how they lived out their miserable existence – we know almost nothing. There is a 16th Century story by Ibn-Batuta who wrote about Kabul that "Before it was a large city but now – a village populated by Afghans". This note gives us a glimpse of understanding how Afghans infiltrated into the countries of ancient culture – Kabulistan and Arakhosia (the area of Kandahar and Ghazni). As the ancient Hindu and Iranian population had been exterminated by the invasions of Turks and Mongols, the Afghans descended from the high mountains and wild valleys and took over the lowlands and lower valleys; they partly continued their nomadic ways of life but partly reverted to farming. The well known and proven ability of the Afghan tribes to assimilate foreign tribes also quickly expanded the number and territorial limits of Afghans. Along with the Afghans the plains and valleys of Kabulistan and Arakhosia were also filled with Turkish newcomers – leftovers of Timur and Genghis-Khan's hordes. Initially it was so. But with time, the Turks took on the Afghan way of life and were assimilated into Afghan tribes. For instance, a fairly large tribe, the Ghilzai or Gildzhi probably are a descendant from the Turkish tribe Khilij or Khalaj which took over western Kabulistan during one of many invasions by the Turkish hordes.

Afghans continued to serve in the armies of the Eastern Iran rulers' armies and were taking on a growing importance. For example, during the reign of Sharukh (of the Timuride dynasty) who ruled Herat, the Afghans received the Kandahar region for their settlements. About the same time, they captured the Bajaur, Swat and Bunir Valleys supplanting the "infidel kafirs".

Thus at the end of the 15th Century, Afghans had already widely expanded their settlements and even had undertaken a number of conquests. Besides subjugating and populating the mountain valleys of ancient Ghandaria (eastern Kabulistan), part of the Afghan people parted from their compatriots, crossed the Indus River and subjugated Punjab, Sindh and areas of the Upper Ganges. There they founded the ephemeral and short-lived Muslim state which temporarily achieved fearsome might. Sultan Babur put the Afghan rule in India to an end by overthrowing the Patan (Afghan) dynasty in 1525.

The same Babur also greatly stressed the Afghans in Kabulistan. Trying to establish peace and security in his state, he immediately ran into the predatory and belligerent

Afghans. He was forced to undertake a number of brutal and bloody wars. He easily handled Afghans living on the plains and valleys. But to pacify those mountaineers who lived in their original motherland – in the gorges and peaks of Sefid-Kuh and Suleiman Mountains – was not an easy task. To pacify them he invaded the Khotan Mountains (the extension of eastern Sefid-Kuh) from Peshawar, went through the mountains up to Kogat and to the upper part of the Kuram Valley. Then he entered the valleys of Suleiman Mountain Ridge and through them reached Ghazni and Kabul. Every inch of the way, he met fierce resistance. But he overcame it and for a long time the Afghans were held down.

But the constraint put on the predatory expansion of the Afghan tribes by that enlightened ruler continued only during his life. The huge Indian kingdom founded by Babur had served as a lever for further strengthening the Afghan dominance of Kabulistan and Arakhosia. The great Mogul dynasty – Babur's heirs – paid scant attention to the poor country that had served their great ancestor as the starting point of his own great kingdom. Further, a large part of the indigenous population [Hindus and Persians] had followed Babur into India. The exodus increased along with growing insecurity in Kabulistan during the reign of Babur descendants. In a word, they politically and ethnically cleared the area for Afghans who did not fail to use it to resume raids and plundering but they also populated the emptied land. That process continued for two centuries (16th – 18th Century) and lead to the situation where Afghans comprised the majority of the population in the districts of Ghazni, Kandahar, Kabul, Jalalabad and Peshawar.

I gave you this long historical information to give you a look at the consistent expansion of Afghan people to the limits of their contemporary territory. That information is quite typical. What does it tell us? The Suleiman Mountains – that poor, dreary, waterless, non-forested region provided the people with a severe upbringing and made them resilient, persistent and proud.

The country did not arouse the envy of their mighty neighbors and if they entered it – they stayed for only a short time. It built a good groundwork for the love of freedom and independence in the young nation. Because the country's resources are very scarce, one had to share with others the little he had and it instilled hospitality as a prominent feature of the people's character.

On other hand, the same poverty forced them to look for means and riches outside their area and to take them by stealth -using raids, robbery and swindling. From this came the greed, robber's instincts, trickery and perfidy as distinctive traits of the Afghan character. The hot and dry climate of the Suleiman Mountains influenced the people to develop a psyche with a fiery temperament. Afghans are irascible, hot-tempered and vindictive.

From the same historical information we see that the Afghans did not expand and grew strong by leaps and bounds. Rather, they did it gradually, adroitly using favorably developing historical situations. In one place they acted as victors (western Dardistan), in another one – as skilful assimilators (Ghilzan) and in the third – as the timely newcomers (lower rivers of the Seistan basin). These gradual moves and the normality of the development gave them an ability to preserve the primary features of their national character and keep them fresh, clean and unbroken. We can consider the nation to be young and viable today.

Origin of the Afghans

I have to say a few words about the Afghans' origin. Most of the scientists agree that they are Aryans and this is supported by the latest research into the Afghan language (Darmstetter). But quite recently some scientists (in particular V.V. Grigoryev, though Ritter and Khanykov previously stood by the Aryan version) considered Afghans (as they themselves think) to be the descendants of the ten tribes of Israel, who were deported by Persian rulers to the eastern outskirts of Iran. This legend exists in connection with a mention in the Old Testament of Khabor (i.e. contemporary Khaiber – Khyber Pass) as the place of exile of the Israeli tribes and with the physical appearance of the Afghan people – eagle-nosed with curly black hair which served as the reason for the preservation of the baseless hypothesis. But I got carried away with the theory. And the Afghans' belief in their Jewish origin has a practical basis. Abdur Rahman talked about it in his autobiography. The ruler of the "God-Given Country" said that Afghans got their name because a part of them descended from Afghan – the Commander-in-Chief of King Solomon's forces and another part – from Jeremy, son of Saul.[8]

If, in the future, you study the genealogy of Oriental peoples you will encounter a number of such legends. You will notice that Turks, Tajiks and many other Oriental nations like to link themselves to a Jewish origin. There is another popular legend among the Tajiks of western Pamir, the Hunza-Naghar (Dardistan) and other mountain peoples – that they (rather their rulers) are the direct descendants of Alexander the Great – and thus they are of divine origin. It is absolutely clear that Alexander the Great is no relative of theirs. But in this case, it is the pride of the people who want to attach themselves to this vessel of history and at the same time – to let an outsider know that they are familiar with literary sources in which they have been mentioned. Without having their own historical data – or having only some dim information – many Oriental nations accept such legends and build beliefs about those who have the most serious reputation and then spread this belief widely. The Bible is the most popular source of these legends. From the Bible, we see traces of Solomon's presence everywhere in Central Asia, his throne (Takhti-Suleiman) near Osh and in the very Suleiman Mountains, etc. From out of this grew the legend of the Jewish origin of one or another of the Central Asian nations. This is fashionable among the Oriental aristocracy.

Now I will move from the historical view of the issue to the anthropological. As early as the 16th – 17th Century, Muslim sources divided the Afghans into four groups – up to 405 clans – which had descended from the afore-mentioned Afghan or another – from the Patan or finally – from the Kerlarni. The works of Elphinstone, Burnes, Yule, Temil, Bellew[9] and among the Russians – N.A. Aristov – were able to figure out the basis of that classification – and it turned out to be anthropological.

---

8 The recorded sons of Saul are Jonathan, Abinadab, Malchisua and Ish-Bosheth by his wife Ahinoam and Armoni and Mephiboseth by his concubine Rizpah. (Translator's note).

9 Mountstuart Elphinstone, *An Account of the Kingdom of Cabul and its Dependencies in Persia, Tartary and India,* 1815; Alexander Burnes, *Travels into Bokhara: Being an account of a Journey from India to Cabool, Tartary and Persia.* Also, *A Narrative of a Voyage on the Indus from the Sea to Lahore* (London: John Murray, 1834; Sir Henry Yule, *The Travels of Marco Polo* (1874) and author of the Encyclopedia Britannica entry on Afghanistan; Henry Walter Bellew, *The Races of*

Let's look into those four groups.

Groups of the Afghan people

The first group – the Karlani includes up to 128 *khels* – i.e. clans. The group includes the tribes: Afridi, Orakzai, Utmanzi,, Khattak, Waziri etc. They occupy all the northern half of the Suleiman Mountain system from the Homul River to the Peshawar Valley and Kabul-Darya. These tribes represent typical Pashtu Afghans – the distinctive fundamental features of the Afghan race shine through them. The prime occupation of the Karlani is livestock raising and farming. They live in small villages, sometimes – in caves; many of the Karlani are nomads. The Karlani split up into small independent tribal communities which are governed by the clan elders' meetings (jirga). The elders are elected and replaced at jirgas and they represent the executive branch of government. During wartime, the communities and alliances elect a dictator.

Here before you is the group of the Afghan people – the clearest and purest in the ethnic sense. This is because, as you can see, they have not left their original people's nest yet. You must be amazed by their beauty and integrity, their free and expedient form of governance. To this group belongs a reply to the Englishmen's reproof that among the Afghans, there are discords, disturbances, bloodshed and poverty and their reply was: "Though we are poor and there is bloodshed among us… It is our internal affair. But we Afghans are first and foremost free".

The same Karlani group is also important since fate has kept them in the very mountain area that is an important link connecting Afghanistan with India. They possess the Khyber and Hamul mountain passes – the keys to which could speedily open the route into the Englishmen's treasure chest – India.

Ethnographers consider that the three other groups are descendants of the Karlani that resettled throughout different periods of time. They mixed with other ethnic groups and settled in new places as separate tribes.

The second group is the Ghourgushti with its leading tribe of the Kakar (around 20 thousand). They occupy the western part of the Suleiman Mountains to the border with Baluchistan. The tribes of the Ghourgushti group are governed by hereditary elders and khans – sometimes with despotic inclinations. There is an assumption that the Ghourgushti tribes are mixtures of the Karlani and Baluchi – and that defines their customs and lower combat temperament.

The next group is the Sarbani. It includes the Abdalli-Durrani, possibly the Yusafzai and other small tribes. They occupy the southern and south-western border areas of the Helmand basin from Kandahar to Herat. Until recently the Durrani were considered the leading tribe. They were in a state of martial law almost constantly. Each household [in the original – a plow] sends a cavalryman to the emir's force. Members of this group are brave and better educated. The main clan of the Durrani tribe – the Barakzai (300 thousand) – has produced emirs beginning with Dost-Muhammad.

Afghanistan: Being a Brief Account of the Principal Nations Inhabiting that Country, Calcutta and London: Thacker, Spink and Co, 1890. (Author's note).

The most numerous Afghan tribe – the Ghilzai or Khilji or Ghilzi (one million) belongs to the fourth group. They are subdivided into the Toran and Burkhan. Masson divided them into western (Otek, Toki, Tereki and Enderi) and eastern (Suleimankhel) clans. They are ruled by independent khans who live east of Ghazni.

Ghilzai occupy a large area from Kabul to Kalat-i Ghilzai. Those tribes have been the most hostile toward the Englishmen. During the 1878-1880 war, they achieved several serious victories over the Englishmen. Scientists think that the Ghilzai are descended from Turkic people, the Khalaj, which settled in the country during Timur's time and have since become completely Afghan.

This anthropological picture tells us that the Karlani group is the most primeval and strong – and possible the most viable – among all groups of Afghan people. The Ghourgushti group, which was spoiled by infusion of slaves' blood, is sluggish and devoid of the necessary vigor. Infusion of Iranian (or some other more recent) blood added a more refined way of life, better education and governance to the Sarbani group. And finally, the Ghilzai group came from common Turkish people and became a little savage and were refreshed by historical experience. Like the people of the Sarbani group, they are capable of a more complex governance system.

National character

Travelers describe Afghans as tall, well-muscled beautiful people with hooked noses, prominent cheekbones and black (rarely light brown) long and thick beards. They wear long – up to shoulder length – hair. Eastern tribes have a swarthy complexion and the western – lighter skin. Afghans are savage, brutal, greedy, and stingy; they are also vain, bloodthirsty, fanatical and perfidious. But on other hand, they are ardent, strongly dedicated to the tribe, clan and country; they are very hospitable. Abdur Rahman-Khan says the Afghans are intelligent, brave, love education and knowledge; they are devoted to freedom and independence, want reforms and enlightenment. They do not have superstitions and prejudice against foreigners and their ideas – such as we see among the Hindu. Many Afghans dress well – like Europeans.

Of course, you could reason that Abdur Rahman's opinion is an example of the educated Afghan's judgment of his own people and nothing else. This judgment has its value as the evidence of deeply engrained pride and a large portion of boasting and cockiness. But the characteristics that we discussed before represent the essence extracted from many opinions delivered by observers of the Afghans. In it we first must note the fiery temperament of the Southerners, their volatility and acerbity; their ability to get quickly carried away with hope but also to lose hope and fall into despair is notable. The wars between England and Afghanistan clearly revealed this peculiarity of the people's character.

You are swaying between the positive and negative characteristics of the Afghan people and ready to look for some middle ground, but this is no easy task. Every researcher stubbornly insists on his own opinion leaning either toward the good or bad side but avoiding the happy medium. If it is an English source – and especially if it is the work of a *political* or *military* scholar – the characteristic of the Afghans would be heavily concentrated on their bad side; the Englishmen feel enmity toward the Asian peoples and are so much gripped by the expectations of vengeance and hate from them that they include a lot of wicked feeling in any characteristic. On other hand, if you read such an essay as "Anglo-Indian Caucasus" by N.A. Aristov – who is an absolutely peaceful person – you will see in his descriptions an excess of the kind vagueness, a desire to highlight the more positive sides – i.e. leaning toward excess toward the good parts. Let your intuition, future study of the works of historians and your practical work in the countries of the Middle East give you a clue toward the intelligent and objective middle.

Population size

Now I am going to move to the issue of the population's size. You remember that the matter of the population's size plays a big role because there is a specific co-efficient *that shows the size of the fighting force that a country could produce during wartime* [Translator correction and italics]. Until now we thought it was 10%, but now the quota should be raised to 15-20%, especially in European wars where even women are taking part.

Afghanistan's population, as with any Asian country, cannot be counted precisely. In the course of last 40 years, most scholars came up with the number five million. Abdur Rahman laughed at those writers and called them "Ignoramuses who are not guilty of their lack of knowledge, but they are insolent when pushing it on the readers". The English Statesman's Yearbook of 1910 declares that Afghanistan's population size is between four million and four-and-one-half million. A.G. Kene came with the number 6,145,000 in 1880 and our encyclopedias stand by the same number. Out of this total number, the true Afghans account for 3,520,000. The Goth's Almanac (1914, page 504) states Afghanistan's population is "about five million people. One of the latest scholars of Afghanistan – Aristov (Anglo-Indian Caucasus) thinks that there are about two million people under the rule of the Afghan emir, one-and-one-half million – in the independent frontier tribes, more than one million – in the British possessions (including Baluchistan); the total number of Afghans is four-and-one-half – five million people. I know Mr. Aristov personally and regard him as a careful and meticulous scientist. I think his account has a solid base.

Now we will talk about the number of other peoples.

Kene and Aristov and others think that other nationalities account for up to three million – a million of Tajiks among them. The Tajik – the descendants of the main Iranian population (farmers and traders) live predominantly in Western Afghanistan and Badakhshan. Turkish people (the Uzbek, Turkmen and others) number up to 500 thousand and they dominate in Afghan Turkistan. The Hazara and Aimak (they reside from Ghazni to Harirud in the north-west and upper Murghab account for 700 thousand. The other nationalities are represented by the Kafir (up to 150 thousand), Kizil-Bach (up to 150 thousand) and Indian tribes (up to 300 thousand) – they live in towns. And finally there are the Baluchi and others small nationalities – up to 200 thousand.

Thus the total population of Afghanistan is about five million – three million non-Afghans among them. If the supposed war effort of the country would be 15%, we can count the maximum military mass at 300 thousand Afghan and 450 thousand non-Afghan (it would be 750 thousand pan-Afghan). It is of course the maximum and the acceptable number would be about half a million.

Before, when we talked about the Afghan nation, I forgot to tell you about their language and the ways of life. I have to mention their language because in our lecture cycle we cannot include this particular language due to the lack of an instructor (professor) as of yet.

Afghan language

Afghans speak the language called "Pushtu" or "Pukhtu". The question of the origin of this language has been developed by the following scientists: Dorn (he was a professor at Petrograd University), the Englishmen – Lich, Trump, and Major Riverty and lately – by the French philologist Darmstetter.

The language represents a serious puzzle and has been such for a long time. Its roots include Sanskrit, Arabic, Hebrew and Persian parts mixed together in unclear proportions. European philologists cannot trace the origin of some words. That fact did confuse the philologists – they could not decide where to place the language. But the final word belongs to the French philologist Darmstetter – the Afghan language is one of the Oriental languages of the ancient Iranian group; though for us the matter is of little interest. As to the "Pushtu" language, it is currently divided into two dialects – Eastern and Western.

The literature of "Pushtu" is quite insignificant. There are collections of legends and folk songs and one can find semi-legendary war stories which are quite interesting. In that deeply national folklore, the main features of the character of the Afghan people is reflected as in a mirror: freedom-loving, proud, boastful, sarcastic, and disliking foreigners – especially the Englishmen. But I repeat – the literature is poor and barely developed. The rest of the literature – the more serious literature of history and politics and other topics are present in other languages, primarily in Persian.[10]

It would be fair to say that, until recently, the Afghan language was a subject of little serious interest to the Europeans – the Englishmen and the Russian as well. You might encounter a legend that an English detachment perished because nobody knew the Afghan language. It felt like conspiracy everywhere, the plans were made and the conventional signs were evident but all that remained a mystery to the Englishmen and their ignorance ended – as we know – with the death of all the detachment in the Khurd-Kabul defile (west of Jalalabad). Only doctor Brydon survived of all his detachment – he rode half-dead to Jalalabad (where an English garrison held the position at the time) to deliver a horrible message.[11] This story [of language deficiency] we must regard as a legend – but we need to highlight the fact that the Englishmen's attitude toward the Afghan language has lately become very serious.

10 The latest information I've received from persons who lived in Kabul (November – December of 1920 and January – February of 1921) shows a strong expansion of the Persian language in Afghanistan; it not only swallowed up the high courts and noble spheres but got into scientific circles, trade interests and general business circles. The real Afghan language is left to the nomads. (Author's Note).

11 Snesarev is referring to the First Anglo-Afghan War (1839-1842). General Elphinstone withdrew his army of 16,000 (3,500 combatants and 12,000 civilian camp followers) from Kabul toward Jalalabad in January 1842 and ended up conducting a 30-mile fighting withdrawal. The force was decimated with only one British survivor reaching Jalalabad. (Translator's Note).

How is the language expressed? The Arabic lettering is used but with some differences. These differences are minor and easily learned. But we should remember that the practical matters of writing are capricious and various. Only long practice will teach you to figure out these involved and capricious scrawls which evolve from simple Arabic letterings. In the future, when you will have to work with trade notes, different documents, love letters, etc. – you will repeatedly see for yourself that what you have is not the same as you see in printed materials or in high-quality calligraphy.

The Persian language plays a major role in Afghanistan. It is the language of the rich and nobility; it is the language of trade and diplomacy. The Persian language is used at the Afghan Emir's court and we will find it in the most remote slums of Central Asia. The courtiers of the influential khans, important mullahs and all generally-educated persons know the Persian language. And if you want to keep something secret, then you must remember that the Persian language is the most widely-used in these circles and you must not use it to reveal your secret thoughts when in the presence of people you do not know very well.

A few words about the Afghans' everyday life. You must make yourself familiar with it at least to some general degree. I emphasize that this way of life, to a large degree, is determined by the fact that you have to deal with Islamic people. As you know, Islam is divided into two large sects; the Sunni and the Shiites. If you approach the business as a European – you have to forget about these sects. The Muslims of the Orient quite often quarrel among themselves and are hostile to each other;[12] for whole centuries they argue about certain rituals and rites, but when you have to deal with them as a European – then there is a Muslim before you – without regard to which sect he belongs to. As a Muslim, the Asian will retain in the depth of his awareness, a stubborn and very particular attitude toward you as to the representative of a different religion and philosophy. You must always remember that. It does not matter how the relations with an Asian are developed, how well he greets you or what friendly attitude he displays toward you – this is evoked by his desire to have you on his side – you must not forget that in reality he feels a very deep mistrust and uncontrollable hostility toward you. These feelings may be put aside temporarily – but so far nobody has been able to remove these feelings for a long while. This kind of attitude toward Europeans saturates all Oriental peoples – and it does not matter if they are nomads or live in villages of two-four houses or even in caves – it is all the same. Figuring out the origin of that feeling would be an unnecessary theoretical distraction. The Asian is by his nature deeply nationalistic. There is a duty of any Afghan: to know his tribe and its eminent representatives; to know his clan, its history, take pride in it and praise it to the sky. And this duty he carries out with great joy and passion. For the Afghan, the nation is his second religion. It is quite obvious then with such a strong, passionate and always one-sided feeling as a background, the people of other nations appear as something strange, distant, hostile and despicable. And the

---

12 To know the phenomenon, it is, of course, necessary to familiarize yourself with the Orient. I have to mention that during reign of Khabibulla-Khan, the clergy were required to say formally to what degree one has to show tolerance toward Afghan Shiites. They issued the verdict: "The Sunni religion is the only righteous one and recognized by Your Majesty as the King of Islam." Based on that verdict all religious rites of the Shiites in Afghanistan have been prohibited. The order had been issued to build all Shiite mosques five feet shorter than the Sunni, etc. (Author's Note).

more distant the nation – the more hostile the Asian's attitude grows in size, depth and passion. And just by this aspect, the European is the opposite of the Asian and consequently is a subject of distrust and animosity.

But this feeling is also reinforced and roused by Islam. Though some of the enlightened and progressive pages of the Koran[13] recommend loving foreign people (something like "... there is no Greek or Jew...") and almost all the world – even pointing toward the hope for universal peace – the general tone of that holy book is overflowing with hate and the most ardent enmity toward everything that is not Muslim.[14] It explains the fact that Islam is the torch which has always inflamed in the Asian's soul the feelings of enmity toward anything foreign into a large wildfire. The Asian does not like, does not trust and to some degree is afraid of Europeans. Do not forget this main trait in his character. Under good circumstances, these feelings could be weakened greatly but under unfavorable severe conditions, the feelings manifest themselves in the form of excesses such as the afore-mentioned massacre of Englishmen in the Khurd-Kabul Valley in January 1842 or the Andijan uprising of 1898.

Personally I do not believe that the Asian could change radically in that regard – at least not in the near future because I completely agree with Le Bone's[15] idea about the stability of the major features of national character. And I regard as rosy dreams the hopes of the researchers who are inclined to believe in near and radical evolutions – as in Asian developments in the Asian's character. With this statement I do not want to denounce the nature of Asian people in general – I am their old friend – but I also do not want to idealize it and try to run unfounded experiments with it.

Now I will talk about some peculiarities of the Afghan's ways of life – those related to Islam. A Muslim lives a double life: closed personal and open official. His women, children, and family are in a world which is locked to you. If a man is poor, then his wife lives in the same house but in a separate closed corner. If he is a wealthy person – she lives in a separate house or *saklya*, separate room. That isolation of a woman, her life and customs certainly represent a very interesting object for research, but you must not attempt to study the matter. If you go to a place to do some propaganda work or you need to conduct military intelligence – in general to carry out any mission – you must reconcile with the fact that your relations should be locked in the man-only circles and you must not try and even consider to get into other half of the house. It is better to pretend that you do not even suspect that the other half of the human race lives in there. You have contacts only with the man. You greet him, settle accounts with him, thank him and you ask him for hospitality. I point at these small everyday factors because they

13 For example Muhammad's dictum "There shall not be faith under duress" or "If God would like He would make all of you (i.e. Jews, Muslims and Christians) as a *single* religious community. But he wants to test you in everything he bestowed on you. Compete with each other in good deeds; all of you will come to Him and He will explain to you your differences. As you know Christ is recognized by Muslims as a prophet and Jerusalem as a Holy City. (Author's note).

14 For example: dictums "Fight the enemy until Islam is firmly established" and "Let all hostilities stop for God hates assailants." (Koran, Surah 2). (Author's note).

15 Gustave Le Bon (May 7, 1841-December 13, 1931) was a French social psychologist, sociologist, and amateur physicist. He was the author of several works in which he expounded theories of national traits, racial superiority, herd behavior and crowd psychology. (Translator's note).

play a big role in their way of life. It is considered improper to ask a man how his wife is. Such rudeness could insult a Muslim as a man and as a representative of the world of Islam. And I will say it again: your policy must be formed on the basis of the pretense that you are totally unaware of the existence of the female half – not just count it sacred – it is completely unknown to you.

I remember one episode during my journeys. In 1904 I went to Kara-Teghin (the easternmost bekstvo[16] of Bukhara). I was met by a local Kara-Kirgiz elder of the volost'.[17] I then spoke fluent Kara-Kirgiz and we soon began to talk freely as often happened in the Orient. He told me that I came too early because if I would pass through two months later, I could be present at his wedding. To my questions, he bragged that even though he was 85 years old, he would have a 12-year-old bride and she was beautiful and came from a decent family. When I returned two months later, I learned that the marriage was concluded (it was his fifth or sixth wife). But when I met the elder later on, I conducted our discourse differently. I ask him, just in passing, about how was the wedding feast was, how much had been eaten and drunk, but I did not even mention the bride. I talked about business, travel, told him what I had done. Thus I left him with the impression of myself as an intelligent, well-mannered and experienced person. I give you this example to illustrate the manner to communicate with these people.

But what was said about women has even deeper meaning than to secure a particular mission's success or the safety of a researcher. As long ago as Aristotle's time, he noted in his *Politics* that transgressions against a woman's chastity often served as a cause for wars or as a case to overthrow a "tyrant". Oriental history gives us plenty illustrations of that. As an example I will point to the fates of harems during wars. And those fates would compose a large and special topic for a researcher: insults of harems (Absalom's behavior during his entrance into Jerusalem)[18] – the most wicked kind of vengeance and terror by the victorious; and quite opposite – the safe and secure preservation of harems in the Orient create an extraordinary aura of nobility and greatness around the victor. In all wars, the timely and reliable protection of harems was a large strategic matter. These facts tell us that the kind of attitude toward women in the Orient has a delicate and deep sense – if it goes as a continuous line through all its history.

I have to say a few more word about women's status and your relations with them. Though you normally cannot see and study the women, you can find some variations with the matter. By Islamic laws a woman must cover her face before a man – there are several mentions of it in Koran. But if you study the issue you will soon find out how the institution of a covered woman varies through Central Asia. For example – in the Fergana region, women are very closely covered; in Eastern Persia and Afghan Turkestan – they are half covered and in Kirgizia and the Hazara steppes, they do not cover their faces. But there are some places where you can see only a woman's fingertips

16 Bekstvo is a region under the rule of a bek – a local ruler. It is about size of a county. (Translator's note).

17 Volost' is a municipal entity in pre-revolutionary Russia which included several villages. (Translator's note).

18 Absalom or Avshalom was the third son of David, king of Israel with Maachah, daughter of Talmai, king of Geshur. (1 Chronicles 3:2). During his rebellion against David he captured Jerusalem and publicly took over his father's harem. (Translator's note).

– so fully is she covered. The issue is interesting itself for study. Why is the definite law followed so differently? Why do Muslims perceive the law in various ways? As experience shows – whether you see the women covered or not depends on the features of the national temperament. The Kirgiz is phlegmatic, has an even temper, he is not jealous. His women are open and you can even talk to them. In the Pamir, where the air is rare and cold, the Kara-Kirgiz is sluggish without much passion – and a woman moves about without full cover and can even display her feelings. But I digress into the theoretical side. Remember, even if you see an uncovered woman – your behavior in regard to her must be very careful. The Asian – as a human being – could stay above the insult, but the Muslim in him will always be insulted.

Now, what should be your regard toward other issues? Say you meet with the issues of politics and religion.

The average Afghan is poorly versed in matters of politics with some exceptions. In religious issues, he is versed much better, he knows much and the knowledge is deep. If in the former, he possesses some free-thinking and a huge curiosity – in the latter he is intolerant and will only allow general discussion and exchange of practical material and facts. What I've said should outline your line of conducting your discussions: when speaking about politics be free, do not limit yourself in choosing the topic but make it colorful. But when speaking on religion – be restrained and tolerant; be able to find and point out the positive sides of Islam – which it has. There is nothing more flattering for the Asian than a nice word about his religion.

One more matter which has a significant practical importance – how should you behave when contacting Central Asian people? As in European countries, you can find lots of differences in Asian countries as well. But you must be prepared to follow certain etiquette, a certain line of conduct – and only then will you be able to gather all the things that you are working for. How should you behave while entering the Asian environment for the first time? If someone (or rumors) put you in a position of a *Prince* or as they say in Asia – a *Big Man* – then continue to play the role: show your importance on your face, take a lead when walking, be the last to dismount from a horse; when leaving a house or yurt, turn your back on those who stay. But if you are a person of small importance – then behave accordingly – humbly. The Orient is hospitable and you must accept (and sometimes – survive) that hospitality. You must pretend that you are flattered by the hospitality and must not refuse it under any circumstances. You receive a cup of kumys – it smells of sweat, the cup is dirty – and it would be very bad manners if you do not drink it completely. I remember an occasion when I visited a wealthy Kirgiz. We ate plenty of mutton, kaymak,[19] pilaf, etc. Then a large course of finely-chopped mutton arrived. The host – my personal friend – took a long time to wash it in a basin of water with his own hands. Then he seized a sizable portion of it with four fingers and moving close to me put the meat into my mouth. I forced myself to swallow it with a smile of gratitude on my face. We must take this into account because only by using tact, carefulness and indefinite patience can we achieve a lot. In the future, you, as military

19 Kaymak, aimak, or kaimak, also qaymar or qaimar, is a creamy dairy product, similar to clotted cream, that is made in the Balkans, Turkey, the Middle East, Central Asia, Iran, Afghanistan, and India. It is made from the milk of water buffalos in the East or from cows in the West. (Translator's note).

researchers or messengers of political ideas, must be able to not only contact the Asian people but also to make them your friends. It will be very helpful if you consider the Islamic surrounding and behave in accordance to it – as much as possible.

Many of researchers of Asia – such as Burnes, Campbell, Alexander, Gardner, Vamberly, etc. – had to pose as Muslims or even convert to Islam. Let's hope there will be no need of such sacrifice on your account. But there are some more benign methods. Say, you do not drink alcohol and one of your confidants spreads rumors that you a Muslim. That would open doors for you. It happened to me during my travel to India. I do not drink at all and naturally did not drink while on the expedition. Someone let out a rumor: "He is a Muslim, but for some reason does not want to talk about it." That had its consequences: when the Englishmen gave me a horse that, at the first opportunity, fell over pinning me to the ground and severely damaging my leg. I had to be put in a bed and I heard that people in the mosque prayed for my recovery.

In Asia, one has to be a hypocrite even against his will. But remember – if you get the incautious idea to pretend to be a Muslim, you will have to follow all the related rites and rituals – and do them accurately and at the proper time, exactly reproducing certain mannerisms defined by Islamic law and not drinking wine, etc. It is very difficult and dangerous and that is why I do not recommend it.

As to the ways of life of Afghans – it does not have specific differences and is common to other peoples of Central Asia. If there are nomads – they live in yurts. The prevalent colors of the yurts are black, white or gray – depending on prevalent colors of nomads' sheep's wool. All everyday life revolves around the yurt: cooking, eating, laundry, animal slaughter, etc. All the possessions of a nomad are kept in the yurt with some safeguards for things in need of special hiding or protection. Animals are kept in places with grass and if those places are not far away from the yurt, then milking cows, mares and she-goats is done nearby. The wives run the household. They erect and strike the yurt, cook and maintain the living area. The husbands conduct warfare, visit other men, protect animals and enjoy the humble delights of the nomadic life. The main food elements are meat and milk in many disguises and bread is used as a supplement.

If the Afghan is a semi-nomad, then his life will differ slightly from this picture. During the winter or periods of poor grass, he will live in a mud hut that is rough, uncomfortable and primitive. There will be some signs of a more settled ways of life such as poor equipment, a prehistoric wooden plow and a badly plowed strip of land. But the everyday life, diet and life style remain clearly nomadic.

And finally – a settled Afghan lives either in a building made of makeshift material or in a cave. Several households (three-four or more in number) create a village. The village size is determined by the availability of arable land or water for irrigation. Whether the land requires irrigation or not presents a serious difference in labor requirements and the peculiarities of the people's character. Irrigation requires sizable and systematic labor efforts, it binds a person close to the land, it makes him timid and dependent – but also diligent and economical. Farming without irrigation is not that demanding and makes a person less dependent. It permits him more leisure time and there is more freedom in the people's character. It makes the person negligent, incompetent – but also more proud and independent. Even today the Afghan takes to farming with little love and is not really too serious about it – they remain nomads deep in their souls. Farming has not yet put its stamp on the Afghan and has not grasped him in its leveling and crushing pincers.

Naturally, the Afghan farmer directs all his attention to farming and keeps just enough animals for minimum economic necessity. Thus his food consists primarily of flour and legume products. A woman cannot easily carry out all household jobs (plowing, making farm tools and equipment, making buildings, etc.) and a man takes on the more difficult of these. This results in a more dependent role for women and among the wealthy and elite, that role comes close to slavery with the complete destruction of her freedom.

The rest of the ways of life are more closely related to ethnography and if you would like to study them deeper, you can find them in works on the subject.

Now I move to other groups of Afghanistan's population. And I will start with the Iranian or Tajik.

The Tajik

The Tajik in Central Asia represent the primarily population of the mountainous regions. Science regards them as stubborn remnants of the ancient Aryan tribe. One can find them in those mountainous areas which are either less suitable for living and nomadic migration or located far from historical routes. Historically, this group of human population became isolated by being gradually pushed out from the rich and accessible regions into the poor ones by waves of victorious conquerors who periodically rolled across Central Asia. At the end, the Tajik was pushed into mountain valleys and canyons which had no interest to anyone or were unknown to most. To find the Tajik today in Central Asia, one needs to look into the most inaccessible regions: take for example Northern India with its cliffs and canyons, the most difficult areas of western Pamir, the far-removed-from-the-historical-route areas of Badakhshan, the Hazaristan which is also located far from peoples' roads. Then there are some corners of Herat province where we can find remnants of the Tajik as in mountainous corners of eastern Bukhara, etc.

In Afghanistan, the Tajiks account for only about a million people. I will dwell on this group mainly because it is the second most numerous after the Afghans. The group definitely represents a settled population. The Tajiks make their living only by farming and though they are oppressed and poor people – they also are industrious to the highest degree and their productivity is very high.

As to their way of life – it is quite monotonous. They usually live in villages adjacent to the working fields. If the area is large, then the number of houses will be sizable, otherwise there will be two-three huts, no more. Specialists state that the buildings' design, shape of doors and windows, utensils, decorations of window curtains and towels come from deepest antiquity. Herded into canyons, the Tajik separated from the rest of the world and preserved all their ancient elements. Looking into their households, you can see that despite the passage of hundreds of years, they still live like their remote ancestors – they build the roofs of their saklyas the same way and work the land with ancient methods, etc.

As to work – the Tajik are primarily farmers. Usually there is very little land and the farmer sometimes lives on a small patch which is not much larger than this room. But he works it very carefully – every inch of it, loosening the soil into powder and encircling every field with stones. The Tajiks grow various grains depending on the terrain's altitude. At altitudes higher than 9,000 feet, they grow naked barley and oats; below that altitude they grow wheat. These are the major sources of nutrition. At the altitude below three-four thousand feet, one can find apricots, grapes and watermelons. The draft animals he uses are oxen and horses and his main tool is a wooden plow. All those elements point to their antiquity. Even with all his thriftiness and industriousness, a Tajik cannot accumulate a sizable surplus and if you find in information about his alleged wealth in some sources– consider this very carefully.

I've forgotten to mention that the Afghans are orthodox Sunni. As to the Tajiks – they are Muslim also but they are Shiites and very often represent a sect of Mowlai or Ismaili. It is a very interesting sect but to look deeper into it would be too specific an issue which we cannot study right now. In the places where power belongs to the majority, Ismaili call themselves Shiites. But if the majority is Sunni, the Ismaili commit "sin" and pretend being Sunni. As the people have been oppressed and subjects for centuries, the Tajiks are a secluded, secretive and distrustful type. They are timid and indecisive and given to hypocrisy. In general we shall note many unpleasant traits in the Tajik's national character and the most unpleasant among these would be hypocrisy and stinginess. It should not be a surprise, of course, because a Tajik has to fight to keep his goods or hide them to prevent them from being taken away. If you meet Tajiks walking on a road, you often will see that they moving barefooted on sharp stones and have slung their shoes (pekh) on their shoulders to prevent damage to them. If the government representative collects tribute (tax) from a field – usually every seventh or tenth sheaf) – you will see such a picture: a Tajik is crying and genuflecting before the official. He cries that he will die along with his wife and the children, if the crop is taken away....But he does that too often and government does not believe him. If a Tajik wheedles something – he does it as a beggar in Naples. This display of stinginess should not deceive you. In some cases, the stinginess covers a great ability to hide a quite sizable surplus of grain and sometimes – even silver and gold. Though due to the poverty of the Tajik, it happens rarely – but nonetheless it happens. From the military point of view – we shall say that the Tajik represent an element of little use. They are too cowardly and craven, but as mountaineers who are well adapted to the local conditions they are useful as guides and porters they often represent very good material. If they are on your side – they can be a significant help. Our expeditions, as well as those of the English, confirm that as fighters in the offense, the Tajik are useless, but in the defense of their homes and holding defensive mountain positions, they can be a formidable force.

If you have an access to a Tajik family, enter his circle of interests – there you will meet the many interesting traits of his character. He is a good family man who likes to dance and will even share his goods with others, not just with relatives.

And of course, while studying those people in more detail, you cannot bypass their *religion and spiritual leaders* – the Ishans.[20] If you want to make sure that the military situation develops favorably for you, if you want the Tajik on your side, if you want access into the depth of people's masses – first and foremost take care to get the Ishans

20 Ishan (Eshon) is the head and mentor of a Muslim community which usually belongs to one of the mystical orders (Dervish or Darvesh). The leaders of the faithful in the Ismaili sect are also called Ishans. A Dervish or Darvesh is a Sufi Muslim ascetic or "Tariqah", known for poverty and austerity. (Translator's note).

on your side. The Ishans are the major engine of the people's life. An Ishan is idolized, surrounded with honor and attention. People kiss his stirrup when he rides a horse. Most of the Ishans are descendants of ancient Persian families who escaped religious and other persecution in the Tajik canyons. Many of them are clearly degenerates as shown by their spiritual and physical qualities. This might be explained by a long idle life spent in luxury for generation after generation without the infusion of outside fresh blood and the refreshing influence of creative work. No wonder that one can find lechers, drunks, opiate users and people seized by any kind of vice among these people. You must keep it in mind that it is not that difficult to tame such an Ishan and have him at your side. In my career, when I was the chief of the Pamir, I quite often contacted the Ishans using methods which corresponded with the situation – and I've had very good spies among them. One of them had a misfortune to be caught in Badakhshan and was crucified on the city square in Faizabad.

Turkic group

The next group I will talk about is the Turkic or more precise – the Turkic-Mongolian. It has three components: one in Afghan Turkestan – these are the Uzbek; the second is the Turkmen who live west of the Uzbeks and crowd up next to the Amu-Darya River and the Persian border. Then there are the Hazara and Aimak which fill up the space of the western spurs of the Hindu Kush Mountains. Of these groups, the Turkmen and Uzbek represent a fairly similar people, so we can examine them together and you probably already know something about them. The differences are small. As to the Hazara and Aimak – these nationalities are isolated and not well known, so we do not have much to discuss about them. Today, science considers them an enigma.

The Uzbek account for about 700-800,000 people, though this number is somewhat hypothetical. Part of the Uzbeks are currently nomads, although during the last three or four decades, due to the influence of the Afghan emirs' policy, they lately have begun to gravitate toward certain winter settlements, i.e. – began to settle. Their process of settling is quite interesting. First, they build small clay huts in the wintering areas and stay in them for several months while looking after their animals. The rest of the year they migrate [from pasture to pasture]. During the next stage – they improve the buildings, make them larger and more reliable and come back to these locations every year without fail. Later, before starting migration, they leave some livestock and working animals with a service team at the settlement. The people of the service team begin plowing land – a little at first, then more and more. As the farming area grows, more people stay there with more animals. Fewer and fewer people leave with their livestock on migrations. Initially, the more privileged part of the population leaves to migrate and the workers stay. As the settling progresses, things turn around. Finally, the former nomads settle down at one place and live there all year around; they start to take farming seriously. The job of herding goes to the servants.

The Uzbeks are still in the settlement process and the Afghan government conducts a very persistent policy to make sure that these people are going to settle. This state policy is driven, in the first place, by the fact that the existence of nomads in a country is non-economical for the state. If a person makes a living by farming, and at the same time keeps animals, then he needs 10-15 times less land compared with the disorganized movement of livestock from one place to another. The animals trample down much more grass than they eat and the land is wasted. Second, it is much more difficult to control nomads and they are less profitable for the government.

A few words about the Uzbek language: it is one of the Turkish dialects. If you know the Sart[21] language, you can easily understand the Uzbek and Turkmen, especially if you live among them. In 1904 I talked to the Uzbek and understood them very well because I knew Sart. There are no difficulties speaking with the Turkmen if one knows Sart. Though their language stands farther off from Sart (in some consonants and tones it is closer to the Kirgiz language), the difference is so small and easily detected that after some practice it will be easy to understand. Among the other Turkish languages, the Uzbek and Turkmen stand out in their purity – the influx of Persian is not that great to disrupt clearly the Turkish basis of the languages. Arabic words represent a small and particularly specific element.

The Uzbek past

The Uzbeks represent the last Turkish wave in the Central Asian theater – a wave that lasted through three centuries (16th -18th centuries) of turbulent conquest. The 16th century was a time when these people flourished and is marked by presence of such names as Shaybani[22] and Ubeidullah.[23]

Those who are interested in Timur's history – or in those who succeeded him – will see that Timur had to fight hard against the Uzbek wave – and this happened during the trying times of his military career when he had organized expeditions into Asia Minor or against Takhtamysh.[24] He was forced to spend several years in the effort to push the Uzbeks back to the north-east before he could move against the latter. Timur pacified the Uzbeks but did not destroy them. Soon after his death, they dominated Eastern Iran.

So, the 16th century was the time when the Uzbeks flourished. When we Russians advanced into Turkestan during the 1860-70s, we found several large and wealthy khanates founded by the Uzbeks. These were Kokand, Bukhara, Khiva, Tashkent and some smaller others. The Uzbek khanates south of the Amu-Darya during that time and even earlier had begun dying out by coming under the rule of Afghanistan. During our advance, the Uzbek as the original nationality generally went into decline. The reason is they turned to a settled life and their nation was divided into individual khanates. But the khanates of Russian Turkestan were more or less powerful at the time and they fell because of the inequality of forces. The khanates of Afghan Turkestan though

21 The Sart is an obsolete name for the settled part of the Uzbek population. (Translator's note).

22 Abu 'I-Fath Muhammad was known as Shaybani Khan (c. 1451-2 December 1510). He was a khan of the Uzbeks (from 1500) who consolidated various Uzbek tribes and laid the foundation for their ascendancy into Transoxiana. He was a descendant of Genghis Khan through his grandson Shayban and considered the Timurids as usurpers of Genghis Khan's heritage in Central Asia. (Translator's note).

23 Ubeidullah was a powerful sultan in Shaybani's Khanate. (Translator's note).

24 Tokhtamysh (died 1405), was the last khan of the White Horde, who unified the White Horde and Blue Horde subdivisions of the Golden Horde into a single state. He was a descendant of Genghis Khan's oldest grandson, Orda Khan. (Translator's note).

were already weak at the time of our arrival. It is significant that the Uzbeks of Afghan Turkestan were the first to settle out of all the groups. Elphinstone, who first collected interesting data on the group, found them in process of settlement.

I deliberately dwell on the nomads' settlement process because I attach a very high importance to it. The fact that the Uzbeks had begun to settle in the early 19th century shows that the people turned toward new ways of life and as a circumstance – toward loosing independence. The situation developed in such a way that the Uzbeks were compressed into the space between the Amu Darya River and the mountains. The Uzbeks were thrown off their territory. They did not have unassailable places to dig into or to build a citadel to support their people during hard times. There was fairly-flat slightly-hilly terrain. The conquerors attacked from the south, north-west or north and, unimpeded, squeezed the people into an iron vise. The Uzbeks soon lost their ardor and today we see a timid, suppressed nation – you can do anything to them. Doctor Yavorski said that the Afghans look at the Uzbek with contempt and consider them unsuitable for military service. There could be some truth in their opinion. The Uzbek are people who lost the active spirit of their ancestors. Now it is almost a completely settled nation that lives in kishlaks but still make some long migrations because the summertime brings numerous insects into the Amu-Darya area which pushes animals to the higher altitudes in the mountains. But during wintertime, there is a lot of snow in the mountains and this requires a return to the tugai.[25]

If you look more carefully into the manner of life of the Afghan Uzbek, you will see the same way of life as our Uzbeks in Eastern Bukhara. You will see a person who looks temporarily settled. His wintering area is humble, like he does not care about large and sturdy buildings. On other side, you see that he is sloppy about farming; his tools and equipment are old and worn and his plow animal is weak. The old habits of the nomads die hard and you can feel it everything. As to specific details of his life – there are the typical characteristics that I have already mentioned to you: he drinks kumis,[26] he likes mutton and, even more, he likes horsemeat –but because horses have become very expensive, he gradually lost his appetite for their meat. He consumes dairy products in large quantities – especially the soured milk varieties. Like all nomads, the Uzbeks are carefree, lazy and love entertainment. Only their wives know where one thing or another is and what is on the "To-Do List" – such is the Uzbek life.[27]

As to his political development, it is astonishing at first glance. During his acquaintance with you, he may take you aback. He will tell you about the White Tsar,[28] the Ottoman Sultan, the British Queen…he will name all the generations of his clan; he will ask you about the Russo-Japanese war. I remember at one of the rendezvous I had with these people, I said that the Japanese are brave warriors. One man asked me if they are Muslims. When I said no, he shook his head – expressing perplexity at the fact

25 Tugai is a Central Asian term for a riparian forest – a forested area of land adjacent to a body of water such as a river, stream, pond, lake, marshland, estuary, canal, playa or reservoir. In Afghanistan, these narrow strips of vegetation are known as green zones. (Translator's note).

26 Kumis is fermented mare's milk. (Translator's note).

27 This pretty well describes both translators and their approach to life. We must have a little nomad in each of us. (Translator's note).

28 The White Tsar is the Russian Tsar. (Translator's note).

that non-Muslims could be brave. But do not be taken in by the Uzbek's wide range of interests. It is the motley and shallow baggage of a carefree, curious person who picked up some information. If you try to question him in depth, then you will notice that he does not know much even about Turkestan and has no idea what is going on north of the Amu-Darya River. True, he knows his clan and tribe, his genealogy – but that is it. Soon you will see that his outlook is narrow, nationalistic and arrogant. Ask him which political side he is on, which side he supports – the English or the Russian – he will not tell you anything definitive; and if he tells you something – do not believe him. It is all the same to him.

This is a little information which could be used to build some suppositions. But the most important for us is the fact that the Uzbeks do not like the Afghans – as the Afghans do not like the Uzbeks. The reasons for that are the same which motivate the Afghans to dislike the Uzbeks. We need to note that the history of the Uzbek is much more ancient and colorful than that of the Afghan – the relative newcomers into Central Asia. The Uzbeks hatred of the Afghans is also that of a currently-subjugated but yet recently free nation. And one could build something based on that hatred.

As to religion – the Uzbek are Sunni Muslims, i.e. orthodox Muslims and they are very religious. Their mullahs' wield great power because it is based not only on religion but also on nationalism. The religion is another factor which needs to be emphasized and which combined with the hatred toward the dominant nation must be taken into account.

We need to mention the food resources of the nation and there we should remember this main fact: the Uzbek are casual farmers. As recent nomads, they have little need of flour and limit themselves to flatbread. So, if an Uzbek subsists on flatbread, mutton and dairy products – what will we find there? What surplus can we hope to find? First – we can find transport: horses (good quality, tall and lightly built) and a large number of donkeys. We can find meat – mutton and other products of livestock-raising. As to farming produce – there we must be wary and careful. It could be that in the Hindu Kush's foothills there is more farmed land than before – then we can count on some surplus of barley, wheat, millet, corn, etc. But we can only speculate on that matter.

I have already talked about the Uzbek language. Now I would talk about the family of Turkic languages and at the same time – about the family of Turkic people because the issue has not yet been discussed in the Turkish languages department.

Turkic peoples and languages

The vast majority of the native population of *Turkestan* belongs to the Turkish nationality; that is how the region got its name – "the country of the Turks". The Turkish people of Turkestan are a part of the vast Turkish world which spreads from the Sea of Okhotsk[29] (Yakuts) to the Mediterranean Sea (the Ottoman Turks). Turks do not represent a monolithic group but are divided into several groups of related peoples. The scientists have not done a satisfactory classification of the Turkic peoples. Among the

29 The Sea of Okhotsk lies between Japan and the Russian Far East. (Translator's note).

existing works, the best are works by the late Russian academicians V.V. Radlov[30] and F. I. Korsh.[31] But even these two classifications do not substantiate with reasonable persuasiveness the placement of the Turkish peoples of all Turkestan into one group or another. The main reason for such uncertainty is that these peoples have not been studied enough – ethnologically and linguistically. Both of the above-mentioned classifications reasonably put the Turkic tribes of the Caspian region, Khiva and Bukhara khanates, Afghan Turkestan and Astrabat province of Persia into a group which also includes Ottoman and Azerbaijan Turks, the Tatars of South Crimea and the Gagauz[32] in Bessarabia.[33] It is called (by Radlov) the south group of Turkic peoples. Both classifications require corrections in relation to the Kirgiz-Kazakh and Kara-Kirgiz. Those two peoples cannot be included into one group. The Kirgiz-Kazakh of the Steppe Region, Syr-Darya and Caspian regions, Khiva khanate and Astrakhan gubernia are more closely related to the Noghai, Bashkir, Volga Tatars, Uzbek and Kara-Kalmyk. The Kara-Kirgiz language shows features related to the Altai and Teleut[34] on one side and to the Sart of Eastern China and western Turkestan on another. The Uzbek of Fergana and Samarkand regions, Khiva and Bukhara khanates and Afghan Turkestan by their origin are more closely related to the Kirgiz-Kazakh. But the Uzbek language is not uniform in its differences from the Kirgiz-Kazakh; it is split into dialects one of which is close to the Kirgiz-Kazakh and the others – to the Sart dialects. The latter could be explained by the long coexistence of the Uzbek and the Sart in various parts of Turkestan. The group called the Sart is the Turk-influenced part of the indigenous local Iranian population. The part of the population that was not influenced by the Turks are the Tajik. There is no singular Sart language because the Iranian-Tajik were influenced by different Turkic peoples in different regions of eastern (Chinese) and western (Russian) Turkestan. The Sart dialects of eastern Turkestan and Fergana and the Syr-Darya regions show the most similarities between them. The dialects of the Khiva Sart gravitate toward the language of the Khiva Uzbek, while showing some of the Turkmen's influence.

By Radlov's classification, which is done strictly on a linguistic basis (and that on exclusively phonetic features) the Turkic languages (and peoples) are split into four groups: 1) Eastern, which includes the small Turkish tribes of Altai, North-West Mongolia (Uryankhai) and Yenisei region; 2) Western, which takes the Turkish peoples from Tobol's banks to the North Caucasus and Crimean Steppes through the Steppe and

30 Vasily Vasilievich Radlov or Friedrich Wilhelm Radloff (Russian: Васи́лий Васи́льевич Ра́длов; January 17, 1837, Berlin – May 12, 1918) was a German-born Russian founder of Turkology, a scientific study of the Turkic peoples. (Translator's note).

31 Fyodor Evgenyevich Korsh (April 22, 1843-February 16, 1915) was a Russian philologist of classic and Slavonic philology, orientalist, and a poet-translator. He was an Academician of the St. Petersburg Science Academy. (Translator's note).

32 The Gagauz people are a small Turkic ethnic group living mostly in southern Moldova (Gagauzia), southwestern Ukraine (Budjak) and north-eastern Bulgaria (Dobruja). Unlike most other Turkic peoples, the Gagauz are predominantly Orthodox Christians. There is a related ethnic group also called *Gagavuz* (or *Gajal*) living in the European part of northwestern Turkey. (Translator's note).

33 Bessarabia is a historic term for the geographic entity in Eastern Europe bounded by the Dniester River on the east and the Prut River on the west. (Translator's note).

34 The Teleut are a small Tatar people living in the Kemerovo region of Altai. (Translator's note).

Volga Regions; 3) Southern – its content we discussed while discussing the Turkmen; 4) Central Asian which includes the Sart of eastern and western Turkestan and the Uzbek.

Korsh's classification is also built on linguistic bases but with the use of morphological, not only phonetic features. Like Radlov's classification, it also establishes four groups of peoples and languages, but the content of these groups differs significantly from Radlov's. One group Korsh named Northern corresponds to Radlov's groups 1 and 2 combined. A special group of Korsh includes Old Turkic peoples and languages: the Uighur, Kipchak or Cumans (Polovtsy) and some other – Korsh named it Eastern. Korsh's third group is completely identical with Radlov's third group but named Western instead of Southern. Korsh's fourth group– Mixed – includes the peoples and languages of mixed linguistic features; Radlov put parts of it into the Eastern and other parts – into the Central Asian groups. Korsh's classification appeared much later than Radlov's and when compared to the latter is definitely more precise – and that is why we would limit ourselves to the discussion of Korsh's. The Northern group is characterized on the phonetic side by such words as "tau" – mountain or "uul" – son with the sound [u] instead of [g] of the Eastern and Western groups ("tag", "ogul") and such forms as "kul-ga"- slave or "al-gan" – I take instead of the form "kul-a" and "al-an" of the Western group; on the morphological side – the present continuous tense type "al-a-myn" – I am taking. The following forms are characteristic for the Eastern and Western groups by Korsh: present tense type "kel-yurmin" or "gel-yur-yum" and presence of the [g] sound in such words as "tag" or "ogul". The difference between Eastern and Western groups is noticeable in the following: "kul-ga" – slave and "al-gan" – one who has taken in the former would correspond to "kul-a" and "al-an" in the latter.

The languages of the Mixed group display mixed features of Northern and Eastern groups.

What is the number of Uzbeks after all? You will find different numbers with many zeros and they fluctuate between 600,000 and 900,000. It is difficult to conduct an actual census because, first off, the people swing between a nomadic and settled life; and secondly, for many reasons the people try to conceal the real number – and that creates ambiguity. The Englishmen say there are 700,000 Uzbeks and I think it is about 800,000. The most important conclusion about these people should be that in the Uzbeks we have old and reliable enemies of the Afghans and that gives us a chance to use them as an advance guard for political and military objectives. Of course, we shall expect that the Afghans are taking measures to hold Afghan Turkestan: we see large garrisons there which are lead by genuine Afghans with well-organized observation systems, etc. It could be that all that just adds bitterness to the Uzbek's hearts and helps us instead of the emir – but who can say for sure?

The Hazara and Aimak

The next large group in the same Turkic family is the Hazara and Aimak (or Char-Aimak). Placing this group– we may tentatively call it Mongol-Turkish –is very difficult because the information on it from different researchers is extremely contradictory. For example – Andogorski points at the line Anar Darreh – Washir – Selim as the southern limit of expansion of these peoples and we shall consider this an exaggeration because it includes land of the Western Ghilzai and some other Duranni sub-tribes such as the Noorzai, Popalzai, etc. The size of the area occupied by the Hazara and Aimak can be defined generally. It represents a parallelogram which has long sides of 400 versts and short sides of 200 versts. The eastern border of the area lays at meridian of Ownay mountain pass [34.467°N 68.329°E] and the western – at the meridian of the line connecting Murgab and Meimene. The northern border lays just a little south of the Band-i Turkestan mountain range latitude and the southern almost coincides with the city of Ghazni's latitude. But again – it is a very approximate picture. The Hazara occupy the eastern part of the area and the Aimak – the western. There is no clear indication where the line runs which divides them.

The Hazara

What kind of people are they? Even today they represent an enigma to researchers. They were described more or less definitively by Elphinstone and a member of his expedition, Macartney.[35] Elphinstone approached the issue with circumspection and drafted about ten pages of unsystematic text of somewhat humorous content. He also presented the first drawings of some representatives of these peoples and tried to find out their numbers. He was the first to study their origin and their religion. The issue of the Hazara's origin is still unclear today; are they of Mongolian or Turkish descent? The term "Mongol-Turkish", which had been in use previously, confused everyone. The wrong nomenclature played a significant role there.

Then, there was a lot ambiguity on the issue of the religion. You will find some clues that the Hazara are Shiites, but I accidently discovered with certainty that they belong to a special kind of Shiites – namely the Ismaili (or Mowlavi).

During the period of my life in the Pamirs, I knew two local ishans who had several kishlaks of their followers in the Hazarajat. They periodically contacted them and received from them their means of living. From the same ishans, I've heard that other kishlaks of the Hazarajat registered with some other ishans and the inhabitants belong to the Ismaili sect. I am inclined to give the fact somewhat wider significance. As I've mentioned previously, there is a definite link between people and the religion professed by them. People adopt not just any religion but one specific religion. Typically, the Ismaili live in inaccessible areas – valleys of the western Pamir, remote corners of India, etc. Their religion contains a great deal of secrecy, mysticism and ritual. For example, they believe that there are some holy books which must be read by ishans only and if an ordinary person read it he would go mad. I've studied one of those books (Ul'-Mul'k-Kitob) and I indeed risked going astray from its half-mystic, half-fantastic but always dark, involved and incoherent content. In a word, the content of the religion is as the people's soul – secluded – it speaks about a cowed, secretive and suspicious entity. Out of the fact that the Hazara profess the Ismaili religion, I am inclined to make some

35 Lieutenant John Macartney, 5th Bengal Cavalry, (1781-1811), mission surveyor and commander of Elphinstone's cavalry escort. See Mountstuart Elphinstone, *An account of the kingdom of Cabul and its dependencies in Persia, Tartary and India: comprising a view of the Afgaun nation and a history of the Dooraunee monarchy*, London: Longman, Hurst, Rees, Orme and Brown…and J. Murray, 1815. (Translator's notes).

ethnographic assumptions. The point is that I've never met a representative of the Ismaili among either the Mongol or Turkic peoples. That religion is professed exclusively by the Tajik or ancient dying peoples of India. And because of that I believe that the Hazara are neither Mongols nor Turks. Or at least they could be Mongol heavily infused with the Tajik blood.

But who are they? In one historical source (Abu-Fazl'),[36] it is said that a group of warriors from the Genghis Khan's troops broke away from the main body and settled in the canyons of the Hindu Kush Mountains– there is a hint that the Hazara are Mongols.[37] But in another source (Babur) we find mention that the Hazara are the Uzbek – thus making them of Turkish descent. In a word – history did not preserve the clues to the people's origin. Outwardly the Hazara looks more like Mongols than Turks, but they dress more like Turks, although they keep wearing hats of the Mongolian type. They are a healthy joyful people. The Hazara are divided into several tribes – Daizangi, Daikundi, Jaghuri and Poladha– the largest among them. Each tribe has its own khan or sultan whose power is unlimited among his people. He acts as a judge, sets taxes and can condemn one to death. Some of the khans live in palaces, dress well and have a brilliant court. There are perpetual quarrels between khans, frequent wars which disrupt the country's peace and undermine its welfare. The absence of unified government and the mutual hostility of these princelings are the major obstacles on the way to development of Hazaristan. As to the Hazara everyday life, it is of little interest and there are various rumors – most of them not proven. Some say they are vivacious and curious people, very hospitable (a man even could offer his wife to a guest – Kuru-Bistoun custom) – the latter, probably, is a vestige of the communal matrimony which existed there before. There is a rumor that if a husband returning from a hunting trip sees a pair of shoes with toes turned toward the door, he will not enter but will quietly go away – so his wife and her guest can continue their discussion peacefully.

The general conclusion is that the Hazara represent a people that are not studied in the sense of their origin or political ideas. The fact that they live in practically inaccessible areas of the Hindu Kush Mountains tells us that they preserved their originality until today.

In relation to natural resources, it is a region with fairly well-developed agriculture; it is not poor but to find out what you can find there in a case of war is difficult. The major occupation of the Hazara is farming and only a small part of them continue to lead a nomadic life.

At the same time we should take into account that it is a mountain region cut by deep mountain valleys with a small farming area for growing grain. The people's industriousness (especially the women's) and favorable climate can hardly compensate for the natural lack of arable land. Also we need to take into account the ability of the inhabitants to hide their animals and grain quickly when it is necessary. Their history tells us that their conquerors have not stayed there for long.

---

36 Abu-al-Fasl'-Mukhamed-ibn-Hussein Beikhaki (995-1078) was a Persian historian and the author of the 30-volume *History of Ghaznevids.* (Translator's note).

37 The Hazara during Babur's time were still speaking the Mongol language, if we believe Spiegel (Spiegel, *Eranische Altertümer,* Vol. 1, p.344). (Author's note).

The Hazara usually settle in villages of 20-200 houses, depending on the size of their irrigated land. The houses often nestle against mountain slopes. Each village has a guard tower which can hold 10-12 people. There is a guard in the tower who beats drums in a case of a threat. The sound is passed from one village to another and people arm themselves quickly. In a short period of time, a detachment of 2,000-3,000 people gather at the threatened place.

The Aimak

West of the Hazara, on the spurs of the Hindu Kush, live a large group of the Aimak. Elphinstone made a number of mistakes in relation to them. He unified under the name "Aimak" the whole mass of peoples, including Turks, Tajiks and even recent newcomers from Persia. Later researchers say that the Aimak on the whole represent the Tajik. I have very serious doubts about that. First of all, the Aimak are fervent Sunni and it is unlikely that Tajiks would have connections with the Sunni. Then, there are connections to the Jamshidi (Chahar-Aimak)[38] who I consider Turkish. Undoubtedly, there are some Tajik in the Aimak group (they consider them as one of the tribes). I think that is impossible to find out how many peoples are mixed up in the group, but doubtless two branches– the Tajik and Mongol –lay in the foundation of the nation. Historical fate has thrown them into regions far removed from the historical routes and merged them into one people that are fairly assimilated.

In his time Elphinstone classified the Aimak into four tribes: Teiman, Hazara (do not confuse them with the earlier described Hazara), Teimur and Zur. The first, i.e. Teiman in turn subdivided into two sub-tribes; Kipchak and Durzi. Hazara is subdivided into Jamshidi and Firuz-Kuh. Obviously the researcher had been confused by the fact that the tribes live next to each other and have some common features and he put them into one group under the name "Aimak".

A similar mistake had been made by the researcher in relation to their language which he named Persian. Works by Gobelentz[39] showed that the Aimak language is Mongolian – closer to West-Mongolian, i.e. Kalmyk but with some inclusions of Persian. It is possible to say that the Aimak (repeating Abu-Fazl's opinion) originated from the remains of a Mongolian host under the command of Nikodar Okhlak sent by Mangku-Khan (the grandson of Genghis-Khan) to reinforce Khulagu-Khan.

The Aimak are fervent Sunni and this provides evidence that they belong to the Turks. They are still nomads nowadays. I think it is their fate and they cannot live a life other than nomadic. Though the emir's policy is to make them farmers, it is hardly achievable with those people. Maybe I accidently forgot to mention that under term "nomad" I consider not only the specific way of life but the whole world outlook, the philosophy.

38 Jamshidi – one of the tribes in the Aimak group. (Translator's note).

39 Gabelentz, *Zeitschrift der Deutschen Morgenländischen Gesellschaft* 1866. This is hinted at in the *Bamberu Ursprung der Maggaren,* Leipzig, 1882, page 199. (Author's note). Hans Georg Conon von der Gabelentz (16 March 1840-11 December 1893) was a German general linguist and sinologist. His *Chinesische Grammatik* (1881), according to a critic, "remains until today recognized as probably the finest overall grammatical survey of the Classical Chinese language to date. (Translator's note).

Just a small part of the Aimak does farming. Most of them migrate while working land in passing and negligently. The Aimak move higher up the mountains in the summer and then return to the lowlands in the fall. One could think that the Aimak are very wealthy.

They could be used as suitable human material, of course, but one has to take into account that they are located far away from operational routes and is difficult to get practical results from them. About the people's character: all descriptions point that they are brave, manly; some of them such as the Zur – bloodthirsty. But then again this could be from an unreliable source. Meat is prevalent in their diet, they especially like horsemeat. It shows their stubborn dedication to the nomadic lifestyle. I was not able to gather what kind of attitude the Aimak have toward the Afghan. I explain it by the fact that the Aimak are an enigmatic people. Lately in the media, information appeared about the resettlement of the Jumshidi into Russian boundaries and the cited reason was the oppression of the Aimak in Afghanistan. It could be so, but it is possible that the bad pasture conditions in Afghanistan pushed the nomads far away from their native land.

The numbers of the Aimak are uncertain. Elphinstone thought that their probable number is 400-500,000.

The Kafirs

With this, I conclude my observation of the peoples of Afghanistan, the Afghan, Tajik and Turks. There are some small groups of peoples in the country, the Kalmyk, Jews, Gypsies, and Hindus but they sink into the mass of the larger peoples. That does not mean that they have no weight in the country – as do, for example, émigrés from India. The Kafir[40] (i.e. "infidels"), inhabitants of Kafiristan, occupy a somewhat separate place among these. That small nation is very interesting from many scientific points of view and until recently represented one of the most interesting geographical mysteries. No other nation produced so many suppositions, legends and myths as the Kafir. In the works of contemporary scientists (especially Robertson) the mystery is uncovered and the nation is described enough today. Islam is making fast inroads into Kafiristan and soon nothing will be left of their old religion which is an interesting vestige of an extremely ancient cult. What has been said should be enough for us because the military and political significance of the Kafir is negligible – as it has been before. That had not prevented Timur from undertaking a most difficult expedition into Kafiristan (under the pretence of punishing "infidels"). In contemporary times, Adur-Rahman also has been forced to undertake an expedition into the region.

In conclusion about what has been said about the peoples of Afghanistan, I will venture to make a political conclusion that they all are alienated from each other and do not compose a single and united family. The Afghan and Uzbek are divided by such a huge gap that it would be impossible to breach it with any bridge. One can consider Islam as the bridge – but only to some degree. As to the Tajik – they are a peculiar and secretive

40 Kafir is an Arabic word meaning "rejecter" or "ingrate." The term refers to a person who does not recognize God (Allah) or the prophet-hood of Muhammad (i.e., any non-Muslim) or who hides, denies, or covers the "truth". The Kafir were the last people to accept Islam in Afghanistan. Today they are known as the Nuristani-from the Nuristan valley which is their home. (Translator's note).

people and they live an isolated life. The Hazara and Aimak are split and divided. What conclusion can we make? By its population, Afghanistan is not a homogeneous monolithic nation and thus it cannot carry out any state mission that requires unity and stability of thought, unity of general sentiments of all the country and comprehensive self-sacrifice. It can work in individual spots, as has been shown by history but not by the united mass. It can work in outbursts but not reliably and not for long. Afghanistan cannot withstand a large and long war and soon would split into a row of quarreling distrustful camps. The Afghan do not like the Uzbek; the Uzbek and Hazara hate the Afghan. The Tajik do not trust anyone and everyone does not trust the Tajik. And that leads us to the conclusion that using a systematic and clearly defined policy, one can tear apart the country into pieces. You say that there is the religion. But there are so many sects: Sunnis, Shiites, Ismaili, etc. And that naturally weakens their religious unity.

From this description one can make a fairly definitive conclusion. If we would try to get closer to Afghanistan and look for a nation that could be used as a base, then we would arrive at the following: it is futile to count on the Tajik; there is no sense to look for the Hazara or Aimak – there are few of them and they live in remote regions, their political weight in the country is insignificant; one cannot count on their promises because they do not have power to support them. I know that in the past, emissaries have been sent to those nations but nothing practical resulted. So we are left with the Uzbek as only our advance guard. Their link to Russian Turkestan, where their fellow countrymen recently were sitting on the thrones of Bukhara and Khiva, is still alive. Their life in Afghanistan under the rule of the Afghans is far from sweet and they hate their masters whom they count as upstarts in the Central Asian arena.

In relation to the Afghans, we can say that they are the dominate people which have realized their weight and learned its value. And if that group would come to our side it would not happen from any sympathy or hope for some specific gain but from some larger considerations of state interests. It is frivolous to think that they simply would embrace us for nothing or would do the same to the British. Such ideas are wrong and careless. Some political consideration could lead (always temporarily) Afghanistan to one side or another but their sentiments will always stay hostile toward any European country. "It all the same if it is a black dog or a white dog, it is still a dog" said Abdur-Rahman. He meant the Russians and the British.

Only a policy which will bring Afghanistan a stable peace, insure its independence and give it a chance for free development in its religious and national venue can count on the support and sympathy of Afghanistan in general and the Afghan in particular.

With this I conclude the issue of the population.

5

Governing forms

Now we shall move to the forms of governance in Afghanistan. I will follow my usual methods and take on the practical side of the issue. On one hand you may be astonished by pictures of excessive cruelty including executions, jail, torture, incarceration, brutal extortion, caning – all kinds of beating. But on the other hand you will be amazed by pictures of freedom, significant self-reliance, political expanse and the start of elections. I'm going to try to use an angle of view of the Asians to reveal some sense of rationality and expediency. The late Abdur-Rahman was well known for cruelty but he said: "One cannot control wild horses with silk reins". And it is the deep truth. Pondering all circumstances and evaluating the Orient carefully and painstakingly will move you to a conclusion that it was a correct thought about ruling such a country. In this case you shall not look with the eyes of an artist or humanist. Your mission is very real and being such it dictates to you a singular scale of judging the governance – it is the scale of expediency and stability.

The essence of the Afghan emir's reign is fairly complex and difficult to perceive. It is customary to call him an absolute ruler or Asian despot – but is it true? First of all the emir is subject judicially and by custom to the country's laws – *Sharia*,[1] common law and the latest legislative norms. Further, his power is significantly limited by the presence of council, suspicious clergy, etc. His personal life and budget are more or less separate from those of the state. All that limits the emir's power to some degree and it forces us not to name him an *absolute despot*. More correctly, he could be considered as the type of absolute monarch found in Europe at the end of the 18th century. He is the ruler of destinies and the problem solver in the country. He begins and ends wars; he has the right to condemn to death or pardon subjects. He personally approves laws and though he called a council of wise men to create them – he is free not to listen to them and if he does not like them, he just dismisses the council. The judicial power belongs to him completely.

It makes serious practical sense to clarify the boundaries which limit and regulate the emir's power. Looking carefully into the roots of his power, you will first see that it is limited by the events in his life and in that regard the emir is a person elected by a group of people who can elect or rather influence the election. How the approval of the emir is conducted– we cannot say but it is visible in a number of facts. A thorough check is run on any new contender and some kind of poll is conducted. It is considered necessary to link the emir to the khans by ties of kinship or some other bond to get support and in

1 *Sharia* is the body of Islamic religious law. It is the legal framework within which the public and private aspects of life are regulated. *Sharia* deals with many aspects of day-to-day life, including politics, economics, banking, business, contracts, family, sexuality, hygiene, and social issues. (Translator's note).

that we can see an indirect approval of the choice. Secondly, the emir bases his policy on the incessant voices of the khans and sometimes even the *maliks* – the tribes' rulers. And as it happens, this is not only with political issues. Then, at the time of every coronation of an emir there is some kind of delay: suddenly it becomes necessary to poll military units; messengers run in different directions; someone's approval is needed; gold flows. Of course, to interpret these limits (of the emir's power) as some level of constitutionality – as the late Abdur-Rahman bragged in his autobiography – is an exaggeration, but some principal of election and some constant dependence of the emir on the Afghan nobility and clergy is certain. Some researchers of Afghanistan – and the people who have done in-depth study – connect the emir with the epithet *Primus Inter Pares*.[2] In practice, the emir's dependence could transform into unrestrained despotism, but it also could lead to the emir's total dependency on the court and clergy. That primarily depends on the emir's personality as well as the developing situation.

Abdur-Rahman was a domineering and stern person. He lived through exile and many difficulties and he was able to create a real governing power in Afghanistan and became the all-powerful ruler. But his son, Emir Habibullah was a much smaller figure. Fat, flabby and lazy, he spent most of his days in the boy's part of the palace (he had eight wives and 100 boys); he did not like matters of state and performed them reluctantly. His laziness and inborn good nature ran their course: the clergy got out of hand, the provinces stopped obeying the center and the Englishmen behaved in the country as if it were their own house. In Central Asia he was said to be the Englishmen's *nuker* – i.e. lackey.[3]

Now Amanullah-Khan reigns in Afghanistan. He is the third son of the late Habibullah, a young man of 28 years. He is not well known yet. He is delicate and amiable, but then again all emirs are like that during early years of the reign. The weight of ruling makes them harder. Amanullah is very cultured. People are saying that the emir is good but his advisors are bad.

Speaking about the administrative structure in Afghanistan, if you study it, you must strictly distinguish between the two sides of the matter: the external side for show – very often coherent and even approaching European forms; the other side – internal – which is quite often concealed from foreign eyes but it reflects the true-to-life essence of the government under which one Oriental country or another lives. And I'll try to discuss the issue using that dual standard.

First of all, what is the general structure of the government in Afghanistan? The country is headed by an absolute monarch. His immediate subordinates and assistants are viceroys[4] (*naib-khukume*) who rule the provinces. There are five provinces in Afghanistan: Kabul, Kandahar, Herat, Sharif and Jalalabad.[5] Their approximate bound-

2 *Primus inter pares* (Latin), *the first among equals*, or *first among peers* is a phrase which indicates that a person is the most senior of a group of people sharing the same rank or office. (Translator's note).

3 Britain (Hamilton for example) attributed Habibullah with a strong stubbornness in his dealings with them on foreign affairs. But it should be remembered that at the time of Habibullah's reign, Lord Curzon was Viceroy of India and he conducted a very hot-tempered and demanding policy toward Afghanistan which insulted the people and even the soft and agreeable emir. (Author's note).

4 The English sources often call them "governor-general". (Author's note).

5 By the latest information, there are five provinces and four regions (oblasts). (Author's note).

aries are as follows. Kandahar province occupies all the southern half of the country and is limited by the watershed mountain ridge of the rivers Adraskan and Fara-Rud in the north-west; by the Siyah-Kuh Mountain Ridge in the north and by a line running from western end of Kuh-i Baba through Ghazni to the Suleiman Mountains. Kabul and Jalalabad provinces lay to the north from the Ghazni Valley with the Hindu Kush Mountains at its north-west and the border of Chitral[6] at the east. All the space north of the Safid Kuh and Hindu Kush to the Russo-Bukhara border constitutes two provinces: Herat and Sharif. The border between them runs along the watershed ridge of the rivers Qaisor and Ab-i Qaisor and further south by the mountain ridge Band-i Turkestan up to Kuh-i Baba. Sharif province is divided by the Kunduz River into two regions, Afghan Turkestan in the west and Badakhshan in the east.

The most important parts of Afghanistan are Kandahar and Kabul provinces. Kandahar province is the source of Afghanistan's power – it is completely populated by Afghans (primarily the Duranni tribe – the emir belongs to that tribe). Troops and militia from the province serve as the major basis of his power. Kabul province represents the political center of the country.

Kabul province is administered by the emir himself and the remaining four provinces by viceroys who represent the legislative, administrative and judicial power. The viceroy also commands the troops deployed in the province but the troops also have a military commander – "*supekhsalar*". In the internal administration of the province, the viceroy is completely independent.

Tribes are governed by khans appointed by the emir and are divided into clans ("*kheil*") which are headed by *maliks* (elders).

In governance there is a large discord between theory and practice, the discord is related to a large degree on the ruler's personality. For example, judicial power belongs to the institution of judges who are directed by detailed regulations of rights and responsibilities in specific parts of the *Sharia*. But that is the theory and in reality all serious cases such as spying, apostasy, political transgressions, etc. go to the emir or viceroy. They may be judged by the spirit of *Sharia* but in practice by the ruler's discretion. And sometimes a ruler becomes the executioner of his own judgment. There were rumors that Abdur-Rahman, during the process of interrogation became so enraged that he would bare his teeth and beat a person so severely that he would be pulled dead from the "judge's" hand. We need to highlight the point that the right to condemn someone to death belongs only to the emir and that this grave right does not extend to others. But in practice, khans and beks also use the right and decide such cases by themselves.

The point is that the emir's order or approval of a death sentence usually is received by a viceroy through secret channels and the latter could always play that circumstance saying that he supposedly received such a decision from the emir. Note that secrets in Asia are kept much better than in Europe. Then there is always a way out for the viceroy by saying that they were forced to kill the person because he tried to hide from judgment or escaped and was killed during pursuit. The viceroy could cite his religious or political indignation while dealing with such an arrogant and blatant infidel or traitor that he

6 Chitral is a district in Northwestern Pakistan, at this time British India. (Translator's note).

could not restrain his noble indignation. In a word there are many ways for a viceroy to expand his jurisdiction and to include the death penalty in it.

Content of legislation

It has already has been said that several separate institutions lie at the foundation of the legislative branch. First and foremost – *Sharia* i.e. Islamic law in general; then there is customary law, especially among nomadic peoples; and finally there is modern law which is developing under the influence of European countries. The modern law, if not produced by European techniques of discussion, is not devoid of some kind of collegiate thinking, agreement and after that – general announcement. In relation to that form of law, Abdur-Rahman brags in his book that a parliament exists in his country, which supposedly does legislative work. But be careful, there is much that is awkward and raw in the "parliament". Abdur-Rahman's words are boastful and embellishments. Afghanistan is just now standing on the path of developing such laws and its attempts are timid.

Sharia

Speaking about *Sharia,* we must remember the historical process that produced that huge and very interesting legislative code. Its beginning goes to the epoch of Mohammed during a time of isolation and the nomadic state of the Arab peoples. The code built up through entire centuries after Mohammed's death and involved a tremendous effort by many people. Several schools developed and through these schools, they took serious care to refine the initial rough form of *Sharia* and extract it from its archaic forms. If you take the time to study Islamic laws, the wild ancient epoch will blow at you from the pages. Say, if you are interested in the relations of a wife and a husband under *Sharia,* then you will find many excessive details and regulations which sometimes get down to immoral details. But in a nutshell, all this leads to increase the rights of the husband and diminish the rights of the wife. But in that law we can find a lot of positive things, even from a scientific point of view, for example how meticulously and subtly some judicial matters were worked out. The same matrimonial law is developed with such a thoroughness which you cannot find in European laws. True, the initial point of the marriage i.e. the moment when the marriage [ceremony] is concluded (by *Sharia* it is a moment of the first coitus) is somewhat strange for European philosophy, but everything that follows from the beginning has been analyzed and instilled with exclusive thoroughness and fineness. And the issues related to the land rights – irrigated and non-irrigated and water rights – about running water, well water, pond water, etc. – all are far more developed then you will find in any other legislation.

The other side of *Sharia* which deserves to be mentioned is its profoundly practical tenor and it's attempt to get into all details of life – beginning with the state and ending with at the family hearth – and regulate it as much as possible. A Muslim's life is scheduled in *Sharia* by minutes and each step is accounted for: when to wake up, go to bed, wash, eat and perform other functions; how to kill game when hunting, etc. It will seem strange to you, but alas, it has its positive aspects. You have to consider the countries which are regulated by *Sharia.* Look closely at the ways of life in Orient, consider what kind of people live there, their temperament, living conditions, points of view, philosophy – and maybe you will see that very often the norms of life and mundane order can only be instilled through despotic means using the pincers of detailed regulations. Then you can agree that only such fully humiliating legislative norms will suit these people.

I will say it again, generally, in your encounters with countries and peoples of Asia, their laws, ways of life – do not rush into conclusions because there are many sides which you will have to think through and even better – to live through. Say, if you would study Islam, its essence, content and tradition – a great deal of the Koran will seem awkward, coarsely naïve, especially in the area of cosmogony[7] and a great deal of it will evoke disdain, even revulsion....But do not rush to judgment: the life of human societies is complex in general and Asia is not Europe.

My dwelling on *Sharia* is short though it is a very important issue. Of course in the future you will have to study Islamic law more thoroughly because it will be difficult to operate without knowledge of it.

As to the customary law, its limits are narrow and we can treat it as some kind of trivia. The emir's government considers *adat*[8] as an unavoidable necessity.

And so, the legislative basis includes three kinds of norms: *Sharia*, customary law and modern law. But how does life interpret these clear and more or less rational norms? What is the difference between theory and practice? Looking into decrees which are attributed to Mohammed himself by legend, you will see that their essence is fairly humane and reasonable. For example, there is a decree to collect a tax, a certain percentage of livestock owned – that tax is called *Zakat* and there also is a tax on grain – *Heradzh*. The Prophet said about the former: "One goat shall be taken for five camels. Of 40 goats which most of the year are grazing on pastures one goat shall be taken and this zakat shall be enough for the number of goats from 40 to 120 inclusively. From 120 to 200 goats – two goats shall be taken; from 200 to 399 goats – three goats and from 400 goats – four goats shall be taken. Above 400 – for every extra 100 goats, one goat shall be taken. It is legal to exchange goats for monetary value. The Zakat collector shall take *average animals* because it is so ordered by the Prophet".

The bureaucratic ladder

I specifically presented this small excerpt to you to illustrate the primary basis that taxation is based on. If in the future, you have a chance to familiarize yourselves with other articles of the *Sharia*, you will see that they are also fairly moderate, tolerant and pretty rational so as not to interfere with the country's prosperity. But, alas, in reality the picture changes and the greed of the authorities ruin the Prophet's deeds. It is repeated in the same manner in Afghanistan, Bukhara or contemporary India. In doing so you will find many tricks, subtle twists and running through all these human inventions is the despicable desire to rip the last shirt off the back of a poor person. And in passing, I do not know who is more inventive in this: an Afghan official, a half-illiterate Asian or a British gentleman educated in England. The Prophet said "average animals" but bureaucrats will

7 Cosmogony is the astrophysical study of the origin and evolution of the universe. (Translator's note).

8 *Adat* is customary law. (Translator's note).

grab the best. The Prophet permitted paying the tax monetarily – he meant the market price of course – but rulers will select the highest price and time the taxation to coincide with the time when a person is in a dire situation. Thus the simple, clearly defined norm of *zakat,* altered through real life ends up completely different – wicked and cruel.

The cause of the tyranny and abuse of power is the result of a huge gap between the rulers and subjects: the government is too far removed from the people, too despotic, too inflexible toward them. Though the emir says: "You are a Muslim and I am a Muslim" in reality this nice formula is an empty sound. As a result, the superior, while standing up on the social ladder, takes as much as he wants, not what the Prophet ordered or what a worker can give. The matter is complicated by the situation when bureaucrats either do not receive pay or the pay is negligible and they live by what they take from the people, and this bureaucratic army is not that small. True, the needs of rulers do not differ that much from those of subjects, but the aforementioned difference in social status makes a bureaucrat uncontrollable and unrestrained, and there is no justice[9] or threat to him from those below. Besides, we should note that the bureaucratic ladder has to deliver such a large sum of money to the emir that it is possible to exhaust the resources of the people through taxation – *and the bureaucratic army must also eat.* Thus the lower the press of taxation goes, the more it penetrates the masses of the people; but it stays sharp and powerful because it always reinforced by the personal interests of the taker.

A fixed sum has to be sent to the emir and not providing that sum threatens a viceroy's position. But the viceroy comes to the job with a wide court of confidants, loyal supporters, and a host of relatives – close and removed, etc. And all that pack must be fed, dressed – and pretty nicely as well. After the haughty needs of the high level bosses are satisfied, there comes a series of second-level bureaucrats: khans, beks, aksakals, amlyakdars,[10] mullahs, etc. who will not forget themselves when working to satisfy the emir. After them, there are even more petty people like the *mirab* (irrigation manager) or the *dargha* (tax inspector), etc.

All that large group of bureaucrats lives by extorting their livelihood from their positions. And since their social status is almighty, the moderate decrees of the Prophet are corrupted beyond recognition and the people are crying under the yoke of taxes. It is possible that now, under the rule of the current emir the situation is different, but I've told you how it was before – the major goal of every ruler at every level was to feed himself and his family well at his assigned location.

The Emir and Viceroys

It is interesting to look into the issue of relations between the emir and viceroys. In relation to the entire bureaucratic world, the emir is a master with absolute power. It is true for the viceroys as well. They are his most devoted people, often – his recent favorites and sometimes – his former intimate lovers. They are his eyes and mind. But everything is so

9 Casual observers – like Hamilton – love to point that in Afghanistan everyone must obey the law and justice is equal for all, even for the emir's relatives. They like to mention a case when the Abdur-Rahman's favorite wife got an order to answer to a lawsuit by a fashionable store. Practice does not support such suppositions and the supposed case is either legend or farce. (Author's note).

10 An *amlyakdar* is a tax collector in Central Asia. (Translator's note).

fickle in Asia and old links break off easily and quickly. The situation where some viceroys are appointed under the influence of that elusive group which forces even the emir to reckon with them helps a bit. These viceroys who got their position that way feel more independent – but these usually are short-lived and quite often they lose their appointed place and sometimes –their earthly place as well.

Because of that, the relations between the emir and viceroy are always somewhat strained and are guided by mutual caution. The emir does not trust the viceroys and the latter are wary about the emir's suspicions and caprices. From the outside, these relations look strictly defined and punctual – all orders are carried out diligently, summons to Kabul are complied with to the minute and implicitly – even if the propects are somewhat alarming. If there is a clear threat to a viceroy's life, he usually escapes it by fleeing the country. The emir's mistrust manifests itself when the newly-appointed viceroy moves to the place of service with his family, large group of subordinates and confidantes – along with them are the emir's special plenipotentiaries – his *oprichniks*[11] – *who are supposed to watch every step of the local government. Those people are usually vested with great power in the event of any confusion, although they behave obediently and even obsequiously. But the emir does not stop there, he usually has spies that are unknown to the viceroy and even his oprichniks.* It could be some *kazi*[12], cook, one of the stable hands in the viceroy's stables or it could be an *ishan* – and they conduct their difficult business very carefully and keenly. Of course, what viceroy does not have his own network of spies in Kabul – to keep up with the political life in the city and keep track of the emir's mood – especially the part which threatens the viceroys' position or even his life?

What are the emir's requirements for a viceroy?

First of all, of course, it is irreproachable political behavior, i.e. dedication to the emir, country and faith – those are the major points which are under constant special surveillance by the emir's oprichniks and spies. Any transgression on his part is punishable by loss of the position, long imprisonment and even the death penalty (though often only as a suggestion).

Then the viceroy is required to deliver a set amount of money on time and in total, he must be active and maintain his prestige and standing. And, only after that, he is required to be just and take care of the population. As you see, the entire administrative system is stood on its head. In our practice, an administrator must be just and humane in the first place – at least that is the requirement, but in Asia they do not brag about it. When I had a talk with a Bukhara *bek* about the ideals of power – how he interprets them – he refused to understand me saying that the Europeans are strange creatures. An

---

11 An Oprichnik (опричник) (plural Oprichniki) was a member of an organization established by Tsar Ivan the Terrible to govern the division of Russia known as the Oprichnina (1565-1572). The Oprichniki were responsible for the torture and murder of internal enemies of the Tsar. Notorious for their violent means of enforcement, they can be compared to modern "death squads" or secret police. Guided by Ivan, they laid waste to civilian populations. They dressed in black garb, similar to a monastic habit, and bore the severed head of a dog (to sniff out treason and the enemies of the Tsar) and a broom (to sweep them away). The dog's head was also symbolic of "nipping at the heels of the Tsar's enemies." They were sometimes called the "Tsar's Dogs" on account of their loyalty to him. They also rode black horses in order to inspire greater terror. (Translator's note).

12 A Kazi is a religious or secular judge in Central Asia. (Translator's note).

ideal ruler – according to him (and to Asia) – is a dreadful one, the boss who terrifies all his subjects. I ask him "Why?" He said "Because everyone must know that the ruler can crush him like a little mouse." So fear is the first and foremost part of power and the other qualities of a ruler come later.

When you read Abdur-Rahman's autobiography, you might think that the situation is very different in Afghanistan than my description indicates and there is a great deal that is new and European. In my time, when I lived in Pamir and heard about such "progress", I could not understand what kind of changes these were. I sent a spy to Kabul. He was a simple man, a wrestler and he could only observe the external situation. He spent two weeks in Kabul and after returning gave me an exact picture of what he had seen. I applied the picture on my knowledge of Oriental customs and concluded that life in Afghanistan has not been changed at all. Everything continues according to the old customs, there are no ministers, there is no constitution and life goes on in the same way that existed under the Great Moguls of India – as it was described by Bernier[13] and Tavernier.[14]

Life of a ruler

Now we are going to look at the ruler's everyday life. The picture will show you that the ruler lives by a scheduled life: he wakes up at dawn, first receives visitors and people with complaints. Then after a walk or a check on his horses, he attends to state business which continues until midday.[15] He eats his meal at noon and after that he rests in the wives' half of the palace. After his rest, he goes hunting or invites interesting people, mullahs and scientists for a discourse. Special events are reserved for the evenings. Sometimes he observes executions – in some cases to make sure that the one executed is the one it is supposed to be. If we look into *Sharia,* we will find the explanation of this regimen: a Muslim is supposed to meet the sunrise, then he must start his day with charity – because each surah of the Koran begins with the phrase "In the name of Allah – the gracious and charitable", etc. The ruler, as a Muslim, also must wake up early, show some charity, etc. These orders are for each Muslim and are mandatory for the emir as well. *Sharia* gives some specific directions for a ruler himself: how to rule his subjects, when he should rest, how to conduct justice, how to expand his knowledge by talks with wise people, etc. All of that is very characteristic and good to know, because it will give you a great deal of useful information. For example, if you know the emir's regimen, then you could observe who visits the emir and who does not, who is in favor and who is not, who has influence over the thin cords of political realities. In the morning, the emir is usually

13 François Bernier (1625-1688) was a French physician and traveler who became the personal physician of the Mughal emperor Aurangzeb for 12 years beginning in 1658. (Translator's note).

14 Jean-Baptiste Tavernier (1605-July 1689) was a French traveler and early commercial trader with India. (Translator's note).

15 Abdur-Rahman had following weekly schedule (it has been preserved by his son Habibullah): Monday and Tuesday were dedicated to mail and the treasury; Wednesday – military affairs; Thursday – state, social and private audiences; Friday – religious holiday; Saturday – sits in judgment as the appellant judge; Sunday – inspection of the army, stores, military supplies, workshops, etc. (Author's note).

visited by his brothers and sons; then his chief of police, spies, mullahs and people who are in favor. I repeat – the knowledge of it could be useful for one or another practical goals. And studying all those people and situation would help you to study the emir's personality seriously– which is, in any case, the most important factor in the life of a country such as Afghanistan.

We need to say a few words about the influential people in Afghanistan and the emir and his close relatives. Of that, B.N. Ivanov[16] – who is present here and who returned from Kabul recently – paints the following picture in his report. As you know the emir has many wives –the late Habibullah had eight of them plus 100 boys. Do not laugh at that curious family appendix. In Asia it is fairly common and is used by smart political dealers such as Englishmen as a specific political factor. In all the mass of gifts sent to an Asian ruler, there are always a number of gifts for the most-favored boys. Asian polygamy plays a significant and complex role in the life of a ruler. History can tell us a lot of instructive stories. Currently the ruling family in Kabul is as follows: The country is ruled by Amanullah-Khan – a young man of 28 years. He is the third son of the late emir. His eldest brother is in jail. The emir has three brothers – the youngest is 10 years old. The young emir's qualities are not clear as yet. To all appearances he is a kind man but with some steel in the character. People speak well of him,[17] though we will not make any conclusions because the real face of an emir never appears early in his reign.

In general, the younger group of brothers has very little influence as of yet, they have not come into real life and have not tasted the poison of politics. This group may be as a political force several years hence. More important is the group that includes the brothers of the late emir. The most important among them, until recently, was Hasrullah-Khan who in his time visited London and was the Afghan army supreme commander. Later he stumbled and has been moved into the shadows; two years ago he was arrested and, by the emir's order, blinded and later – executed. His next uncle – Muhammad-Omar-Khan is a sick person and I thought he was dead, but in Got's almanac (1914) I found his name again. Right now he is 31 years old. In his time he was thought to have a great future due to his noble origin on the maternal side,[18] but I think he will not last long. His next two uncles are younger and do not have any significant importance.

Until now, when speaking about Afghanistan I've told you that the center of gravity, influence and power belongs to the ruler. There is a first minister or, if we use old words, vizier.[19] Practically, this is the real major spring of power. But in recent literature we see

16 Boris Nikolaevich Ivanov was a Soviet intelligence officer who worked in Afghanistan in the 1920s. (Translator's note).

17 My latest information adds a great deal of interesting things about the current emir. He is infused with serious reformist ideas and takes Peter the Great as an example. He was able to enact a law on monogamy (mandatory from the moment of declaration) and he has only one wife. He is very curious and accessible. He adapted the Morse code to the Persian language and he drives a car himself instead of using a chauffeur. As to religion, he is fairly liberal. At audiences, he speaks fast and powerfully (in Persian). (Author's note).

18 His mother was Wabi-Khalima – the favorite wife of Abdur-Rahman, the daughter of Sakhib-Zade-Allikullah-Khan and granddaughter of the Emir Dost-Mahomet on the maternal side. (Author's note).

19 A vizier is a high-ranking political (and sometimes religious) advisor or minister. The term literally means "burden-bearer" or "helper". (Translator's note).

mentions of ministers, somewhat akin to European ministers, and I need to turn your attention toward this new Afghanistan institution.

Ministers of Afghanistan

In that regard I have the report of B.N. Ivanov, who is a very observant and interesting researcher. He did find a number of ministers in Afghanistan. As I've said, the current Afghan ruler and his brothers are young people and do not represent any influential political group. They have not gone through political testing. The uncles, who were sizable figures even if they lost their luster lately, are another matter. But next to these people who are related to the emir (it is the major source of their power) there is another group of people. In Ivanov's report, they are called ministers: minister of interior, trade minister, minister of exterior, etc. I shall tell you my sincere impression about that cabinet.[20] Ivanov mentioned several times in detail the interior minister and said that he is a very influential person who holds all the reins in his hands. When the emir is absent, that minister answers in his stead, asks his own questions – the rest of the ministers only nod like pawns. And the question is, is this really a cabinet of ministers with a prime-minister at its head and whose ministers lead a specific branch of the state apparatus, or is this a parody of the institution of ministers in Europe? Asiatic rulers often behave coquettishly toward Europe. When only one minister speaks and the other ministers arrive in a group and sit idly in the waiting room and obviously do not play any significant role – all this leads me to think that the institution of ministers is merely a facade which is supposed to show Europe that there are ministers in Afghanistan. In reality, the old system of power is still in place in Afghanistan.

In Asian countries, there was always a situation where the head of the country had to be an absolute, all-knowing, all-penetrating ruler who held everything in his hands. By law, custom and practice, he was supposed to personify everything and everyone. But because life puts obstacles in his way, the ruler cannot carry out all the functions that fall upon him even if he has all the qualities which are necessary for the job. And, if he is a weak, depraved and dissolute man, he is even less able to govern. As a result, in Oriental countries the institution of viziers developed through long practice (you can trace it through the Mongols, Turks, Great Moguls and Muslim countries in general). The viziers are the emir's assistants who are the beginning and the end of all *practical* rule in the country. They are something akin to the *majordomo*[21]of medieval French kings. The institution of viziers developed in the Orient because of essential and inevitable

20 According to Abdur-Rahman's biography, the emir's cabinet included: Ishik-Agasi (something like a Lord Chief Staff Master of British court), counselor, major secretary and several other secretaries, ranks of the emir's guards, treasurer of the emir's personal treasury, state military secretary (military minister), state secretaries of the North, South, East and West, postmaster-general, commander-in-chief or his assistant, chief stable master, "kotval" or palace secretary, quartermaster-general, chief of the royal apartments, superintendant and heads of trade and education departments. (Author's note).

21 Mayor of the Palace was an early medieval title and office, also called majordomo, from the Latin title *major domus* ("superior of the house"), used most notably in the Frankish kingdoms during the 7th and 8th centuries. (Translator's note).

necessity. Their real power is quite often transferred into legal power and that is why in Oriental history there are cases where a vizier usurps the power and creates a new and sometimes long-living dynasty. You can find such cases in the history of the Turkic dynasties of India and the same in Gazni, in Khiva, and elsewhere.

You can find the institution of viziers everywhere in Central Asia under different names: in India they are First Ministers; small rulers in remote regions of Dardistan still keep Viziers, in Bukhara the old Turkish name Kush-Begi is still preserved. And it is hard for me, who is accustomed to these facts, to admit to a new institution in Afghanistan – the institution of ministers. I think it is a translation from European – and a false one at that. My life experience tells me that now – as it was before – an almighty vizier runs all things and the emir only applies his high hand where needed. If an emir is such active and decisive a man as the late Abdur-Rahman, then he would work actively and a vizier would only help the emir, moving temporarily into the shadows. But if an emir is a lazy and carefree person, such as Habubullah-Khan, then he would spend most of his time in the boy's part of the palace and a vizier would rule with full power. And in fact, as noted by Ivanov, the interior minister has the most serious influence in Afghanistan's government – he speaks for everyone, suggests solutions for the emir and generally behaves with undue familiarity. In him I see my old acquaintance –the vizier who has now dressed himself in the toga of a minister. And in that institution which Ivanov called new, I find the existence of the old institution of vizierate, which I have mentioned before. In Ivanov's list of ministers, there is one very interesting note: he divides all ministers by their political sentiments into two categories: Anglophobes and Russophiles. For example, the trade and industrial minister is a weak adversary of England, the finance minister is a fierce Anglophobe, the interior minister is a strong Anglophile and the commander-in-chief (the emir's uncle) is a Pan-Islamist.[22] I have to dwell on this situation. In your calculations and conclusions, you must clearly understand what those terms mean: what is an Anglophobe, Russophile or Pan-Islamist and what is at the roots of the phenomenon? If you hear that an Oriental person is on the England's side, you would probably try to explain that by the person's deep believe in British ideas or his sympathy to English politics and hope that fate will kindly side Afghanistan with England; or in the world outlook of an Asian Russophile you would look for the main belief that Afghanistan's good fortune is to go along with Russia, i.e. against England. You would be seriously mistaken. If one is saying he is an Anglophobe and another one – that he is an Anglophile – in the first place this is determined (as Ivanov correctly noticed) by selfish goals. Of course the fact that a wealthy and intelligent person could become a flagrant hireling of England is kind of strange, but it is a common occurrence in Asia. Anyway, all those political signboards are not the result of a deep philosophical outlook or diligent political thinking – they are the result of an incident, habit, convenience, fear and mostly – self-interest. As to the Pan-Islamists they are a different category of people. In Asia, any privileged person – and especially high-born – cannot escape choosing a political platform, but it is not becoming for him to be an Anglophobe or Anglophile – he is too noble, proud and independent. But

22 This is one of the mysteries of Snesarev. His two categories appear to be five: Anglophobe, Anglophile, Russophobe, Russophile and Pan-Islamist. (Translator's note).

the political coloration is required and he most often takes the most advantageous and respectable out of them: as a faithful Muslim and follower of the Prophet's commandments he most probably will become a Pan-Islamist. And you will find out that most of the Asian aristocracy belongs to Pan-Islamism, i.e. they dream about the convergence of all Islamic peoples into one union. By the way, I would say that I admit to a significant sincerity in that philosophy, to a possibility of impulses and I think we can build something on the base of these political-religious sentiments to some degree. But I need to point out in advance that their world outlook and their representatives – especially those mentioned in the press – have never seriously understood it in a practical sense. I think that the Pan-Islamist movement is characteristic of ideology and far-remote hopes. But in a practical sense, related to politics or business as we see it in literature – it is still groundless and lifeless. And because of that I cannot agree either with Englishmen or with other Orientalists that Pan-Islamism represents a serious threat to Europe and we need to consider it as such *right now*. I would repeat that Pan-Islamism, so far, is only an ideological movement and it could only move onto practical plane once it is based on a strong organization with certain financial support.[23] In any case, I thought that I needed to mention it because Pan-Islamism is in an evolutionary stage as yet and you will have to watch it, think about it and make some conclusions.

It is interesting that among the Afghan political groups, there are representatives with a Turkish (a very intriguing) orientation.

Turks – escaped prisoners of the past war [World War I] – built a small and very close family of orthodox Sunni. It was at first good for them to find a place and subsequently to integrate into the Sunni mass of the Afghans. But later some other political movements were incorporated into the Turkish colony. As the Germans' allies, the Turks brought into Afghanistan a deep hatred of Englishmen, which was heated up by some information from India and they became representatives of a very strong Anglophobic movement. We can attribute the sympathy toward Soviet power in that group in part to these [anti-British] sentiments. In fact, the Turkish people in Afghanistan are not only sympathizers, but propagandists and defenders of the Soviets. I feel that Ivanov's observations are correct and we need to attach great significance to the fact of the Turkish sympathies toward Soviet Russia. In that very active and passionate group, Russia has unexpected friends and a ready and united advance guard for wide political endeavors.

Departments of the Administrative Machinery

Now, it is interesting to look at how the administrative machine works in Afghanistan from a technical point of view. I will mention that the sum of the administrative institutions is divided into two categories: military and civilian, though there in no clear dividing line between them, especially if they are under the command of a "prince of the blood". Again, while studying the issue, we should not forget the duality of everything Asian – a beautiful and logical exterior and a rough interior. For example, there is a whole assortment of departments: public works, medicine (health), mining, etc. And

23 One could argue that Snesarev foresaw the possibility of Al Qaeda. (Translator's note).

here is a quest for you – to look at these establishments: are they really well organized departments of ministries like in any European state or are they badly translated from the English words? I can tell you definitely that when I've studied the issue, I could not come to a clear conclusion. Take the department of public works for example. You will see that its' efforts built the roads from Herat and Mazar-i Sharif to Kabul, but the Kabul to Peshawar road has been under construction for 10 years. This latter road is the only well-built one. So, the department worked hard, but if you personally look at these roads –their condition, maintenance and repair – you will see something unexpected. Take, for example, the road in Badakhshan which is on the right bank of Panj River. One can ride it on horseback; our scouts confirm it, but look at it carefully. In some places, especially where it is needed the most, the road practically does not exist; large bumps are not smoothed out, there has never been any kind of repair and nobody looks after it. This is a complete difference from our mountain roads in Turkestan or those of the English in India. I think that these so-called roads from Kabul to Kandahar or Herat are pure fantasy and maybe only the road from Kabul to Peshawar through Tang-i Karun represents something real. And that leaves us with the conclusion that the department of public works effectively does not exist because there are no result of its work and the department is only a signboard. I've heard that the road from Mazar-i Sharif to Kabul is maintained reasonably well, graded for bumps and systematically cleaned of snow, but knowing Afghanistan's backwardness one would have his doubts about it.

Take for example the health department – you think about it and you begin to laugh. There is no more or less organized medical help in Afghanistan. There might be a British[24] doctor – either male or female – who has lived in Kabul for a long time or it could be a doctor from India. And all the population goes to them with internal sicknesses, eye problems, nervous diseases, etc. We recently received a request from Afghanistan to send an obstetrician to Kabul due to a grave situation among the women giving birth. What kind of a health department it is? Old midwives probably send 50 percent of birthing women to the other world as has happened since time immemorial and the population continues to go to various quacks for help. There is no department and is only a signboard – because there are no doctors or obstetricians. Take a doctor with you on your mission and you will personally see how badly the Afghan population needs medical help. From all sides and at all stops the mass of sick will flow to your doctor.

As to the department of mining – Martin, who spent eight years in Kabul, says that there is nothing like that in Afghanistan. He tries to explain why this is so, to fence off the situation, but these are only words. There is one department that is really working, the economic department or as it was known before, the treasury.

And so, there are no institutions on the European scale in Afghanistan. It has its own old Asian establishments[25] – disorganized, accountable to no one, with the whole

24 The following English doctors were in the emir's service: Mr. O'Mira – a dentist (from 1887), Mr. Grey – a surgeon (1889), Ms. Hamilton a female doctor (1894), Ms. Daly (from 1895), Major Cleveland (1904) and the Brown sisters (1904). Currently, there are probably no British doctors in his service. (Author's note).

25 Judging by Abdur-Rahman's autobiography, before his ascension to the throne, the complete civilian administration consisted of 10 scribes; public institutions did not exist and all administrative meetings were conducted in functionaries' bedrooms. There were no journals and all

mass of mirzas.[26] Those are primordial establishments which do not accept a system or a strict organization. If you need to get some papers from them, you will have to wait a while until you can get some results. I would not recommend having to deal with these "departments". Thus I believe that if any kind of new institutions are born in Afghanistan, they are in an embryonic state and most elementary. They have no plans, documentation, systems, statistics, control, etc. Sometimes the emir gets a report that whole provinces were robbed, but by whom and how – to discover any clue is extremely difficult. There is an interesting saying by Abdur-Rahman: "In our country one quarter of taxes are paid voluntarily, another quarter we must beat out with a stick, another quarter sticks to dishonest hands and nobody knows to whom the last quarter goes." I will say it again, all named institutions are only signboards and behind them you will find the old Asian establishments known since the Great Moguls.

Regime

I will say a few words about the regime. If we put aside an impression of some logic and the appearance of legality and look into the essence of the matter, we will see that an Asian regime – whether it is in Afghanistan, Khiva, Bukhara or Dardistan – cannot withstand any critique from a humane, economic or moral point of view. Before you there is a whole mass of evil, suffering and tears – Ivanov, an emotional person, noticed it and described in his report how much suffering and abuse there is in Afghanistan. But a person who has gotten wiser from observations and who is accustomed to the Asian perspective will react to it much calmer. I have to admit that the regime is terribly brutal, often unjust; it contains much trickery and evil, spies are everywhere, punishments are bloody and excessive. But unfortunately, all that is tied to the nature of the Asian world to such a degree that we need to look at that as something unavoidable and to a great measure expedient – at least until the country will move to a new order and the people will change.[27]

In particular if you have more interest in regimes, you can find a sufficient description of those executions and tortures which are used in Afghanistan in Martin's book. The Englishman writes about how arms are twisted or how a person is slowly pressed in a vise and describes the tools of torture and so on. He simply savors it. I will not dwell on these details and tell you that I've seen these things multiple times with different beks of Bukhara, of Kulyab, Shughan, etc.

---

documents – incoming and outgoing documents were registered on separate sheets of paper – to find any of them one had to go through all of them. Abdur-Rahman, by his own words, started all over and accomplished a lot. But I think he did not do much *new*, he just fixed what was really bad in the old. (Author's note).

26 A Mirza is a functionary, scribe or secretary in Central Asia. (Translator's note).

27 Kaye, a historian of the First Anglo-Afghan War, spoke well about this when describing the personality of Dost Mohamet. "Falling into the course of Afghan politics, a man (leader) must fight or die. The hand of every man is raised against him and he must direct his own against everyone...The Afghan sovereign must accomplish many acts which are the enemy of our humane feelings. He must rule with severity or abdicate his power. Such severity is unavoidable in ruling such a people." Kaye, *History of the War in Afghanistan*, Volume I, 123-124. (Author's note).

That they exist is not important; what is important is the understanding of their idea, so to speak – the philosophy of torture. Once I visited a bek and he decided that I was an important person and according to the Asian customs he began to offer me rugs, a horse, etc. I refused, but trying to utilize the host's generosity I told him that if he wants to do something pleasant for me, he could throw away all the torture tools I had seen in his principality. On that remark, he decisively and coldly replied that he cannot, because *without those tools there is no power.* We began to discuss power and its methods and I got a clear impression that we were standing at the opposite poles of world views, that we could not agree and he would not yield at any price. He agreed to show me the jail. It was something terrible. A huge pit had been dug out in the corner of the bek's yard. It was three-four sazhens deep and I cannot say how wide. A narrow, almost vertical, stairway led down. The small square opening – ¾ of arshin[28] on the sides – was the only way for air and light to get inside. People stayed in that pit without a break, some not seeing daylight for several years. Of course, only the strongest survived. Mortality in the jail was practically all inclusive – the prisoners mortality rate was almost at 100 percent. Naturally, people ate, drank and performed body functions in the pit. I wanted to go into that horror of human existence and I asked the bek to let me in. He refused for a while to let me in, but when he was certain that it was my personal wish out of curiosity, he agreed. I began to go down and stopped three or four steps down the stairway. Dizziness from the terrible stench had overcome me. I fainted and was pulled out to the surface. I asked the bek if he would release someone in the honor of our meeting. He agreed and a man more than 80 years old was pulled out from the pit. He was a total disorder, stunk terribly, his gray hair looked like oakum (fakirs in India had something like that). When I approached him to explain that he was free now, I saw a madman who wildly squinted his eyes at the daylight. I helped an insane man.

And after all, I need to say that a person who weighs the issues carefully, a thinker and a practitioner at the same time, will admit that as much as it may look brutal –in the nature of Asian countries, unruly Asian peoples and their wild and uncontrollable temperament, one can find some sort of justification for the brutality – an unavoidable concession to state order. It is dangerous to let out of your sight this sometimes-hard principle of state expediency – and in Asia applying a sentimental-abstract scale is the most dangerous course.

28 Arshin is an old obsolete Russian measure of length equal to 0.71m or 28 inches. (Translator's note).

6

Economy of Afghanistan

Now I'll move to the elements of the state economy of Afghanistan. I've already talked about taxes imposed on the Afghan population. Now I will look into the issue of how countries like Afghanistan conduct economic activity and the methods of their economics. In research papers you will find a brief mention of the two parts of its entire treasury: the means of the state and the personal means of the emir. In reality, these sums do not always stay separate. This means that the treasury remains at the old stage where the personal wealth of a ruler and the state's treasury are mixed and confused. The emir hardly understands what belongs to the state and what his own personal wealth is, but he tries to make a show of the difference. The major sources of state income are the following: 1) Land, orchard and livestock taxes; 2) Customs duty on export and import; 3) Postal income; 4) Stamp duty; 5) Income from state land; 6) Rent from state housing and stores; 7) Fines; 8) Confiscation; 9) the British subsidy to the emir – 18 laks of rupees (1,800,000 rupees).[1] The list will tell any person who has an elementary knowledge of economics that this is a fairly primitive economy and that, with such a budget, the country cannot move far either in the wide economic sense or in the organization of a prolonged and difficult war.

What is the sum of Afghanistan's income in the present financial system? There is no definite answer. Approximately 50 years ago[2] (1876) it was about seven million rubles and today some researchers think it is about 15 million rubles. But here only the monetary part of the budget is defined. We need to note that in Afghanistan, up the present time, taxes are paid with money or in kind[3] (the government is trying to change this situation to more monetary payments as it is more convenient and less cumbersome; but for the population it would be more oppressive). As it is, payments in kind represent more than half of all paid taxes. Usually, taxes paid in kind go to support the military and the emir's and viceroys' courts. If we are going to count the taxes paid in kind, then

1 The sum has presumably been increased to 24 laks beginning in 1916. (Author's note).

2 The Stoletov mission was able to approach this difficult question during the reign of the Emir Shir Ali Khan. (Author's note). Nikolai Grigorevich Stoletov (Столетов, Николай Григорьевич) (1834-1912) was a general in the Imperial Russian Army. Stoletov graduated from the General Staff Academy in 1859. In the 1860's, Stoletov took part in the Russian conquest of Turkestan and was a major participant in the Russo-Turkish War of 1877-78. During this conflict he commanded the Russian and Bulgarian forces at the Second Battle of the Shipka Pass. After the end of the Russo-Turkish War, Stoletov was made Lieutenant-General and appointed commander of the Turkestan Military District and participated in a diplomatic mission to Afghanistan. (Translator's note).

3 Every level of treasury in Afghanistan has two departments: 1) Monetary operations; 2) Operations in kind. (Author's note).

Afghanistan's budget goes up to no less than 40-50 million rubles. The following entities control the treasuries' income and expenditures: the viceroys' administrations, clergy, municipal offices and trading houses (I am forced to use this European term for want of something more precise).

As to the matter of how the general income is divided into expense items – there is no clear information. Everything that is depicted by Englishmen has very little credibility. Absence of a budget estimate, mixing personal funds with state funds, absence of proper accountability and taxes paid in kind, etc. – all these makes it impossible to do any kind of definitive accounting.

Among the aforementioned income sources are some special ones which require more detailed look. The fines, confiscations, etc. are relatively small and are dwarfed by the major ones, those which are prescribed by *Sharia*. We need to dwell on the main two, *Zakat* and *Heradzh.*[4] After studying their size and content, we will approach the essence of Afghanistan's state economy and its income. And in conclusion, we can estimate the financial load which could be used to build the Afghanistan's armed forces. Both Zakat and Heradzh are major types of taxes not only in Afghanistan but in Bukhara, Khiva, and some regions of India and therefore deserve our undivided attention.

Zakat

Now, let me approach the matter in more detail. Zakat[5] means "*purification*" in Arabic. Muhammad said with all certainty that every Muslim must give away some part of his real estate and wealth to support the *poor*. In that law we can see three principles: 1) It is the duty of every faithful Muslim to share a certain part of his income with others; 2) That share was intended for the poor; 3) The tax was taken from surplus beginning with a minimum amount – for example a person who owned less than 40 goats was not supposed to pay zakat. This example shows that zakat is a modest and rational tax, and judging by it we can conclude that Muhammad was a good politician and lawmaker. In the case of zakat, he did not forgot the important principals of the limitation and taxation of increasing property, i.e. the animals which are grazing on free ranges, free grass and proliferate naturally. By the spirit of the law, horses used for riding and limited in number by natural proliferation cannot be taxed by zakat. In Afghanistan, taxation by zakat applies to camels, sheep and goat which graze freely on its fertile grass ranges. These are the judicial and spiritual basis of the law. But life and practice have corrupted these principles into something unrecognizable. The prophet intended zakat for the poor and while he lived and under his first sincere successors it was so, but later it had been taken from the poor by those of nobility and influence and became a state or municipal tax. The prophet ordered that average livestock be taken, but in reality the best are taken away. The prophet permitted payment of zakat with money instead of paying in kind, but this also became a source of grief and a major injustice in the reality of the abuse of

4 It is interesting how shallowly the Englishmen looked into the Afghan economy – they almost always keep silent about these undoubtedly larges items of the budget. (Author's note).

5 Anyone who is interested in learning details of this interesting Muslim institution can find information in the book *Khidaya Commentary of the Islamic* Law, translation from English by N.I. Grodekov, Tashkent, 1893, 4 volumes. "About Zakat", vol. I, 69-130. (Author's note).

power. Anyone who is interested in details can find them in my works *India as a Major Factor of the Central-Asian Issue* and *Eastern Bukhara* and in the works related to the ways of life and ethnography of Central Asia.

And that is the first major form of taxation which is in the basis of the Afghanistan's financial system. If you will recall that the slopes of Hindu Kush are filled with livestock and that the Afghans primarily raise livestock – you would understand that zakat is one of significant forms of the state income. I will repeat only that in Muhammad's law there is a lot of sense and economic calculation – he thought to support the poor people and not to destroy the wealthy households. Even today, these ideas produce a sense of rationality and ethic beauty. But the surplus of households has been captured by the wealthy taking it away from the poor. They perverted the prophet's ideas and through the ages turned a law that was beautiful in its essence into a severe and deeply unjust tax system.[6]

Heradzh

Now I will move to the second type of taxation. It is a tax on ripened grain. Muslim law says that from each un-irrigated desyatina, 1/10th of the crop shall be taken and from an irrigated desyatina – 1/5th of the crop. This tax is collected in Afghanistan, Bukhara, Western Pamir and some other Oriental countries, but as it is with zakat, the prophet's plan of heradzh was corrupted by the evil will of man.

Here is how heradzh is collected. After the grain ripens and is harvested, the entire crop is moved to the threshing floors. Usually several people use one common threshing floor where all the grain that needs threshing and also those that do not require it are stored. Of the latter, only sesame is stored in sheaves for control. Only flax seeds are used for oil production and its fibers are used for animal feed.

As soon as the farmers start threshing, a special class of people appears on the stage. They are subordinates of the amlyakdar and named the "darga"[7] in Bukhara. Their numbers in every "amlyakdarstvo"[8] vary depending on the area and population. Every darga must see *that not a single portion of any product is hidden before the total account of the harvest is taken.* In part they are aided by the fact that several people use one threshing floor and there are also snitches. Every darga has several assistants who *watch* the threshing during the daytime and *guard* the threshing floors at night.

When the threshing is completed and all the kinds of grain are gathered into piles, they are sealed with the darga's stamps. The stamps are made out of wood and shaped

---

6 Zakat was intended to be a voluntary donation without government interference. Normally the donor would first give zakat to needy members of his extended family and then outside the family. There was no requirement of records and the matter was between the donor and his Creator. However, many governments at different times have inserted themselves into the process and collected zakat as a tax. The government distribution of these monies, naturally, is different. (Author's note).

7 Our chronicles corrupted this word into "darugi" or "dorogi" – the name of the Tatar tribute collectors or general administrative personal of the Tatar administration in ancient Rus'. See S.F. Platonov, *Lectures on Russian History*, Saint-Petersburg, 1909, 6th issue, p.110. (Author's note).

8 Several kishlaks – something akin to our 'volost'". (Author's note). The volost' is an obsolete Russian administrative unit that included several villages. (Translator's note).

as rectangles (with sides two vershoks long[9]) or round discs (two vershoks in diameter). The owner's name or some sort of marking is carved in the stamps. The sealing process is as follows: several lumps of moist clay are used and one side of these is stamped with the stamp. Then these lumps are inserted into a grain pile at a certain height from the ground. All the piles are separate with a certain distance between them with the stamped side visible. After the sealing is finished, they cease guarding the piles. If grain is stolen from a pile, (displaced lumps will show that) the owner of that pile bears all responsibility.

When all piles are sealed, the dargas report to the amlyakdar. Then amlyakdar goes to these places to make an estimate of the amount of grain in the piles.

The local measures of grain are different in different regions. Usually the amlyakdar, after looking at a pile, tells the owner how much grain is in the pile – and looking out for the treasury's interests (more probably, for his own) routinely overestimates the quantity. The owner, who knows the administration's habits very well, most often disagrees with the amlyakdar and insists on lower numbers. A prolonged argument ensues. An "amin"[10] acts as an arbitration judge as he is the most experienced person in such deals. He normally takes an average number between amlyakdar's and owner's estimate and announces his decision. In most cases, both sides agree with the amin's decision. But if the amin cannot reconcile the arguing sides, they take scales and weigh the entire pile. When the quantity of one product or another is determined, the amlyakdar writes the quantity of the product which the person is supposed to give as the heradzh payment.

The collection of heradzh – as it is with zakat – is done in monetary form instead of payment in kind. The payment of heradzh is done during the winter based on set prices approved by the government.

The set prices are determined by members of the judicial branch of power in every district (kazi-rais).[11] The latter observe prices on products of the new crop at local markets during certain periods of time and then calculate the average price which becomes the set price. The kazi-raises send these set prices to the government for approval. The government, after approval, sends the prices back to the kazi-raises who in turn send them to the district rulers. The latter send the prices to the amlyakdars. The amlyakdars announce the prices to the population and request that they now pay the heradzh.

There are many dark spots in the picture I have painted, although they are well hidden from the casual observer. For example, the prices are established by a certain person who is a bureaucrat in his essence. As a member of the administration, he makes living by his ability to inflate the prices – at least the government is encouraging him to do so. He is trying to catch the moment when prices at the markets are up and establish them as *the average*. He sends these prices to his boss who changes them – most often an increase – and sends them to the viceroy who has the right to approve them. When the viceroy examines the various prices and he picks the highest one of them and if all the prices look too low to him, he will increase them by 10-20% or even 30%...As a result, the prices

9 Vershok is an obsolete Russian measure of length equal to 4.45 centimeters or 1.75 inches. (Translator's note).

10 Village elder. (Author's note).

11 Kazi-rais in Central Asia controlled compliance by Muslims with *Sharia* laws in everyday life, provided public services in towns, road maintenance and controlled the correctness of measurements and scales. (Translator's note).

will be significantly higher than those defined by real life. We will not talk about other abuses in the heradzh collection – there are enough of them. In the end, the farmer pays much more than Islamic law requires.

At any rate zakat and heradzh are the main taxes and if one needs to calculate the available resources of an Asian state, he should figure out the amounts of collected zakat and heradzh. I emphasize that the calculations must be done according to real practice (if it is possible) without regard what the law requires. It is not possible to tell you the correct approach to the solution but it is very important to figure it out practically. By chance, one could find out the quantity of grain or livestock in a separate small area and with some corrections make a conclusion about the larger region – with some scientific precautions. If one can figure out the total quantity of taxes in kind in one area or another, and familiarize himself with the process of collection (how severe or lenient it is), then one can fairly easily translate it into a monetary value knowing the average market prices.

On other side it is possible to find out through a mirza or other source how much money in zakat and heradzh had been sent to the emir from certain area during particular year. After that, one has to go through the verified average prices of the quantities of zakat and heradzh in kind (though it is more difficult), i.e. to find out the quantities of animals and harvested grain. Knowing the collection procedure, one can calculate the total wealth of the province (region, district) in livestock and grain. In the first case, it is possible to identify the largest item of income in the Afghanistan's budget and in the second – the country's wealth in livestock and farm produce.

I'm only telling you the method[12] which can be used for the accounting, but there are many possible corrections and individual methods. Say, if the viceroy's data shows a certain sum, you will need to lower it about 20-25% to get the more realistic number, etc.

After discussing two major typical kinds of taxes I do not want to dwell on other smaller taxes. But to describe the taxation situation of a person in Central Asia, I will talk a little about other taxes using Bukhara as an example. I will not go against the truth, because Bukhara and Afghanistan are much alike in their administration and economy. The small taxes may have different names in Afghanistan, vary slightly in details, but their essence will be the same – and that is most important. There are the following secondary taxes.

Secondary taxes

Zakat-chakana. This tax is for people who do not pay real zakat – those who have less than 40 sheep or goats. To collect the tax, every spring the bek sends a representative to

12 In the works related to Afghanistan, the data gathered by such questioning is present quite often and they produce some results. For example D.A. Mel'nikov has been able to find out that in Afghan Turkestan (in its steppe areas), 300,000 desyatinas are sowed and that the wheat surplus in Khodzh-Nakhr (18 aryks of Balkh) and Tash-Kurghan is up to 1,358,000 puds, but the author correctly thinks that those numbers are only an approximate estimate of the arable land and not produced crop. See D.A. Mel'nikov. *The Area of Operational Routes from Termez to Kabul.* Tashkent, 1907, pp.126-130. (Author's note).

every amlyakdarstvo who goes through every household not paying zakat and collect a half of ten'ga[13] (7½ kopeks) for each sheep in the household or a quarter of ten'ga (3¾ kopeks) for each goat. *All collected tax* goes to the bek.

Kosh-puly. Each spring before field work begins, every farmer must pay four-eight ten'gas for each pair of plowing animals (oxen or horses). The amount of the tax varies depending on the soil's quality and therefore, its fertility. *All that money goes to the bek.*

Yak-sirah. Besides paying the *kosh-puly*, the same farmer must pay the price of one butman[14] of wheat. No one is exempt from that tax – even a family which has one sorry animal must pay the cost of a half-butman of wheat. *This money also goes to the bek.*

Kafsan. An amlyakdar is the second administrative person after the bek. He also gets a sizable portion of taxes. Each farmer gives to the amlyakdar one pud (panj-seer) of the crop from every butman of grain (the paid heradzh excluded). The panj-seer is the name of a stone which weighs one pud. And so, the amlyakdar gets six to 12 percent of the crop.

Mirab-ana. The mirab is a person who is in charge of irrigation in certain areas. He is appointed by the bek. *It requires a great deal of work and attention by a mirab* to distribute water to the users timely and justly, so that no one will be offended. The mirab is a very important person to the farmers. And he receives his deserved payments. Every farmer with irrigated rice fields must give him one butman of rice for each pair of working animals or pay its cost monetarily.

Kafsan-darga. The above-mentioned dargas have not been forgotten. There is no established tax for them but they receive payments from farmers by mutual agreement.

Other taxes. After paying all these taxes, where a farmer gives every bureaucrat his portion – either deserved or undeserved – one would think that he is now free to go to market with his surplus of product (if any is left) and sell it. Not so. He again must pay a special tax for the right to sell – the "amin-ana".

Amin-ana. All the markets of Hissar bekstvo are rented to three renters (the "amin-anachi"). For example – the same amin-anachi rents markets in Hissar, Kartahen, Khanaka, Gazimalek, Shurian, Ak-Kurghan, Regar and Sufian. He is responsible for keeping the markets clean and maintaining the markets' scales. Annually, he pays the bek 50,000 ten'gas (7,500 rubles) as the rent for all these markets.

The two other renters pay the bek yearly rents of 70,000 ten'gas (10,500 rubles) and 13,000 ten'gas (1,950 rubles) respectively.

Let's look what that gets the renter. He receives: three ten'gas for each butman of any product sold; two ten'gas for each camel or horse sold; one ten'ga for each ox or cow sold; ½ ten'ga for a sheep and ¼ ten'ga for a goat.

Naturally, the renter has a significant number of employees to control sales at the markets. And considering the fact that sales could be conducted outside of the markets in any kishlak, the renter keeps special agents in all kishlaks to get his payments. These agents carefully watch all transactions and will not miss any sale without getting the fee.

Assiya-puly and Abydzhuvaz-puly. Every bek, being more or less a greedy person, establishes by his own will in his bekstvo taxes on various mills. There is a tax on

13 Ten'ga is the old monetary unit in several Central Asian states. Presently, it is the monetary unit of Kazakhstan. (Translator's note).

14 The butman is different in each bekstvo and varies between eight and 16 puds. (Author's note).

flour-making mills of 20-100 ten'gas per year. The tax on cereal-making mills is equal to one butman of rice cereal or two butmans of raw rice (shalah). The tax amount depends on the productivity of the mills.

Tunal-puly and Alyaf-puly. The bek will not forget about fruit orchards and clover fields which bring some income to the owner by selling the surplus. On each tanap (60 square arshins[15]) of fruit orchard, he will set a tax of 16-18 ten'gas per year. Each tanap of clover fields is taxed at the rate of four ten'gas per year.[16]

I told you this entire story not to evoke a sense of pity or outrage but to create the actual picture of the little person's situation in Afghanistan. That person is interesting to you in two aspects. First, he represents the work force. If you are interested in the person – you will see that he lives and feeds his family even under the press of huge taxation and, undoubtedly represents a great productive force. And really, watching him – especially a farmer – will make you wonder – how can he work so hard and long? On the other hand, even in his slavery, he is still a political factor. As you can see, this person suffers a great deal, deals with a lot of hardship and keeps his disenchantments hidden – that person must have a few rosy dreams in the depth of his soul. That tells us that the governance system in Afghanistan should not rest on the presumption of its stability. There is a huge gap between the working masses and those in power and that gap always can be widened. The oppressed masses always can realize their potential freedom and rise in revolt. This is why I wanted to tell you about all the grievous details, from the political and economic points of view. A farmer of an Asian country represents a variety which can silently work much, create much and suffer much. But the process of the oppression creates discontent, rebellion and the existing order of thing may be broken.

With this, I end the issue of the administration and economic system of Afghanistan. I would like to highlight the fact that the official part of taxes – i.e. that is paid to the emir or goes to the armed forces – can be found out very precisely and one can make all accounts from the top to the bottom down to a single chicken. But everything that is taken above that measure is stolen and extorted – all that cannot be accounted for – and these are huge sums. With this, I want to tell you that in your research you can determine what the general tax resources of Afghanistan are, but how much goes to the real needs of the country and how much – to the administrative apparatus –is impossible to find out. And because of this, any conclusion about the general economic potential and its military-economical abilities will be very difficult to make.

Military-industrial activity in Afghanistan

While speaking about industrial activity in Afghanistan, I touched upon it very briefly and casually. But it does exist, though in a rudimentary state and in the form of military industry. I was right then, because when speaking about people's activity, I had to

15 One square arshin is equal to 0.5 square meters or about 5.56 square feet. This means that the tanap is 333 square feet. (Translator's note).

16 I have not named all the taxes. For example, there is the Dzhozie – a tax paid by Jews and Hindus; the Badzh – a fee for caravans or for driving animals to market, a river crossing fee, etc. (Author's note).

tell you about that which involves the mass people's actions, not the actions by only the government or one or another particular group.

Now, when I approach the more specific military assessment of Afghanistan, I need to talk about that industrial activity due to its great importance for the Afghan Army. Some attribute the creation of factories and industrial plants to Abdur-Rahman which is true. And the following information is taken mostly from that emir's autobiography, although many specialists consider it greatly exaggerated.

There is no doubt that Abdur-Rahman did a lot. He founded a special state department of State Secretary ("mirmunshi") which collects and processes reports on all workshops founded by foreigners or in the emir's service. The department also does translation of books related to industrial issues, chemistry, physics, mathematics, etc.

Abdur-Rahman signed contracts with British, Hindus and other foreigners on the condition that they can leave their positions only when their students are be able to work on their own. Thanks to that idea, various industrial branches are completely in the Afghan's hands. Here is the history of the creation of the military industry.

At first, practically the entire industry in Afghanistan was oriented toward supplying the state with military items. Because of that, they initially purchased equipment and tools for making rifles, cannons and ammunition. In 1885, they selected a plot located on the Alam Handzh River near Kabul for construction. There, they built mechanical workshops and installed metal lathes, drills, equipment for making moulds and minting coins as well as cutting machines used in cast-iron workshops. They were powered by steam engines of three, six and eight horsepower. All that equipment was purchased in Calcutta and was served by 22 Hindu master artisans. In reality, three British engineers, especially Mr. Salter Pine, established this industrial process.[17] The process grew step-by-step, existing workshops were expanded and new one were built. The industry began general purpose production. Further, the equipment for making Henry-Martini and Snider rifles and the cartridges for them was installed along with machines for drilling out the barrels of cannon and rifles. Then they added 100-horsepower steam engines with boilers, steam presses with boilers as well as machines for sewing leather, making rifle powder, making soap, making candles and minting coins. They also built wood-working workshops and lumber mills.

Further acquisitions included machines for processing and dying leather along with agricultural equipment and tools. After that, they purchased machines for making cold steel weapons [knives, swords and bayonets], and machines for casting and processing mortar and heavy artillery shells, making rifle cartridges and other equipment. The number of machines grew steadily year-by-year as did the number of plants and factory workers, road builders, miners and others. Five years ago, the number of the people working for the government approached 100,000.

In 1894, because of the British government's interference that prevented delivery of rapid-firing Hotchkiss cannons that had been purchased by Abdur-Rahman from abroad, the Kabul plant began to make them using blueprints. Later there was a rumor

17 Many technical specialists, especially artillery specialists went to Kabul. Those are: S. Pine, Akkin Martin, Jerome, McDermot, Casheron, Sorenton, Clements, Middleton, Stuart, Walter, Grant, Donovan, Edwards, Tasker, Riches, F. Martin, Finleyson, Fleisher and others. Most of them are British. (Author's note).

that they had begun to make Maxim, Gardner and Gatling cannons. Electricity and telephone communications were introduced during the last decade.

The mint in Kabul can produce 80-100,000 rupees per day. The minting tools also are made there. The Kabul masters can make up to 10,000 cartridges daily for rifles of any system and in a case of acute necessity – twice as many. As to making rifles – their production was set by Mr. Casheron who worked at a government-owned factory in India. About 15 years ago, the plant was making up to 15 Henri-Martini rifles daily. From beginning of this century, they have been making the latest model Lee-Metford magazine rifles. English engineer Stuart built and organized an artillery factory. During its construction, huge pieces of equipment were transferred to Kabul – boilers and machines up to 28-foot long – and all that in the absence of railroads!

Besides the military plant, there are facilities for the production of other merchandise (distillery, tannery, soap manufacture, candle making and other plants). There is also an optical industry (to make telescopes, optical sites, artillery rangefinders, and heliographs) as well as woodworking and architectural industries.

To complete this section on military industry, I am going to read to you an excerpt from Ivanov's work – it is the most recent material. As to reliability of the data, he writes carefully and in a restrained manner; in our discussion he told me that at the time he had undertaken all measures to check all collected information.

"The Afghan army is supplied by the Kabul military plants. Comrade Kulikov has been able to inspect them. Of course, our military personnel were not allowed inside. The inspection was conducted hurriedly and was far from complete.

The plant produces cannon, machine guns, rifles, powder, cartridges and woolen cloth. There are also the mint and printing house at the plant. The plant was founded 40 years ago by British engineers. Today it is managed by a Turk-émigré. The plant has a 100-horsepower two-cylinder engine and two dynamo-machines. It produces up to 350 Peabody rifles and carbines per month [obviously – per year: Author]. The work quality is good. Cartridge cases, cartridges, bullet jackets and complete bullets are made by the same plant – up to 10,000 per day. They use brass as the bullet jacket material. The workmanship is fairly good. Percussion cups are also made there. Supposedly the plant makes three-inch and six-inch rapid-fire cannon, but Kulikov saw only two cannon. One, judging by his description, is a three-inch with wedge-type breech mechanism and the other is 'very long', something similar to our four-and-one-half-inch gun with the wedge-type breech mechanism. He also saw two machine-guns: one was undoubtedly a Maxim. It was said that the plant makes 24 machine guns per year. It produces up to 350 artillery shells per day [obviously – per month: Author]. Airburst fuses are made out of brass. The plant makes only black gunpowder for the ammunition. It is stored at the plant until it goes into ammunition. The plant makes shashkas[18] and bayonets of an average quality – if I can judge by the shashka I've received as a gift from the emir. The mint can make up to 60,000 rupees per day. Up to 300 meters of wool coat cloth is produced per day. A military tannery produces leather, leather goods and footwear for the army. It has a traction engine of 12 horsepower which serves all units and the sewing shop. There are no more than 100 vats with the capacity of 20 hides each. The plant makes sole leather,

18 Shashka – Cossack name for a saber. (Translator's note).

full-grain leather and a kind of our "bolgara"[19] leather. The sole leather is of high quality; full-grain and bolgara – of average quality. The tanning process continues for 40 days. The tanning is done with an extract of apricot bark, ink and tanning nuts. Vinegar and rusted iron are used for dying leather black. The plant produces up to 50 tanned hides of all kinds per day. Footwear is manufactured by machines. The special stamps cut leather parts of a shoe or boot and fix heels. They use steel nails in the footwear production. The plant makes 100 pairs of footwear per day. There is a special workshop which makes about 30 pair of shoes daily for officers and bureaucrats. Four English saddles are made per week by handwork. The same plant makes belts, straps and other things which are necessary for military equipment. There are many small workshops in Afghanistan which produce belts, holsters, etc. The two named plants employ about 1,500 people (though we were told that the number is 4,500). The laborer's wages are about 30 rupees per month and the top management receives up to 500-600 rupees per month. Everyone receives food rations from the government.

Up to 40 automobiles of different make are at the emir's disposal. There are some motorcycles. Telegraph communication do not exist. Official offices in Kabul have telephones. It is said that there is a phone line between Kabul and Jalalabad".

I will not give you my assessment of the information given to Ivanov. Some of the numbers are quite old – I saw them in Abdur-Rahman's autobiography or other old sources: evidently mirzas thought it was safe to give out old, well-known numbers. But many numbers are undoubtedly fresh. The story of the phone connection between Kabul and Jalalabad (and possible Peshawar) is probably true – I've heard about it from other sources.

With that I finish the general overview of Afghanistan … I will move to the study of its armed forces, fortresses and operational routes.

19 Leather made by complex technological process in Russia and Central Asia. It is dark brown in color, very soft and extremely durable. (Translator's note).

7

Military qualities of the people

Now I will continue with a study of the armed forces and keeping to our principles of the illuminating the issues, I consider it necessary to point out how important it is for a military geographer to get a clear view of what people and what other elements constitute the army of one country or another. Relevant to this is the fact that military geographers divide peoples into two categories: the warlike and the peaceful. This idea is best developed by the British.

Into which category does most of the Afghan population belong to? Undoubtedly, it belongs to the warlike category. During this course, I have had a chance to tell you why the Afghan nation, through ethnic interbreeding and trials of history, produced active, proud and freedom-loving people. War requires of people the following qualities: patriotism,[1] equanimity, courage, physical abilities, endurance and patience. An analysis of the Afghan personality shows that he possesses all these qualities. Certainly, the Afghan has some negative features: he has difficulties accepting discipline, he is a rebel by nature; he is not inclined to follow general directives and prefers to act as a guerilla; he is also proud above measure and arrogant. All these positive and negative qualities are explained by his history. Looking into the Afghan ancestry, we find that he is first and foremost an Aryan – that is why he is courageous. Then, the Suleiman Mountains served as his original homeland, obviously for a very long period, and that increased and perfected the warlike qualities of the people by adding endurance, love of freedom and a hot temper. Add to this, the fact that three-fourths of the Afghans are nomads – and that means horsemen – which adds to their quality as natural warriors.

So you see that nature and the history of these people made them warlike and militarily effective. Those people will easily withstand any rigors of war. They are capable of building a state and increasing its territory. They can defend their independence among other nations – if we believe their history.

Army size

What is the numerical strength of the Afghan army? Foreign yearly almanacs in the 1890s gave the number of 35,000—which was severely mocked by Abdur-Rahman. The number stayed at that level for a while and only recently, in 1904, the *Statesman's Yearbook* increased it to 44,000, including 7,000 cavalry and 360 cannon.[2] Russian

1 Love of the Motherland and in a wider sense – acceptance of the general attitude of a country. (Author's note).

2 The 1910 almanac gives the Afghan army number as 60-90,000 people, including 9,000 cavalry and 360 cannon. (Author's note).

information of the 1880s (Sobolev[3]) concerning the numerical strength of the Afghan army, founded by Shir Ali Khan, put it at 50,000 in 1878 and included 68 infantry battalions (600 soldiers each), 16 cavalry regiments (500 cavalrymen each) and up to 300 cannon. But from our point of view, it was more like a throng, not military units; but they could be commanded and controlled fairly well at times. Also there were up to 80,000 mounted militia and 60,000 foot militia.

Ten years ago, Russian sources gave the numbers of Afghanistan's regular army as above 90,000 people in all branches.[4] The latest British sources also agree with 90,000 people in the regular forces.

As to the size of the irregular forces (militia) and armed clan paramilitary forces – the numbers are completely hypothetical. Abdur-Rahman thought that the country could count itself safe and secure if it had 1,000,000 trained warriors. We can be pretty sure that Afghanistan cannot field such a number right now and will not be able to do so in the near future.

We can calculate the militia and paramilitary numbers as follows. Statistics consider that one-tenth of all males are in the proper age groups and are fit to bear arms. Counting the entire Afghan male population of the country, we have 125-150,000 people. We need to add the same number of non-Afghan males which comes to 300,000 people. We also have to take the population of the north-west frontier [inside British India] into account who will, in the case of a holy war, come to help their comrades. Military specialists determine the size of the north-west frontier reinforcement as 100 thousand people. The total number of militia could be up to 400 thousand people.

The central command, which is located with the emir in Kabul, consists of several departments. The departments control different sections of command and control and logistics, but in general responsibilities overlap in government departments and the military departments run some civilian affairs.

Building up the Army

The issue of recruitment and manning of the Afghan army is also murky. The most recent observer of the Afghan army, B.N. Ivanov, says that the army is staffed with volunteers. It is hardly possible. Against this supposition is the information we have from various sources.

An attempt by Abdur-Rahman[5] to staff the army based on universal compulsory military service evidently failed, though there was a serious attempt in 1895 to coerce a

3 L.N. Sobolev was a Russian geographer and historian on the 19th Century. (Translator's note).

4 Hamilton (p.321) gives the total number in the army as 148,000, but that includes 30,000 police and 30,000 clan militia. (Author's note).

5 Abdur-Rahman's autobiography is inclined to give him a credit for re-creating the Afghan army anew which is incorrect. The initial organization was established by Sher-Mahomet-Khan – using an officer of the British-Indian army. Campbell was his true name. Taken as a prisoner of war, he converted to Islam and built the Balkh Army for the Balkh Khan Muhammad-Afzull-Khan (Abdur-Rahman's father). Emir Sher-Ali (1863-1879) took a lot from the Balkh Army and continued improvements taking the British-Indian Army as example. Abdur-Rahman only successfully continued the work of those two. (Author's note).

meeting of the khans to accept such a system. At any rate, the issue of manning the regular army and foot militia is fairly well organized. But the existing rules and norms of various provinces and clans are different and that makes it difficult to speak about a unified system.

In Herat province, for example, induction goes by villages or irrigation sectors and is done in proportion to the number of people. The lists of inductees are made in the presence of witnesses from among the local people, special authorized officers and civilians. The buying out an inductee (bribe) is accepted, so the poorest class of the population goes to the army. Other provinces have different systems.

There is a rule that military service is mandatory for all the population with exemption of the Uzbeks[6] who pay a tax, because they considered unfit for service. Those who are not on the active service go into the reserve; there are records of the reserve personnel. Those in the reserve receive a small compensation which can be paid with food rations.

The draft age is 18-35 years, although the law establishes it at 21. The enlistment period is 18 years and this excludes the possibility to have young army reserve.

The regular army is stuffed predominantly with people from Afghan [Pashtun] clans and the militia – with people of other clans which are supposed to provide military service. The regular troops are usually located outside of the area of their clans; the militia stays in their areas. The foot militia is manned similarly to the regular army and the mounted militia – by the decisions of the khans who are obliged to provide it.

The armed paramilitary forces include people aged 17-70 who are able to carry weapons. In order to reinforce the regular army and have ready reserves, Abdur-Rahman, in 1896, ordered the induction of one member of each family of seven-eight people for army training for a short period of time. The recruit, after the training, had the privilege of taking a rifle with him to the village. The late emir Habibullah ordered the conduct of inspections of these trainees in the villages and to take them to firing ranges for firing exercises. All that information has appeared in Indian newspapers, but our specialists say it only exists on paper and in reality the organization of the work with reserves is extremely unsatisfactorily.

Now, this is the vague picture of the manning of the Afghan armed forces which one can determine from information from different sources. Lately, there have been rumors that the provinces with predominantly an Afghan [Pashtun] population have switched to compulsory military service, while other provinces keep the voluntary system, but these rumors require serious examination.

To that picture should be added the miserable conditions of soldiers, the pitiful pay for their dangerous work, the acceptance of bribes and replacements instead of service, frequent leaves which are poorly controlled and poor control of personnel in general – all that leads to the situation where only losers, the homeless and people who do not like working stay in the army. One can find a soldier of almost any age in the Afghan army – from a beardless 15-year-old to a white-haired and weak old man. The soldiers are

6 But the information from the Hazara Khan Muhammad-Azim of Mazar-i Sharif and Deidadi states that among the seven total seven paltans (regiments or battalions) there were two: "Mazar-i-Jadidinavi" and "Mazari-i-Kunagi-Turki" manned by Uzbeks. At the time (1898), the khan's information made quite an impression, but examination showed it did not deserve serious attention. (Author's note).

dressed poorly and in mismatched uniforms. In general, the appearance of an Afghan company makes a most unflattering impression. In a word, the dregs of society go to the army– not the best part.

Everyday life in the army is fairly primitive and badly regulated. Troops are stationed in barracks in large cities; in other cases they are billeted among the civilian population. The latter is considered as an exception, but very often is practiced as a punishment. If any kishlak or house commits an offense, such as not paying taxes, hiding a criminal, etc. – a military unit or a detachment is sent to the place for billeting. The soldiers' behavior is so insolent and rowdy that the population considers the billeting as the worst kind of punishment by the emir and tries to avoid it at any cost. The fact is interesting as an illustration of the morale among Afghan army personnel.

Living in the barracks is not mandatory and the major reason for that is the absence of collective allowances. Everyone receives an individual allowance and is responsible for his own sustenance. Usually a soldier joins his comrades or attaches himself to a family or even more often, sets up his own family where he eats. All this makes the barracks a place only for official training, duty details, etc. Clearly it does not help build camaraderie and unity in the army.

Training in the Afghan army involves the most rudimentary drills: marching, shooting, turns, running, bayonet attack, assembling and disassembling rifles. Besides this, there is some training in moving in an extended line and maneuvers with blank cartridges. There is no information about combining the existing peacetime tactical units into more complex formations or bringing together units of three branches into a single detachment. One could think that lack of money and primitive military views are the obstacles to the more complex types of military practices.

This characterization is related to the regular army. As to the reserves, our information is even murkier. There are two major issues related to the reserves: the level of training and the time required and reliability of their readiness during war.

It has been said that two emirs – Abdur-Rahman and Habibullah – took care of the reserves' preparation, but did they achieve their goal?

Taking into account that the Afghan clans, in their native regions, are fairly independent and the power of the center is weak in relation for peripheral areas, we can think that the attempts of training hardly have been accomplished. Add to that the lack of weapons and it is clear that if the reserve training muster can gather all the trainees, it will produce very little because the training will be with bare hands. Most probably the reserves represent a raw mass of people who are completely untrained. But we should not go too far in our criticism of the reserves. Do not forget that the Afghans are, by their nature, warriors and cavalrymen and even if they do not have tactical skills, are poorly trained and not completely united for maneuvers – they will carry out their missions due to their natural skills with weapons and horses, their familiarity with the terrain, their patriotism and their bravery. They probably will occupy designated points, important positions and will become the covering force for defensive lines, thus providing serious assistance. And the field army will be the moving hammer for decisive strikes at the enemy or prevention of the enemy's attacks.

Officer Corps

The officer corps is the most vulnerable part of the Afghan army. Abdur-Rahman complained about the problem in his autobiography.

The Afghan officer corps is staffed with: 1) Aristocrats; 2) Soldiers who distinguished themselves in battle or in some special service to the government and also those who served a long time with excellence; 3) Those who passed a specially- established exam at the military school in Kabul or graduated from the school.

All these measures so far failed to provide the army with reliable officers – and there are few educated men among them. Many of them are practically illiterate. We must keep in mind that the social situation of the officers in Afghanistan is sorrowful. The money allowances are pitiful and are paid irregularly. The population's attitude toward officers is bad…all these factors are not helpful in creating great command personnel.

Ivanov had a chance to observe the Kabul military school which was founded 10-15 years ago with a six-year course of training. Entrants are 10-12 year-old old boys. Some sharp tongues say the boys are all illegitimate sons of Habibullah-Khan. All instructors in the school – except the Russian language instructor Slivitski – are Turkish-émigrés. The training is extremely poorly organized. The school commandant is a former Turkish poruchik[7] – a clever courtier, who appeared there about twelve years ago. He does not have either the necessary theoretical knowledge or combat experience. Ivanov had a chance to see the school personnel during recess and found out that the military bearing of the higher grades is good though it is far from that of our former military schools, even in drill and ceremonies. The school has not produced a sufficient number of officers yet and it make difficult to judge the results.

The same observer has noticed that appointment to command positions is very rarely earned by excellent service but usually purchased with money. The prices of promotion are, in his words, 55 rupees for the first officer rank; 2,000 rupees is then enough to buy all the following ranks up through korneill.[8] The observer finds that the officer corps is amazingly unprepared and of low intellect.

We need to note that the emir's relatives or members of Barakzai[9] clan are appointed to the top military posts.

Foreign manuals and instructions are translated into the Afghan language[10] [Pashtu], but observers say that the translation has been done poorly, many terms are just invented and some phrases sound funny. A lot of time and effort are spent training the officers but the results are poor. We have seen that the pupils are abysmal but the real misfortune is that the instructors are also no good.

7 Rank in the old Russian Tsarist army equal to First Lieutenant. (Translator's note).

8 Colonel. (Translator's note).

9 The Barakzai clan furnished the rulers for the last ruling dynasty of Afghanistan. (Translator's note).

10 The latest information available to me shows that the Persian language is now used as the tool of teaching. (Author's note).

Discipline

I will say a word or two about discipline. This issue requires a very careful approach because in military institutions, discipline reflects a people's spirit and their way of life to a larger degree than any other thing.

Discipline, as we understand it, does not exist in the Afghan army. Discord among clans quite often produces internecine squabbles between different units located in the same town.

Relations between soldiers and junior officers are simple and unceremonious, but while on duty, blind obedience is the rule. The high cost of living and the small allowances paid lead to abuses and often bring on disciplinary violations. The kinds of punishment are jail, monetary fines and in serious cases – the death sentence.

Thus, there is no discipline in the form we are accustomed to in European armies. Off duty, all the ranks are mixed together. The officers smoke with the soldiers passing the kal'yan [hookah] from one to another, their circle of interests is the same. It seems like there are no commanders or subordinates. But this should not deceive us. The Afghan army has many elements embedded in it which can substitute for our European discipline. First of all – this army is a united family of devoted Muslims and it is ready to stand up for the Prophet's banner – and make no mistake – the banner will be raised in any war. Then the Afghan love their native land and freedom fanatically and that characteristic will strongly unite them during war. Finally, their iron discipline will not be forgotten during wartime.

Besides maneuvers, troops carry out garrison duty in the cities and towns, maintain fortresses, build roads and governmental buildings and sometimes help to collect taxes and recruits. Uprisings are a common occurrence and their suppression serves as good school for combat for the troops.

Organization of the armed forces

The armed forces of Afghanistan are organized as follows: the regular army includes infantry, cavalry, artillery, sappers and auxiliaries. The infantry *(nizami)* is organized into *paltans* – regiments or battalions with the strength of 700 men each, but there are four guards *paltans* with a strength of 1,000 men each according to its table of organization. The British (Chirol) and our specialists count 80 infantry regiments or battalions. The *paltans* are named after the provinces in which they were formed (Herat, Kabul etc.) or their clans.[11] The *paltans* are divided into companies *(kompani)* of a 100 men each. The number of companies in a *paltan* varies between six and ten. A company is divided into two half-companys *(kambu)* and each half-company is divided into squads *(paira)* of six men each. The *paltan's* commander is *"Korneill"* (Colonel), a *kompani* – *"Kiftan"* (Captain) and a *paira* – *"Haval'dar"* – a non-commissioned officer [Sergeant].

A mullah plays an important role in a paltan. He reads the Koran and teaches the men to make them literate; he also teaches command language to the officers. There is also a physician *(hakim)* and a surgeon *(jerraj)* in each *paltan.*

11 Paltans "Alyuku-Zei-Kandahari", "Siyakh-Push", "Mazari-Kunaghi-Turki",etc. (Author's note).

The regular cavalry (*suvare*) is organized into regiments (*rissale*) of 400 men each, except the guard *rissales* whose numerical strength is 800 men each. A cavalry regiment is divided into "*turpa*" ("hundred" – 100 men each) while each *turpa* is divided into two half-*turpas,*[12] *which in turn are divided into squads (paira)* of six men each as in the infantry. Our and British specialists count 40 regular and three guard cavalry regiments. Each cavalryman buys his own horse – stallions only – same as in our Turkestan squadrons.[13]

The artillery is divided into: 1) *Jelavi* – field artillery with six-horse teams; 2) *Katyri* – mountain pack artillery; each cannon is carried by four animals; 3) *Fili* – heavy artillery (9-10 pounders) pulled by horses or oxen; 4) *Ghavi* – fortress artillery. Today, we count up to 100 artillery batteries *("toop-khane")* of the field and mountain artillery with six guns in each battery. A battery is divided into platoons with two guns in each. A gun crew has six men. The personnel of the field, heavy and fortress artillery are combined into paltans of 700-1,000 men each.

There are two paltans of sappers ("*safar-mainei*" – sapper-miner) of 1,000 men each with the same organizational structure as the infantry. Sapper companies apparently are sent on assignments to different cities.

During peacetime, the regular forces of the three branches do not create large combined arms units but in wartime they create detachments composed of several different branches. Commanding the separate detachments and garrisons in peacetime are several generals who have a questionable ability to command combined arms elements in maneuvers, but they are undoubtedly proficient in commanding expeditions to put down rebellions and suppress riots.

In peace time, the regular army is billeted in the most important inhabited and strategic locations. On our border, the strongest garrisons are located in Herat, Mazar-i Sharif and Faizabad. The bulk of the armed forces is concentrated in Asmara, Jalalabad, Kabul, Ghazni and Kandahar.[14]

Auxiliary troops include non-combatant commands: administration, warehouses and depot personnel and also field trains. All these commands are manned predominantly by Tajiks.

Armament and equipment

The Afghan army has a mix of various designs of modern and obsolete weapons. And although details of our information are somewhat unclear, the essence of the situation is clear. Since 1899, the Kabul armory workshops produced more than 3,000 five-cartridge magazine-loaded rifles of British design per year. Besides that, England delivered a significant number of .303 magazine-loaded rifles with several million cartridges. So we can reason that about half of the Afghan army regiments were armed with magazine-loaded

12 In Badakhshan, turpas are named "rodjmata". (Author's note).

13 Most cavalry forces preferred geldings since stallions are always fighting and the presence of a mare in estrus could turn an ordered cavalry charge on stallions into a steeple chase. Since the Afghan cavalryman bought his own horse, he wanted to eventually be able to breed it. (Translator's note).

14 It is useless to figure out how many *paltans* or *rissales* are located at any given point because they are moved often. For a long time, 13-15 *paltans* were located In Afghan Turkestan, three in Mazar-i Sharif, four in Deidadi, two in Banu, two in Meimene and three in Badakhshan. (Author's note).

rifles at the beginning of our century. The rest of the army is armed primarily with Martini-Henry rifles *("novegi")* – partially Afghan-made and partially imported from abroad. There are regular regiments armed with Snider and Lee-Metford rifles from the Afghan government's reserves.

The infantry militia *(hassadar)* is armed predominantly with percussion-cap and other older-model rifles, because the newer models that were turned in by the regular army during weapons upgrade have been designated for the militia, but kept in depots out of fear.

The regular cavalry is armed with Martini-Henry carbines and other carbines and also with sabers, pistols and daggers.

A militia cavalryman *(havalsar)* must have his own armament: a flint-lock rifle, saber and pistol. But some of them have replaced their flint-lock rifles with percussion-cap or even breech-loading weapons.

The artillery equipment went through the same metamorphosis and there is also no uniformity.

The Afghan government evidently wanted to create some uniformity at least for mountain artillery. In 1903, 12 rapid-fire mountain cannon, 18 field cannon and two howitzers were sent from Essen to Peshawar along with an adequate amount of ammunition. The same shipment included a large number of German-made steel blocks – the Afghan were supposed to make their own rapid-fire cannons from them using these samples.

But the English, who did not trust the Afghans, have not let the shipment through and so there is no rapid-fire artillery in the Afghan army.[15]

The regular army is equipped with breech-loading cannons called "*Dumbalya-Nur*" which were made in Kabul using English blueprints and samples.

Yak Kobza system three and four-pounder mountain howitzers and the 13-pounder field howitzer are transported by ten horses. They have one trunnion on the lower part of the cannon, an elevating screw, a screw-type breech mechanism and a central striker. The muzzle has a screwed-on barrel-sleeve. The *Yak Kobza* system three and four-pounder mountain howitzers, six and 13-pounder field guns have a wedge-lock breech mechanism.

The fortress guns are mostly smoothbore, but there are some rifled cannon. For example, there are six 10-inch fortress guns in Kabul. They are mounted on gun platforms and move on rails. The same cannon are present in Herat and Deidadi.

All breech-loaded cannon use fixed rounds [a unitary round, not separate powder bags and projectile]. The six and 13-pound field guns have grape-shot rounds. The cannon carriages are made out of steel.

Also there some older muzzle-loading cannon still present. These are as follows: The *Dakhan-Pur* system has three and four-pounder mountain guns; six-pounder field cannon and nine or 10-pounder heavy cannon. The *Kobza-Pech'* system (dismantleable) has three and four-pounder mountain guns. They disassemble into three parts for transportation.

15 This happened during the rule of Viceroy Lord Curzon who had a very aggressive posture toward Afghanistan. The reason for holding up the shipment varied. Once it was "A large amount of ammunition for heavy artillery" which Abdur-Rahman officially gave up; or some cartridges with explosive bullets were found and "they are prohibited by the Hague Convention", etc. Such a mix of military precaution with feigned philanthropy is very typical of the English. (Author's note).

All these systems are rifled with three lands and grooves. The latter systems have elevating screws and the former use wedges for elevation. Muzzle-loading cannon use iron shrapnel shot with a time-fuse located in its head.

Shrapnel rounds for breech-loaded artillery systems are unitary rounds. They use iron shrapnel with the time-fuse set in the base of the projectile. There are also single-barreled (120 rounds-per-minute rate of fire) and double-barreled machine-guns.

The country has three arsenals. The main arsenal is in Kabul, another one is in Herat (it repairs cannon and makes small arms) and the third one is in Mazar-i Sharif (it repairs cannon and small arms).

There are probably two gunpowder plants located in Kabul and Mazar-i Sharif. In Kabul they make smokeless propellant. About four-five years ago, the Kabul plant employed up to 3,500 people under the management of an Englishman and 100 *desyatniks* (foremen) from India.

Uniform

The uniform of the regular Afghan army (officers and soldiers) has some system to it, but it is extremely complex and not necessarily followed. The government-issued uniform is worn while on duty and personal civilian clothing is worn off duty. The cost of the uniform is subtracted from money allowances. Other equipment is also issued by the government.

In peacetime, infantrymen and sappers wear ammunition belts (30 cartridges) across a shoulder. During wartime, they add three ammunition pouches (12 cartridges each) onto a waist belt. It comes to 66 cartridges per each person in total.

Each infantryman has a bread bag (with a three-day supply) and a tin canteen for water.

Sappers carry a pick and an axe. Shovels are transported in unit transportation.

Feeding the troops

Now let's look at the issue of feeding a soldier in the Afghan army – the immediate task in the supply train organization and the more expanded task in the organization of the quartermaster service.

The army has only pack animal trains. Each paltan is allowed 100 pack horses. Thus one pack horse is assigned to five-six soldiers.[16]

However, there are some paltans which do not have pack animals and, when marching, these battalions use pack animals taken from the local population using a special government indent. The cavalry has no allowance for pack animals from the government and it purchases the animals on its own – one horse for seven people. In the artillery, there is one pack horse for each gun (six people).

Abdur-Rahman established a general pack animal reserve in the army for mobilization. Until recently, it had 24,000 government-owned horses and a large numbers of elephants, mules and about 60,000 camels. There is a breeding horse farm in Kabul

16 These horses are used for moving soldiers' personal belongings. Other horses are supplied for moving army equipment. (Author's note).

with 2,000 brood mares and 80 stud stallions. It has several thoroughbred horses of the English and Arab breeds. There are several horse farms in other places as well.

Quartermaster service during peacetime is a fairly easy task because each soldier is supposed to take care of feeding himself. The troops give receipts for appropriated products and this will be deducted from future taxes. The receipts then go to accounting offices. In some cases, the population is ordered to provide for the soldiers – and that is really a heavy burden, as I've said before.

Special warehouses and depots have been constructed to provide wartime logistics. During peacetime, these serve to rotate supplies and in some cases to control prices. In this case, they play a general state role. The most significant logistics facilities are concentrated in Kabul, Herat and Shadian [near Mazir-i Sharif].

This is a primitive army logistics system. Maintaining large pools of transport animals in concentrated herds of government-owned horses is one of the worst methods economically. Naturally, the horses are poorly fed, many of them are stolen, a lot are hurt by inadequate care and the best go to the aristocracy as draft horses for their carriages. As a result, in a crisis, there will be a shortage of transport and all the mobilization plans will go nowhere. As to the quartermaster's service, it is in a rudimentary state. The practice of billeting troops on civilians, soldiers feeding themselves, those receipts – all these are vestiges of the past which are rejected by contemporary armies, allowing such practices only as rare exceptions.

Monetary allowances

When discussing logistics, we need to take a separate look at monetary allowances. They are really miserable. The monthly monetary allowances differ in different provinces. Evidently the allowance's size depends on the cost of living in a particular province.

For example:

	Provinces					
	Herat			Mazar-i Sharif		
Ranks / Branches	Infantry (rubles)	Artillery (rubles)	Cavalry rubles)	Infantry rubles)	Artillery (rubles)	Cavalry (rubles)
Sepoy	4.00	–	8.00	5.20	5.85	13.00
Khavaldar	5.60	–	12.00	6.50	8.85	–
Sunakhdar	8.60	9.60	16.00	14.95	–	39.00
Kiftan	14.60	–	24.00	22.75	39.85	52.00
Kumaidan	36.60	–	40.00	58.50	–	–
Korneil'	80.60	–	–	71.50	–	130.00
Birgit	120.60	–	–	130.50	–	–
Djarneil'	160.60	–	–	385.50	–	–
Naib-Salyar	260.60	–	–	650.50	–	–
Supekh-Salyar	400.60	–	–	975.50	–	–

It is difficult if not impossible for an infantry soldier to provide for himself and a family on five rubles and 20 kopeks and for a cavalryman – on 13 rubles,[17] especially with the existing system of fines. And this is the major reason for the low state of discipline among the troops. The allowances of company-grade officers – eight-14 rubles in the infantry and 16-52 rubles in the cavalry – push the officers to fine the soldiers and accept bribes from them. They do the same to the local population while on assignments. Some provinces – Kandahar, Hazaristan and others – help their recruits with money and payment in kind.

The militiamen's allowances are even smaller. Ivanov gives other rates in rupees which are about three times higher than I gave you, but how reliable his sources were, I do not know.[18] Some increase in allowances is possible because the cost of living in Afghanistan has gone up and Abdur-Rahmans' rates (he was the first to introduce monetary allowances in the Afghan army) would be too low today. Besides, there was information that the emir Habibullah-khan, at the time of his ascension on the throne in October 1901, made a 25% increase of the allowances of military ranks: for example – for an infantryman from eight to 10 rupees; a cavalryman from 20 to 25 rupees; a militiaman from six to eight rupees. But it is hardly possible to triple the allowances since the reign of Abdur-Rahman.

The numerical strength of the Afghan Army

Now that we have figured out the organization of the Afghan army, let us look into its general numerical strength. I think that during peacetime, we can talk about 90,000 people in the regular army – we and English specialists agree on this. There is no information on the reserve, although we cannot reject its existence. I think that the reserve's number can be found in an oblique fashion. The population of Afghanistan is about 1,500,000 and they can produce 150,000 soldiers (10%). As we understand the emirs' policy, all that mass is supposed to go through military service one way or another. If we count 90,000 in the regular army and assume that the majority of these are Afghans [Pashtun], then the difference between 150,000 and 90,000, i.e. 60,000 is be the approximate reserve strength.

Even more difficult is to find out is the numerical strength of the militia. In 1894, Artamonov determined it to be 23,000, but that author has no credibility. We only know that the militia is divided into footmen *(hassadar)* formed into commands (*bairak*) of 100 men each and mounted (*sarkari-sur*) also formed into hundreds (*turpa*). The militia is very poorly trained and it would be correct to place it into the paramilitary category as some specialists do.

Finally, the number of the paramilitary force (including the militia) can be estimated at 400-500,000.

17 Although the population is obliged to sell products to the troops at established lower prices. (Author's note).

18 Hamilton gives the allowances in Kabul rupees and it is equal to what I gave you. M. Grulyov, on the words of a Hazara khan, gives same numbers. See M. Grulyov *Rivalry of Russia and England in Central Asia*, St. Petersburg, 1909, p.189. (Author's note).

The following table shows the Afghan army's numerical strength in wartime.

	Total Strength
Regular army – peacetime	90,000
Reserve	60,000
Paramilitary and militia	400-500,000
Total:	550-650,000

Ivanov assesses the capability of Afghanistan to put up 900,000 troops at wartime; he proceeds on the wrong estimate of the Afghan population as 11-14 million people. Abdur-Rahman, in his autobiography, mentioned one million as an ideal number of trained warriors. That number has some symptomatic meaning, but to base a strong conclusion on it, as on Ivanov's number, is difficult. At any rate, our number of 550-650,000 is sooner underestimated rather than overestimated. These numbers are calculated based on the numbers of tactical units and their organizational strength.

Ten years ago, the organizational strength of the Afghan army was determined fairly correctly. What it looked like you can see in the following table:

	Categories				
	Officers		Soldiers		
Units	Field-Grade	Company-Grade	NCOs	Privates	Non-combatants
Paltan (Infantry battalion)	2	12	66	600+	3
Rissale (Cavalry regiment)	2	12	66	300+	18
Artillery Battery	–	1	11	92	2
Sapper company	–	1	9	74	2

At the same time the numbers of the tactical units were as follows:

Infantry – 80 battalions (paltans);
Cavalry – 40 regiments (rissoles);
Artillery – 100 field and mountain batteries;
Engineer troops – 2 regiments (20 companies) of sapper-miners.

Ivanov's talk about tactical units is not clear. He give "about a hundred" total number of paltans with about a quarter of them of cavalry. That means 75 paltans and 25 rissales. But in his table of the units' locations, I find their number equal to 94 (and there is no mention of the cavalry regiments among them). The unit distribution by garrison is as follows: Herat – 20 paltans; Mazar-i Sharif – 12 paltans; Meimen – six paltans; Kandahar – 16 paltans; Kabul – 22 paltans and Jalalabad – 18 paltans.

Third Anglo–Afghan War

For a complete characterization of the Afghan army, I would have to turn to one of the wars conducted by Afghanistan to show you how that army behaves at war, how its mobilization works; what its strategy, tactics, logistics, etc are about. But the lack of time forces me to give up the notion. To make up for this [information] gap, I will give you an excerpt from Ivanov's report on the latest Indo (Anglo) – Afghan war in May-June 1919.

> "There were formed three fronts: 1st (Eastern) – Yahistan sector (commander Sapekh-Salyar Sali-Mahomet; 2nd (Southern) – Kandahar sector (commander Nadyr-khan[19]) and 3rd (Northern) – Chitral sector. The most importance has been attached to the Southern front. It had the largest number of the best regular troops – up to 12,000 not counting a significant number of local guerillas. At first the Afghans achieved quite significant success there. The troops captured six towns, including Kurma, Tutkai, and Tal'. In the latter, they captured a large amount of trophies, especially rifles. The Afghans at that front lost up to 5,000 men and the English – 6,500. It was the Eastern sector that proved to be fatal for the Afghans. There were 12,000 troops acting on the Afghan side in the sector – mainly local guerillas primarily from Afridi clan. At first they had marked success. The English withdrew to their line of forts. Peshawar faced the threat of attack. But soon the English recovered from the shock on their own familiar terrain and went over to the offensive deploying all their machines and using airplanes.
>
> Among other operations, the airplanes struck Jalalabad where they burned a market on May 11. On May 02, the first day of Ramadan, the British airplanes flew over Kabul and dropped six bombs. One struck the military plant without damage; another damaged a fence in the emir's palace and the third killed or hurt 40 horses in the royal stables.
>
> The Afghan army turned to a shameful flight. Their *Djarneils* and officers showed cowardice, all weaponry and machines were left behind – the airplanes inspired sheer terror among the Afghans. Their losses in that sector came to 3,000 men, including 1,000 soldiers of the regular army lost in a single battle. The English lost about 4,000.
>
> The sector commander Sali-Mahomet has been blamed for the failure (it said he was bribed) and he is currently in jail.
>
> In the Northern sector, the Afghans had up to 10,000 men, including 3,000 of the regular troops. The Afghans' losses amounted to 2,000 men while the English– up to 3,500.
>
> It is interesting that the Germans, our former POWs and members of the German-Turkish mission, offered their assistance to the emir early in the war. With their typical conceit and distrust toward the Turks, the Afghans rejected the offer. Only after the Eastern front was routed, the emir hastily sent several German officers and sergeants to Jalalabad in automobiles and they stopped the panic flight of the emirs "warriors" with some difficulty.

19 Currently the Military minister has the emir's attention. He is one of the few Russophiles (among the aristocrats and bureaucrats). (Author's note).

> The hostilities continued only for a month and a half. The total absence of unified command and control, officers' helplessness, the disorganized supply of the army for everything, the dire state of the treasury which lost the major source of revenue – import and export duties and the acute fear of airplanes by the Afghans – all that pushed the emir to rush into peace talks. The peace treaty had been concluded on the conditions far from advantageous for the Afghans, but less harsh than one could expect. Afghanistan's independence had been recognized."

With this, I conclude my short (by necessity) review of the Afghan armed forces. The Afghan army is strong in its spirit, resilience, patriotism and terrain knowledge. But anything that improves the army on the technological side is only in a rudimentary state. Thus we shall think of that army as a small army of Asian people – poor and backward – though brave and freedom-loving – and not an army of the European type.

8

Strategic Points of Afghanistan

Now I will move to the issue of the strategic points in Afghanistan, its fortresses and routes of communication (operational and others).

First we will talk about the strategic points. If you look at the map of Afghanistan, you will see an irregularly-broken quadrangle which contains a first-rate mountain range running diagonally and splits into three branches. In the south, south-west and north the mountains of the ridge are transformed into plains. Thus the military-geographical center of gravity related to the country's defense is positioned in the triangle of mountain heights with the apexes in Herat, Kabul and Kandahar. All the history of Afghanistan's defense has been based around that triangle. If you look at the country's defense from that particular angle then you will have a clear picture. And do not forget that the mountainous part of Afghanistan is passable only by narrow and difficult roads, through specific mountain passes of the Hindu Kush at specific times, i.e. the term "passable" there is a *very conditional* one.

Long ago, the people of the East knew about incalculably rich India[1] with mountainous Afghanistan barring the road to it. And how to overcome that bulwark was always a historically important Central Asian topic. That mission, though linked to the conquest of India, was itself a very *big item* which represented the first and unavoidable stage in the process of India's conquest. Alexander the Great, Genghis-khan, Timur and many others worked on the problem of how to conquer Afghanistan. To do so, one needs to capture its vital center. The center has not been constant but its most stable area is the Kabul region. True, in the early 11th Century, the center was near Ghazni, but later moved into the western spurs of the Hindu Kush Mountains; Herat thrived for some time. But in most cases, the Kabul area was the center of gravity.[2] That is why the first mission on the way to India has always been to capture Kabul. For example, Babur – the

1 And the Western nations also heard about it. Paul Centurione from Genoa and Marko Foskarini from Venice came to Moscow in 1520 and 1537 respectively with the goal of establishing a trade link with India. If we believe the anonymous author of *Relatione dell Imperio di Moscowia*, the same thought also occurred to Ivan the Terrible. And there are practical goals before you. The rumors about India in Europe always were quite strong and with the Crusades, they were clarified. The issue of contacts between India and the West during ancient times has been wonderfully developed in H. G. Rawlinson's work *Intercourse Between India and the Western World*, Cambridge, 1916, p.192. (Author's note).

2 There is no better illustration of the Kabul's importance than the story of the long struggle for Afghanistan and more precisely – for Kabul – between Babur's sons Ghamayun and Kamarad. The city changed hands between them several times. And only final conquest of Kabul gave Ghamayun a chance to look toward India and return to power there. See Malleson, *History of Afghanistan*, p.p. 122-180. (Author's note).

founder of the Great Mogul dynasty, moved by a snow-covered Hazara road – sometimes chest-deep in snowdrifts –to attack and capture Kabul by surprise. This makes us understand that among all the points of interest in Afghanistan, Kabul – the current capital of the country with its 60,000 population – has been and still is the central point. Its significance today is greatly increased by its being the center of power and political life of the country; and its eternal significance is determined by its location at the crossroad of the routes from Afghan Turkestan and Herat province across the Hindu Kush and its spurs, which then go as a complex bundle toward Ghazni (Kandahar) and through the passes of the Suleiman Mountains to the Indus River. The city is surrounded by an old wall with seven gates and it has an old citadel. Today the wall and citadel's significance are about zero. The surrounding heights have good, strong positions with a significant part of the latter represented by the small fortifications on Shir-Pur – two miles north of the city. We do not possess detailed knowledge about these fortifications, but we can surmise that on the heights one can find a number of small forts and prepared artillery positions.[3]

But to reach that vital center from the north, one needs (today as always) to cross the Amu-Darya River, go through the Hindu Kush foothills and then cross the Hindu Kush Mountains themselves. And so this triple barrier created three lines of defense and the third line, the Hindu Kush is naturally strong and accessible only at limited times of the year, so they were usually left practically without fortifications. Presently, the Amu-Darya has lost its significance as a barrier for historical and lately – for technical – reasons. But in old times, it demanded attention and the remains of fortresses, such as at Termez, tell us about their ideas to hold the northern enemies at that barrier by all possible means. The main idea was to stop the enemy in the northern foothills of the Hindu Kush while he was openly marching – deployed and highly visible. He was supposed to overcome sandy expanses near the river and move ahead leaving behind the dangerous barrier of the same great river. This idea from time immemorial has forced the rulers to fortify steppe towns such as Shebergan, Balkh, Mazar-i Sharif, Tash-Kurgan [Hulm] and Kunduz and they still have their military importance today. But the old somewhat-incoherent idea, is now simplified and condensed in the fortress of Deidadi [Kala Jangi] on one of the most important operational routes 56 versts south of Termez and eight miles south-west of Mazar-i Sharif, the main administrative center of Afghan Turkestan and a junction of roads from Amu-Darya to Bamian and Kabul. In the design and location of the fortress, we can see the strong influence of European-style fortifications. The bastion fronts are aptly adjusted to the terrain and the fortress' profile approaches those of Europe. The fortress commands the terrain and provides a strong frontal defense. The fortress should be considered as a serious obstacle for the advance toward Kabul.[4]

But naturally the line of steppe cities did not prevent incursions of the enterprising enemy into the foothills of the Hindu Kush and that was a reason why there were so many small fortifications sprinkled all over. These fortifications, which were entirely adjusted to the capricious and peculiar relief of the terrain, did not create any line or

3 One can find detailed information about Kabul in the works of Hamilton, Grulyov, Martin and – generally – in any English work on Afghanistan. (Author's note).

4 Appendix XII (Author's note). Never published (Translator's note).

systematic position; they are spread all over at spots linked to important mountain passes or historical defensive areas. Some of those fortifications are still functional today and keep their significance.

Of the most interesting I have to mention are Sar-i Pol, Gheibag, Gardan-Diwan and Banu.

Finally, to our knowledge, there are no prepared fortified positions in the Hindu Kush itself. Of the old forts, the small fortress Sarkari in Bamian has survived. It used to control a junction of important routes (some of them accessible to wheeled transport) leading from Mazar-i Sharif and Herat to Kabul. Also there were rumors about some fortification activity by the Afghans in the mountain passes – but for right now they are just rumors.

In relation to those ancient relics of the military art, we have to say that they would amaze us with their modesty and primitivism; they are a child's play for modern artillery for example... but how would modern artillery get up there? The significance of any of these small forts is its location which controls a specific road. Imagine that on the fortification's sides are forts and artillery will be placed there at the critical time – then you have to force the defile. All these small fortresses have their importance through the thought put into their creation and by the terrain at the locations. If the modern military art is not too late reinforcing those ancient fortresses with technology (and obviously the Englishmen will take care of it), we will have well-secured hard-points facing us.

Thus the northern face of the mountain massif which is open toward Russia is secured to some degree first by the Amu-Darya River, then by the line of steppe towns with the group of forts in the foothills and finally by the fortifications which could be in the mountain passes. If Englishmen, with their equipment and money, are able to get there on time, our movement toward the Hindu Kush will encounter a significant obstacle. We have to take that into account.

But the Hindu Kush can be outflanked on the west by a circuitous route to Kandahar or crossed from the west by the Hazara road. And at the beginning of either route stands Herat, which is the second most important city after Kabul.[5] First of all – it is the main

5 The information about Herat can be found in the same sources and the same authors (except Martin) that we looked at for information about Kabul. A more recent reference is in *Sytin's Encyclopedic Dictionary*, vol. VII – my article (With Shwartz) about Herat. We also can find considerable information from the British authors about the fertility of the valley and Herat's significance. Conolly was awed by fertility of the valley and thought that a whole army could sustain itself there for years (Conolly, *Journey to the North of India*, vol. II, p.324). The historian Kayl describes Herat's importance briefly but expressively repeating an old nickname "Gateway to India" and describing the valley as the "Breadbasket of Central Asia" (Kayl, *History of the War in Afghanistan*, vol. I, pp.212-213). It is necessary to mention the words of W. McNaughten – the extraordinary envoy to Afghanistan in his letter to Oakland -the Governor-General of India. He wrote: "We could consider Herat as an axle around which all operations directed to overthrow our might and interfere with our interests in India would rotate". Later visitors gave us the same impressions of Herat and the valley (Lemsden, Yate, etc.). G.B. Malleson wrote a book dedicated to Herat named *Herat the Granary and Garden of Central Asia*. In his other book *The Russo-Afghan Question*, he dedicated several vivid lines (pp.122-130) and while describing its importance he refers to such authorities as Napier of Magdal, Hamley, Rawlinson, Roberts and McGregor. (Author's note).

city of Herat province, which is the wealthiest in Afghanistan and which we may want to consider as a forward maintenance area of our advance. Second– it is a large city with a rich history. And today it is a big political and administrative center. And finally – Herat stands on the junction of routes from the Trans-Caspian region to Kabul and Kandahar. In political works, Herat is customarily called "The Key to India". The old saying goes "Whoever owns Herat – owns Kabul. And whoever owns Kabul – owns India". Presently Herat is a fairly large city with population of 18,000. The city is encircled with an adobe wall – 18 feet tall and 9-14 feet thick. The wall has $7^1/2$ foot tall banquettes, embrasures and flanking towers. The wall has five gates. There are two citadels on the northern face of the fortress: one is old, shaped as a rectangular Asian *kala*[6] with flanking towers – it is not greatly defensible; and another is a new one built as a rectangular protrusion of the wall with an outside moat and flanking towers. As I've already mentioned, Herat is the second most important city after Kabul and it requires serious attention.

Besides Kabul and Herat, the following are more or less prominent in a military sense:

Kandahar is on the junction of the routes from Seistan, Herat and Hazarejat into the Indus Valley. In the past, it was the Afghan capital. Today it is a center of boiling political activity.[7]

Faizabad and *Zebak* are junctions on the routes from the Amu-Darya River through Hindu Kush's mountain passes toward Chitral – an open flank of the British fortified border.

Sabzevar [Shindand] is located near the exit from the 100-versts mountainous and barren area which encircles the Herat Valley from the south.

Farah and *Lash-i Joveyn* are located at the flanks of a narrow gap between two adjoining mountain massifs Kain and Siyah-Kuh. The area's topographic features and fertility provide a very convenient sector for active defense.

Gereshk is on the junction of the routes from Herat and Hazarat to Kandahar. It also dominates the route from Seistan to Kandahar.

Qalat-i Gilzai [Qalat] and *Ghazni* control the routes from Kandahar to Kabul. Ghazni also is a starting point of the best routes through Suleiman Mountains toward Indus River.

6 Kala means a fortress in many Central Asian languages. (Translator's note).

7 One can find details in Hamilton's works or the authors who wrote about 1st and 2nd Anglo-Afghan wars. History supports the importance of Kandahar. The city was captured by Babur before his march on India and from it, he sent a special detachment to secure Babur's right flank. Nadir-Shah needed to capture Kandahar and built a base there before he could launch his attack on India. Kandahar played a prominent role in both Anglo-Afghan wars. Witnesses are saying that today the life in the city – especially with trade – is very lively and it is on a par with Kabul. (Author's note).

Communications routes

Now I will move to a description of Afghanistan's route of communication. There are two possible points of view when one studies the routes of communication of Afghanistan: to study them as only a part of all the routes available for future moves toward India; or to study them in relation only to Afghanistan itself. You will find that the first point of view is prevailing in this researchers' works. If we study the routes of communication in relation to Afghanistan only, we will have to limit ourselves to the study of those that lead to Kabul or connect to some important points within the country only. In fact, the researchers who study the routes of communication extend them into important regions of India or, at least, to the Indus River. Why they are doing so? Because they see Afghanistan as the *territory of approaches to India*, considering such a method as the only correct one while doing military research. And I consider that point of view – studying the routes of communications in Afghanistan as a network of routes leading to India –the only true and rational one. It is difficult to imagine that there is any reason ever to undertake a military campaign in Central Asia only for the sake of Afghanistan. Afghanistan is a poor country. Conquering it will result in the hatred of a proud and freedom-loving people. It would be very difficult to keep the country under rule and that is why I think that idea of a future war for Afghanistan only has no sense at all. If there will be any actions in Afghanistan, they will be related to India and its future subjugation.

No one can say that it will be easy, but do not forget that all of Central Asia, including Afghanistan, are of interest only due to how the world values India. I further state that this military mission will be the most difficult in the world. We cannot forget the immense value of India to England and the strong and continuous exertion that England will make to defend their precious colony from any encroachment. It was not for nothing that Lord Curzon, while Viceroy of India, stated that every English family would send their only son to protect England's most valuable possession. You may have heard a widespread British aphorism: "What is more valuable to England – Shakespeare or India?" Usually Englishmen do not answer the question, but the comparison of these two great values – spiritual and material – speaks for itself. And because of these reasons, I have always thought that we should study Afghanistan's communication routes as they pertain to the approach to India. We cannot limit ourselves to the routes that end inside of Afghanistan, but need to continue our study into India. We also should study some routes inside of our own borders and not forget those running alongside Afghanistan – through the Pamirs for example.

In any modern country, we have to study three kinds of communication routes: railroads, water routes and ordinary – i.e. ground routes. But Afghanistan is so poor and backward that the first two kinds of communication routes are absent. There are no railroads and no water routes. We cannot seriously consider some sections of the Kabul River or the left side of the Amu-Darya River as navigable waterways. Of course, I need to look into the railroads and waterways of Russia and India adjacent to Afghanistan but due to lack of time I will skip the issue – I will describe it in the appendixes to my lectures.[8] And now we will talk about ordinary routes of Afghanistan.

8 Appendix XIII. (Author's note). It has never been published. (Translator's note).

Ordinary communication routes

The common (ground) routes are of major importance in Afghanistan because only they cross the country's territory and many of them coincide with the operational sectors that exist between our Central Asian possessions and the Indus River.

All these routes are divided into longitudinal routes which cut Afghanistan from north to south and link our Turkestan with India (routes of advance) and traverse routes which cut the country from east to west – these link with the longitudinal routes and serve as communication routes.

In turn, the ordinary routes are divided into three groups: Western or routes of the Kandahar sector – from our Kushka region to British Baluchistan through western Afghanistan; Central or routes of the Kabul sector – from the Amu-Darya's banks to Kabul and Peshawar through the Western Hindu Kush; and Eastern or routes of the Pamir sector – from the Pamir Uplands to Peshawar through the Eastern Hindu Kush, Chitral or Gilgit.

Western group of communication routes

The western group of routes is a fairly thick knot of roads which are cut into two segments by Kandahar and Herat and are very important routes of communication. But since the number of roads in the different segments varies, we should study them by segments: from our border to Herat; from Herat to Kandahar; and a brief study of the segment from Kandahar to the Indus River.

There are five routes[9] leading from our probable concentration areas in the Kushka region (*Ak-Robat, Kushka* [Serhetabat or Gusgy] and *Tahta-Bazar*) to Herat. They cross the Parapamisus Mountain Range in the sector from Khumbow mountain pass to Zarmast mountain pass (about 130 versts wide). The mountains of the Parapamisus Mountain Range are highest in the sector between Ardevan and Zaramast mountain passes and lowest – between Chashma-Sebz and Khumbow mountain passes. The mountains become higher west of the latter.

The easternmost and westernmost routes are the longest (220 and 222 versts) and the central route (through Ardevan mountain pass) is the shortest (114 versts).

Two western routes (from Ak-Robat through Khumbow and Chashma-Sebz mountain passes) are long (up to seven long day marches[10]), and they are accessible to wheeled transport without additional improvement. But there is no supply of water, food and fuel in the area. Two eastern routes (from Kushka through the Khazaret-e-Baba mountain passes) are shorter (six regular day marches) but they require additional improvement for wheeled transport passage: the Ardevan route – at the mountain pass and the Khazaret route – all over. There is supply of water on both routes, but no food and fuel. Local resources will be available on all four routes only after coming into the Harirud Valley.

Considering that the goal of our troops' march to Herat will most probably be to capture the city before the arrival of reinforcement of Anglo-Indian troops, marching

9 Appendix XIV. (Author's note). It had never been published. (Translator's note).

10 The number of day-marches is determined by the locations of inhabited points with water sources. (Author's note).

speed becomes paramount. And because of that we shall give preference to the Ardevan route as the shortest one (114 verstas) which requires only insignificant improvement work at the pass to move wheeled transport. Moving by that route, our infantry could reach Herat in six or even five day-marches and cavalry would be there on the third day. But the troops would stretch out for several day-marches while moving on only one road. It would be to our advantage to move the troops on two middle routes simultaneously: from Ak-Robat through Chashma-Sebz and from Kushka through Ardevan. If both columns start moving on the same day, they will come to Harirud Valley at the same time – on the sixth day (one – near Rosnak and another one – near Herat) on a 50 versts front. On the ninth or tenth day, all forces will be concentrated around Herat.

Besides these four routes, there is a fifth one: from Tahta-Bazar to Herat through Kala-Now and Zaramast mountain pass. It would take eight long day-marches (222 versts) in the mountains. It is accessible to pack-animal transport only and the pass is difficult. There is very little food, water and fuel on the route. This route is not suitable for moving a large detachment with a supply train, but several hundred troops with horses could move through successfully during the springtime since there would be plenty of pasturage.

Thus, on the way to Herat, the terrain is fairly accessible and has no strong-points capable of holding up the advance. But it lacks water, food and fuel up to Harirud Valley. The population consists of mixed nationalities with the Afghans [Pashtun] having no more than one-fifth of the general population.

When you study in detail the length of the routes and the number of related day-marches in Asia, this one thing will amaze you. For example, you see that the route through Khumbow is 220 versts and requires seven day-marches while the route through Cheshma-Sebz is 209 versts but requires eight day-marches – i.e. the fewer versts require more day-marches. You will understand this after becoming more familiar with the specifics of movement in Asia. Calculation are not done using European methods – taking into account only the route's length because the terrain is the same on average as well as its accessibility. In Asia, the road goes from a well to another well, from one kishlak [village] to another. And these restrictions strictly define the day-marches: in a day you have to move 10-12 versts or up to 50. The organization of day-marches does not depend on distance or ground conditions – it primarily depends on the location of inhabited points [which have water] and water sources.

There are significantly fewer routes between Herat and Kandahar than before Herat. The sector has only two through roads which widely vary in quality and accessibility in different segments of their long length. The towns of Sebzevar [Shindand], Farah and Geresk are located on routes through fertile and densely-populated valleys of the rivers Adraskan, Farah-Rud and Helmand. They naturally create a series of intermediate bases that help to alleviate the difficulties of the march.

Two routes are available for moving from **Herat to Kandahar**. They go south first – to Farah-Rud, and then turn south-east. The first route (first western, then southern) goes from Herat through the Senghua-Kissak canyon to Sebzevar, from there to Farah, Delaram, Geresk and then to Kandahar. The total length of the route is 570 versts. The second route (first eastern, then northern) goes from Herat through Shakh-Bid canyon and Adraskan to Jembran; from there – to Daulatabad, Vashir, Haiderabad and Kandahar. The route's length is 540 versts. The length of both routes is almost equal and would take 24-25 day marches or about a month of marching. They are almost parallel to each other with the distance between them around 30 versts. Both routes are crossed by rivers Adraskan, Farah-Rud, Khash-Rud, Helmand and Arghandab. All these rivers are passable by wading in summertime. During the spring and fall, the rivers are at a high level and require building bridges.

To hold the advance the enemy could use positions at river crossings, especially near Geresk, Sebzevar and on the line Farah – Lash-e Joveyn.

With the exclusion of the initial six-seven day-marches (from Herat to Sebzevar) where routes go through the spurs of Siyah-Kuh, the rest of the way goes across slightly hilly plains. *Both routes from Herat to Kandahar are accessible for wheeled transport.* There is no fuel. Food and water supply is poor on both routes and is spread out very unevenly.[11] There is no water and food on both routes from Herat to the Adraskan River (six day-marches) and from Adraskan to Khash-Rud (eight day-marches) food and water can be found in very small quantities on the first route and are practically absent on the second. From Khash-Rud to Helmand (five day-marches) one will find a little food and water on the second route but the first route lacks them completely and from the Helmand River to Kandahar (five day-marches) during a good crop year, one can count on finding some food and fuel supplies from the local sources because the area is densely populated and well developed.

The distance from **Kandahar to Quetta** is 220 versts or 12 day-marches. During the first seven day-marches to the Khoja-Arman Mountain Range, troops can move by the English highway and several dirt roads accessible for wheeled transport.[12] Further movement is going to be by the English military road. The conditions of the march will depend on the level of deliberate damage done to the road by the Englishmen who built the road.

Multiple rivers which cross the routes serve as obstacles with good rear guard positions in the sector of first seven day-marches. Then there is the Khoja-Arman Mountain Ridge with three passes guarded by English forts. And finally the routes are blocked by the Pishin fortified camp. There is plenty of water on the routes but there is also a shortage of food.

Totaling up everything we've said about the Kandahar operational sector, we shall conclude that the distance from Kushka to Kandahar through Herat is about 700 versts or 31 day-marches.

The advantages of using this sector are:

---

11 Because there is practically no *grain surplus* across almost all of Afghanistan – only enough to sustain the population during a year, the small quantities of the grain which could be found by the troops after harvest must be considered not for immediate use but as necessary for the sustainment of the population. The population most probably will not voluntarily sell it because that would produce famine. Thus, in case of necessity, for one reason or another, one would have to resort to *requisitions* in order to use local supplies. One must not forget that such actions by Englishmen lead to mass uprisings by the population (1879-1880) and that made it very difficult to guard communications. (Author's note).

12 The English improved and constructed the highway from Quetta-Kandahar during the 1878-1880 Second Anglo-Afghan War. (Translator's note).

- The ability to move troops by railroad directly into the assembly area near the border and the presence of a strong point there, the Kushka fortress.
- Troops can move on two parallel routes (30 versts distance between them) which are accessible for wheeled transport. The terrain along the routes is generally flat, without major natural obstacles and with fairly populated areas.
- The routes will bring us to Herat in six-seven day-marches. Herat is an extremely important point and the surrounding Harirud Valley is the only Afghan region that abounds in grain. Use of this approach also permits us to base out of the richest Persian province – Khorosan.[13]

But there also are some disadvantages:

- The significant distance.
- The absence of food, fuel and water supplies on all of the routes except in the Herat Valley.
- The threats of strikes at our flanks: a) from Seistan; b) from Hazarejat; and c) from the sea through Baluchistan – this is possible to some degree, considering British naval superiority and their influence over Baluchistan.[14]
- The route is barred by the fairly strong Herat fortress and it comes up against a well-fortified sector of the British border.

Together we came to Quetta. It leaves us with 370 versts from Quetta to the Indus River (Succor). Leaving detailed description of the route to the appendix,[15] I will only say that the route is difficult by its very nature and also in relation to possible actions by the Englishmen. The major obstacles on the route are the Bolan mountain pass from which runs the road runs 94 versts to the town of Dadar through narrow valleys and canyons squeezed by steep mountain slopes (sometimes up to few dozens of steps wide) and the waterless and incredibly hot Tap desert. Presence of these obstacles forces us to find and use bypass routes: the Pitin military road (Gharnai station – Loralai – Fort Munro – Dera-Ghazi-Khan on the Indus River); a highway of 335 versts and the bypass road through Kalat (Quetta-Kalat-Cotra-Handowa-Larkana ferry across the Indus River) which is very long (589 versts) and very difficult.

Central group of routes

For our convenience, the routes of the central group from the Amu-Darya River to the Indus River can be divided into segments: from the Amu-Darya to towns of the steppe

13 There are 130 versts distance from Herat through Khusan to Persian border with two roads accessible for wheeled transport. (Author's note).

14 It sounds somewhat strange, but nevertheless the idea to advance toward Herat from the sea is quite often found in the current military literature of India. I would point to a detailed article in *The Pioneer Mail* published 20 years ago and written by a top officer of the Anglo-Indian army. And one can find many such articles. (Author's note).

15 Appendix XVI. (Author's note). Not published (Translator's note).

zone of Afghan Turkestan and from there through the Hindu Kush to Kabul and then from Kabul to the Indus River.

Ten routes run from the Amu-Darya's river crossings to the steppe towns:[16]

- Kerki – Andkvoy – Meymaneh – 220 versts (eight day-marches).
- Kerki – Shebergan – Mazar-i Sharif – 242 versts (ten day-marches).
- Kerki – Aqchah – Balkh – Mazar-i Sharif – 227 versts (nine day-marches).
- Kerki – Bossaga – Ak-Tag – Nimlik – Mazar-i Sharif – 129 versts ((nine day- marches).
- Chushka—Guzar – Shar-Tepe – Maidan-Dival –Mazar-i Sharif – 72 versts (three day-marches).
- Patta-Hissar [Termez] – Mazar-i-Sharif – 56 versts (two day-marches).
- Patta-Hissar – Tash-Kurgan [Khulm]– 70 versts (three day-marches).
- Kabiadin river crossing – Tash-Kurgan – 32 versts (one day-march).
- Takhta-Quwat – Kunduz – 54 versts (two day-marches).
- Hazarat-Imam river crossing – Kunduz – 55 versts (two day-marches).

These ten short routes do not provide any serious obstacles for wheeled transport – with the exclusion of small sand patches making moving a bit more difficult. Using these routes, the troops could quickly move from the Amu-Darya river crossings to the line Mazar-i Sharif – Tash-Kurgan –Kunduz for a subsequent move across the Hindu Kush into the Kabul Valley and further to the Indus River. But for further advance, there are fewer accessible routes because the terrain, up to the approaches to Peshawar, is a system of high and barely accessible mountain ranges.

Routes which connect the steppe zone of Afghan Turkestan with the Kabul Valley can be divided into two groups: Bamian – which leads to Kabul Valley from the west through the Bamian mountain pass bypassing the Hindu Kush; and Charikar – which crosses the Hindu Kush, descends from the mountains near the town of Charikar and enters the Kabul Valley from the north (through the Kuh-i Daman Plains).

The Bamian[17] group in turn includes the two following routes:

- Mazar-i Sharif – Dekhi – Zardigah mountain pass – Bamian –Ownay mountain pass – Kabul (526 versts or 23 day-marches).
- Tash-Kurgan – Gheibag – Kurgan – Dwab – Kara-Kutal mountain pass – Bamian – Ownay mountain pass – Kabul (496 versts or 20 day-marches).

Both these routes are accessible for wheeled transport only at some segments and are generally difficult to negotiate. Moreover, during some periods of the year – wintertime and during snow melt – they are practically impassable. The advantage is that there is plenty of water, pasturage, wood and frequent inhabited points.

In my presentation, I highlighted the idea to pay serious attention to the Hindu Kush mountain passes and not the passes of its foothills and spurs still, those also could seriously hamper movement and they shall be taken into account.

16 Appendix VII. (Author's note). Not published (Translator's note).

17 Appendix XVIII. (Author's note). Not published. (Translator's note).

Take for example the first route – it is full of mountain passes. Before you can get to the Bamian Gap you need to go through five mountain passes: Dandan-Shikan, Dumby-Ushtur, Chakhar-Asman, Zardagao and Shibartau. The first two of them (and Dandan-Shikan in particular) are especially difficult and barely accessible for wheeled transport. And after passing through the Bamian Canyon, the series of mountain passes continues. Before you reach the fertile valley of the Kabul River, you will need to negotiate three large mountain passes: Kashka (Lesser Iraq – 8,570 feet), Greater Iraq (13,443 feet) and Ownay (11,300 feet). The route has eight mountain passes in total.

The road from Dehi-Darvaz to Dwab through Balagali mountain pass could serve as a communication route. The route goes in a south-eastern direction through mountainous but well-populated terrain and permits the use of wheeled transport.

The Charikar group also consists of two routes:

1) Tash-Kurgan – Aibak [Samangan] – Seihtut – Dushi – Chardara mountain pass – Ranghar – Charikar – Kabul (371 versts or 16 day-marches).
2) Kunduz – Aliabad – Jui-Kalan – Yaram – Khavak mountain pass – Charikar – Kabul (416 versts or 17 day-marches).

Both routes are difficult but their advantage is that they are accessible for wheeled transport. Their accessibility is limited to eight-nine months per year. But if the information about winter snow removal at the Khavak mountain pass is correct, the second route should permit moving troops year round. The other advantages of those routes are plenty of water, food, pasturage and wood.

Two routes lead from Kabul to the Indus River:

1) Kabul – Butkak – Hurd-Kabul – Jagdalak – Jalalabad – Khyber Pass – Peshawar – Attok (373 versts or 20 day-marches).
2) Kabul – Sheikh-Abad – Kushi – Shutur-Gardan mountain pass – Peiwar-Kotal mountain pass – Kuram – Tal – Koghat – Kushalghar (447 versts or 23 day-marches).

Both these routes are accessible for wheeled transport though in some places they require improvements (Shutur-Gardan mountain pass, Khurd-Kabul canyon, etc.). The better (and shorter) one is the first route through Jalalabad and Dhaka. These routes have serious tactical barriers, such as the Khyber Pass on the first and Fort Kuram and Fort Tal on the second. The tactical impregnability of the Khyber Pass forced creation of two bypass routes: one north from Dhaka along the Kabul River (between the river and the Tartura Mountain Range) through Loi-Shil'man, Shakhidmian and Shakhgai to Peshawar – 66 versts from Dhaka in total. The second one – to the south – goes from Ali-Madjid to the area south-west of Shara and Chin and then futher through Bezar Valley, Sis-Obi mountain pass to the Afghan village Chinar (47 versts).[18]

The study shows advantages and disadvantages of the central group of routes.

The advantages:

18 See details in a book *The North-Western Border of India* by General Staff Colonel Polozov. (Author's note).

- The possibility to move troops directly into the border strong points of Kerki and Termez by railroad,[19] i.e. to move large masses of troops into forming-up areas for our deployment with the Amu-Darya securing the areas. That would give us the ability to capture the steppe town's line in one-two days.
- This is a significantly shorter distance in comparison to the Kandahar sector.
- The routes lead to the Afghan capital of Kabul.
- The mountains prevent strikes at our flanks by sizable forces.
- There is a good supply of water and fuel.
- There is a fairly sufficient supply of food.

The disadvantages:

- The sector's routes are blocked by some fearsome obstacles to troop movement and logistics. Only two routes allow the use of wheeled transport – at any rate, field artillery will have difficulties.
- It is not accessible year around.
- The strongest fortress in Afghanistan (Deidadi) and several fortifications in the mountains block the only available routes for the troops.
- The routes come to the highly fortified segment of the English border.

That is what we can briefly say about the routes of the two operational sectors – the Kandahar and Kabul. We see their advantages and shortcomings. Let's compare them.

First, the Kandahar sector is longer than the Kabul sector: the distance from Kandahar to Kushka is 700+ versts and from Amu-Darya to Kabul is 400+ versts. There is no water on the first route and plenty on the second. Then we have a shortage of pasturage on the first route and enough of it on the second. The Kandahar routes have very few inhabited points and the Kabul routes have many of them. But the Kandahar routes are fully accessible for wheeled traffic and the troops can move with all their supply transport and artillery while on the Kabul route one needs to go across the Hindu Kush and use pack animals. Also the Kandahar operational routes are open year around and the Kabul routes are closed during wintertime. So, before you are two sectors and each has its own advantages and disadvantages. But when you extend both sets of routes to the Indus River, the assessment becomes even more difficult. Each extension to the Indus River also has its own advantages and disadvantages and this complicates the matter even more. The only clear thing is the difference in distances. Add the distance between the Amu-Darya and one of the steppe towns, than between the town and Kabul and between Kabul and the Indus River and you have 800+ versts. If you make a similar calculation for the routes of the Kandahar sector, then you will a distance between Kushka and the Indus River of about 1250 versts. So, the Kandahar sector's length is 1250 versts and the Kabul's is 800. The former consists of 60 day-marches and the latter

19 The latest information tells me that the railroad is damaged, stations are destroyed and that in many places track have been removed. But, certainly, this is a temporary problem. (Author's note). This destruction occurred during the fighting in the Russian Civil War between the Reds and Whites. In this section, British forces backed the Whites. The fighting surged along the rail lines. (Translator's note).

40. Weighing that and leaving the rest out, we see a serious difference in the marching time. Marching to the Indus River through Herat – Kandahar requires two months while doing so through the Hindu Kush and Kabul would take only one month and ten days. The difference here is almost a month.

If you ask me which sector is preferable – I will leave it to you to decide. It is a difficult question because you lack complete information for clear choices. Science in such cases recommends extending the scale of research. One of the best ways to do so is to ask history. And history will tell you that despite the fact that the Hindu Kush is a first-rate mountain ridge with difficult-to-negotiate valleys, steep slopes, winter blizzards and threats to the flanks – almost all the victors went through it. If I am not mistaken, history does not provide a single example of a large expedition into India which was not completely confined to the Kabul sector. Alexander the Great – after the conquest of Bactria (currently Afghan and Russian Turkestan), Genghis-Khan in his invasion of India in the summer of 1221, Timur in his early spring and summer of 1398 expedition, Babur in many of his expeditions and others – they all used the Kabul operational sector.[20] The only invasion of India that has been attempted through the Kandahar sector was that of Nadir-Shah.[21] But he did not have any other options – all his support base was in the west.[22] But that is not all. The conquerors not only preferred the Kabul sector to the Kandahar sector– they even preferred it during the time when the Hindu Kush is inaccessible – as one might think. I've already listed Babur's operation on the Hazara road and Timur's expedition – an old man at the time – who was lowered from the mountain slopes on ropes and animal skins.[23] These examples show us that military

20 For those who would like to familiarize themselves with the expeditions of Asian military leaders I would direct them to raw data and immediate sources (there are no well-edited finished works): I. W. M'Grindle, *The Invasion of India by Alexander the Great*, Westminster, 1896 – there are excerpts from works of Arrian, Curtsius, Diodorus, Plutarch and Justinus; M. I. Ivanin *The Military Science and Conquests of Mongols and Central Asian Nations during reign of Genghis-Khan and Timur*, St.Petersburg, 1875; Babur's Memoirs (or Babur-Name's) – they are published as the original by Il'inski, Kazan, 1857 – translated into Persian by Abdar-Rakhim-Mirza-Khan in 1590. The English translation from Persian has been done by John Leyden and W. U. Erskine in 1826. There is a French translation from the Turkish original by Pavet de Courtieill. Only a part of the work has been translated into Russian – and badly at that. (Author's note).

21 Nāder Shāh Afshār the Great is also known as *Nāder Qoli Beg* or *Tahmāsp Qoli Khān* (November, 1688 or August 6, 1698-June 19, 1747). He ruled as Shah of Persia (1736-47) and was the founder of the Afsharid dynasty. (Translator's note).

22 You can find details in the work of S. O. Kishmishov *Nadir-Shakh's expeditions into Herat, Kandahar and India*. The work itself is fairly weak, because it is based on weak works such as Malcolm *Histoire de la Perse*; Mirza-Mekhti *History of Nadir*, etc. There are mistakes aplenty everywhere. For example it says that Babur was born in Faizabad (p.150), that Akbar is Babur's son (p.150), his description of the Suleiman Mountains is pure fantasy (pp.152-153); Genghis-Khan's expedition into India is placed in 1197 (p.162), etc. (Author's note).

23 There is one more revealing example. During the prolonged struggle between Babur's sons – Hamaiyun and Kamrad (in the 40s of the XVI Century) each crossed the Hindu Kush several times and during different times of the year. Among those crossings, the most outstanding was by Kamrad in the winter of 1547 when the prince went through deep snow, blizzards and snowstorms. He went through Char-dara mountain pass. Malleson, *History of Afghanistan*, pp.141-142. (Author's note).

leaders went through the Hindu Kush even in wintertime, overcoming huge difficulties but surprising the enemy with their unexpected appearance. And that gives us a chance to conclude that the Hindu Kush sector should have preference and if we have to operate there – the main forces should go by it and only small – diversionary – forces should go by other directions.

Eastern group of communication routes

Now what is left for us is to study the eastern group of the routes. Some researchers, for the sake of convenience, split them in two segments: from Pamir and the Amu-Darya to a line Chitral-Gilgit and from there to the vicinity of the Punjab. Others divide these routes into two sub-groups: Badakhshan and Pamir. I will not make an assessment of their research methods, but I will mention the most important of them briefly:

- Kulyab – Samti-Baloh – Rostak – Faizabad – Zebak – Dorah mountain pass – Chitral (446 versts or 20 day-marches).[24]
- Alay Valley (Daraut-Kurgan) – Ters mountain pass – Aghar – Takhta – Ghorum – Kara-Bulak mountain pass – Mardjanai mountain pass – Khorghosh – Kala-E-Panj – Ochil' mountain pass – Chitral (636 versts or 32 day-marches).
- Alay Valley (Sarytash) – Kizil-Art mountain pass – Pamir Post – Borogill mountain pass – Darband – Chitral (673 versts or 33 day-marches).
- Alay Valley (Sarytash) – Kizil-Art mountain pass – Koshebell mountain pass – Tash-Kurgan – Myn-Teke (Kilik) – Ghunza – Gilgit (626 versts or 32 day-marches).
- There are two routes available to reach the Punjab's northern approaches (near Nowshera and Rawalpindi):
  - Chitral – Dyr – Miankala – Malakand mountain pass – Nowshera (225 versts or 10 day-marches).
  - Gilgit – Bunji – Astor – Kamri mountain pass – Tragbal mountain pass – Srinagar – Murree – Rawalpindi (490 versts or 20 day-marches).

When I counted these routes I gave a tribute to the thoroughness of research, but you must have a clear picture of all the routes. Only someone who has never been in the area and moved along these routes, someone who has not seen the wild and bleak terrain which these routes cros – could calmly count and classify them into groups of a specific operational sector. But for a person who has been there, all these classifications are lifeless and hardly reliable bookkeeping items. What is possible to say about the sector in general? Their lengths vary from 700 to 1100 versts. There are 450-600 versts from the departure area to the Chitral – Gilgit line and another 200-500 versts from there to the Punjab. But when speaking about the Pamir routes, one should put the topography first. The area is located at high altitude – 12,000 feet average. This altitude forces your body to adjust; it requires more energy and an increasing number of blood cells. It races your pulse. A traveler cannot sleep on his left side, any move quickens the heartbeat. It

24 Appendix XXI. I will discuss the Pamir routes at other time. (Author's note). Not published (Translator's note).

takes about three weeks to adjust to those heights. When we were preparing our Pamir detachment, we conducted special tests for the candidates before the expedition. They were ordered to run a specific distance, climb a wall and after that say a prayer to the Lord thrice. Those who did that were accepted. Accidents happen if precautions are forgotten. One of my officers on the way from Osh to Pamir doubled the distance for the day's march – and died near Bordaby from a heart attack – he moved to high altitude too fast. Do not forget that in the Pamir sector you will need to cross eleven mountain ranges through passes at 16-17-18,000 feet altitude. After crossing the Hindu Kush, you will descend into such out-of-the-way places of which the ancient Chinese travelers said "Dragons live there". Consider the situation when trails go by cornices – often broken by gorges, there is no bread or wood and extreme cold persists for nine months – all this should make us cautious. To think of using the sector as operational routes and imagine sending over 300 cavalrymen there is equal to pure fantasy. Science takes that operational sector into account – but only for the sake of the wider picture. History though has mentioned one case of crossing there in a half-fairytale expedition by Ughuz-Khan to India. It says that he with 40,000 cavalrymen had crossed the Lesser Tibet (Mustag and Kara-Karum mountain passes), went by northern foothills of the Himalayas and like an avalanche descended through the southern slopes into the then capital of Northern India – Delhi. Scientists are skeptical about this case – if it happened at all, but then again – in the military history of Asia, there is always much that is legendary and unbelievable. Of course, we cannot base our plans on such extraordinary cases.

Finally we should remember that there are no more than 1,800 Kara-Kyrgyz living in the area who are barely able to sustain themselves by moving from place to place and who must withstand hunger and severe cold. Having considered all the facts, we should not put the Pamir sector in the same category as the Kabul and Kandahar sectors – we should leave it to the role of a secondary or diversionary approach. But I have to tell you that the Englishmen apparently look at the Pamir with some alarm and apprehension. They spent a lot of money on Dardistan and the Gilgit Agency, conducted much reconnoitering of the terrain, conducted special wars (the Ghunza-Nagar for example). And Durand, in the beginning of his work, directly warns against some future Skobelev-like "cutthroat" who could suddenly invade Northern India through the "Pamir Bridge" and inflame the whole country.[25]

All of these factors forces me to conclude that the Pamir sector is difficult and barely accessible – but for Asia in general and for India in particular, it could play a significant role with a sudden strategic surprise…we should not reject it completely because at war we should not miss any opportunity.

Lines of Communiation

Now we shall discuss intercommunications or longitudinal routes. I will mention three of them, leaving out some of the less important:[26]

25 *The Making of the Frontier* or my translation Созидание Границы; pp.36-37. One can find there (in the text or my notes) what measures the English have taken to secure the northern border. (Author's note).

26 Appendix XXII. (Author's note). Not published. (Translator's note).

1) *Bala-Murghab – Meymaneh – Shebergen – Mazar-i Sharif – Kunduz – Faizabad* (733 versts or 30 day-marches). This route is very important as a link between columns advancing from our territory. Almost the entire route is accessible for wheeled transport with some minor improvements needed in few areas. The mountain passes on the route (Shebaqli, Arganeh, Lateh Band – and the somewhat-higher Yan-Darya, Aluchakham, Teshkan and Dariam) are not high, but they might create some difficulties as they are not prepared for wheeled traffic. The terrain varies: besides the ordinary mountain-steppe areas, there are also sandy regions and as an exception – marshy lowlands. There are farm lands all along the route and there is plenty of water and pasturage. Collecting food in many places should not be difficult, especially at large inhabited points. The locals' attitude toward us should be more friendly than indifferent, but not hostile.
2) *Herat – Jengelzabad – Hermab – Mushak – Gzharmez – Kabul* (632 versts or 28 day-marches). This is the so-called Hazara Way. The route has been the subject of rapt attention at the former Turkestan military district's headquarters which received plenty of rumors about the building of the Hazara road and telegraph line along with some supplemental works near the road. They continued until a special agent went by that road from Herat to Kabul and clarified the situation. It turned out that the road is a natural way improved in some places but not that much. Almost all the road is accessible to wheeled traffic and, in those places accessible only by pack-animals; it can be fairly-easily improved for wheeled transport access. The route has plenty of water and pasturage. Inhabited points are frequent and food collection should be easy. The locals' attitude toward us is unclear, but we should take all precautions as they are freedom-loving Mountaineers.[27]
3) *Kandahar–Kalat-i Ghilzai –Ghazni – Kabul* (474 versts or 23 day-marches). This is a very well-known route that has been used by the English more than once. You can find the descriptions of the route in the works on the Anglo-Afghan Wars and in materials collected by travelers. This entire route is good for wheeled traffic and it is suitable for siege artillery transportation. The inhabited points along the route are frequent and there is plenty of water and food. The population is pure Afghan [Pashtun] – proud and vindictive brigands – our relations with them must be very careful in everyday issues and in military matters.

I will not talk about secondary routes or local roads because this does not fit the scale of my presentation. You can find the information in the sources I indicated at the beginning of our course.

General conclusion on routes

There is only one general conclusion on Afghanistan's communication routes: the country is badly lacking in them. There are practically no railroads, waterways or highways. There

27 Our specialists recently traveled on the road and they generally confirmed what has been said. Of course, there is no telegraph or telephone, the road improvements are absent – only some clearing of obstacles, bridges are of the "Caucasus" type; but the works are fairly sizable. The wheeled transport would first go six-seven day-marches from Herat. (Author's note).

are primitive ordinary roads – the country uses what nature gives to it and in the shape that nature gave to them. The road network is extremely sparse. There are some areas that are not crossed by a single road as, for example, the area bounded by Bala-Murghab – Obe – west of Kuh-i Baba – Meymaneh or the area bounded by Herat – Kandahar – Ghazni – the Harirud River.

Undoubtedly, with such pitiful road conditions, Afghanistan can only live a semi-barbarian life without culture and industry.

As to the military aspect of the country, the absence of developed roads makes it practically inaccessible and unassailable. It is impassable in many places. It deprives the advancing troops of communications between separate detachments and generally makes the country very suitable for passive resistance. The people's proud and freedom-loving character and the huge mountainous areas make very difficult to conquer the country and especially difficult – to keep it under control.

9

Political Significance of Afghanistan

In the wrap-up to my presentation, I need to look into the political significance of Afghanistan. Before we begin the political examination of one or another subject, we need to establish, quite definitely, what the real, un-embellished value each subject represents in relation to the international situation and what its intrinsic spiritual and material values are. And only after we establish such an evaluation, we can move to an attempt to resolve the political issues in one direction or another. Further, in my presentation, you will see that we made several attempts to advance on Afghanistan and, to tell the truth, they were pitiful and awkward. As to the Englishmen, in addition to their innumerable research works and their extravagant expenditure of money, they were also forced to conduct three wars with Afghanistan: the first Anglo-Afghan war (1838-1842), the second (1878-1881) and the third (two years ago – it lasted a month and a half during May and June [1919]).

The question comes instinctively: What is the reason for all these efforts to gain influence in Afghanistan or even to conquer it?

Besides these wars, there is a centuries-old history of open and secret quarrels and a long and unceasing political struggle between England and Russia over influence in Afghanistan. There is a huge mass of literature (especially in British sources) which stubbornly repeats the same ideas about the role and significance of Afghanistan. A person who is not familiar with the content and spirit of that literature, especially with its high-strung and cocky self-assurance, runs the risk of becoming totally confused by it. The point is that the literature is purely political – i.e. nervously prejudiced, covert propaganda, quite lying and far removed from being scientific, balanced and honestly objective. But its abundance (I mean the English literature), its monotonous repetitions and self-assurance – all this undoubtedly should influence any reader. I will tell you more. That monotonous and stubborn literature influences all of Europe – if not all of the world. It especially has an effect on widespread (and world-wide) opinions about India. Of course, Afghanistan represents a much smaller issue and it is the province of specialists. Those who needed to know the truth understood the one-sidedness and deep egotism of the British political interpretation long ago. Some of them even attempted to liberate European thinking about Asian politics from British domination.[1]

Now, let us move to the real assessment of Afghanistan. Can Afghanistan be of value by itself? We have a country of five million people, very poor, primitive, without

1 See the leading article "L'oeuvre du Comité", page 2 in *Bulletin du Comité de l'Asie Françise*, Avril, 1901. (Author's note).

machinery and culture. It does not make sense for either us or the British to pursue control over such a semi-barbaric, unbalanced and always agitated country. What would we achieve if we controlled it? There is nothing to say about mineral wealth – it is negligible and not yet explored. It is possible to make agriculture more modern – but that will take a very long time and huge expenditures and will have modest results. And what about their population of five million? A sizable portion of it is nomadic – and so they are semi-barbarians with weak work habits, who are negligent and indifferent toward the economy. Clearly, Afghanistan itself does not have any significant value. But that is not all. This is a mountainous country without roads and mechanical equipment with an estranged and unreliable population.[2] And that unreliable population is also proud and freedom-loving. The latter circumstance will lead to the situation where, after subjugating the country, keeping control over it may prove very difficult. Organizing administration and establishing order will take enormous resources and the country will not return those resources – it does not have anything to return.

So, we most definitely have to say that Afghanistan, in itself, did not play any significant role in the centuries-old struggle between England and Russia. Its value always was an *indirect* and *conditional* one. Serious thought about the political value of *Afghanistan* concludes that its main value lies in the fact that the *country* possesses the operational routes into India. History brilliantly illustrates this fact showing that there were 20 great invasions into India during the last four millennia. All of these invasions show that, since time immemorial, powerful peoples tried to get into India – usually with the goal of enrichment – and they always went through Afghanistan. There were no other ways. And since Afghanistan has these key routes, it is politically valuable, gives a certain disproportionate weight to it and provides the key to resolution of the question about the main cause for the political struggle between England and Russia. There is a phrase attributed to Alexander the Great that only India would give him the key to retaining power over Asia.[3] That idea was clearly understood by his predecessors and his followers. And India's importance is always reflected back onto India's unavoidable country-threshold – Afghanistan.

And because of that, my illustration of the political significance of Afghanistan will reflect the view that Afghanistan itself is not important either in a financial or an economic sense – or any other sense for the matter; but in being the permanent threshold of India (the significance of that position has not been diminished since and will never be lost) it represents a formidable political factor and sizable political entity. India has always been an object of greedy desires and conquests and India is still the same object today –the country that enticed past conquerors to capture their treasury will naturally lead them to do such again today.

Let's remark that the conquerors did not stay in Afghanistan for long and they did not meet any strong resistance there, but at the time it did not diminish the political significance of the country. The major conclusion is that Afghanistan is the only threshold of

---

2 "The Country of rocks and stones" is how the English refer to it. For example, see Thorburn, *Asiatic Neighbors,* p.93. (Author's note).

3 It is mentioned in the work of V. Kryazhin *The Twilights of the Orient*, Moscow, 1919, p. 4. (Author's note).

India – and there is not any other one. Look at the map and evaluate the roads leading to India. Let's start with Baluchistan.

From history, you know that Alexander the Great made his withdrawal from India along the seashore and that cost him a lot of work and hardship. The first Arabic conquest of the late 7th Century was also conducted by the same route – but those two singular cases are the only historical exceptions – no more. Besides, in both cases, ground operations were combined with naval operations, i.e. as strategy defines it, these were complex operations. Obviously, Baluchistan cannot lead to the conquest of India. It is extremely difficult to get into India through the Pamir and even more difficult to cross the Himalayas. Earlier I've said how difficult it is to move detachments through the Pamir sector. Speaking about the Himalayas, we would paint an even bleaker picture. Thus, that leaves us with Afghanistan as the only bridgehead for the invasion of India. Strictly speaking, all attempts to capture Afghanistan usually were only preparation for the conquest of India, but it always has been concealed for political and military reasons. Englishmen are also trying to hide the real political role of Afghanistan and the significance of their work in the country. In my time, when I made a public presentation in Petrograd in 1908 related to the British-Russian Convention of 1907 that discussed Tibet, Turkestan, and Persia – but nothing about India – I emphasized the manner of British political hypocrisy. The same thought I put in my work "India as a Major Factor of the Central Asian Question."

And I'm saying it again, Afghanistan represents an interest only as a neighbor of India and primarily because it contains the only road network that leads to India.

There are some indications of a larger scope to the political significance of Afghanistan – in the past at least. For example, Charles Simond in his works[4] mentioned an ancient geographers' thought (this is also mentioned in Elesée Réclusb Geographic universelle, L'Asie anlerieure) that between *Turan* (contemporary Turkestan), Iran (Persia) and Hind (contemporary India) is an "intermediate country" – and through that country peoples pass into one of these three mentioned territories and it is a barrier on the way to any of them. Of course, that grand thought has been proven by the long pages of history and it is impossible to argue against it. But for the current historical moment, when Persia and Turkestan have very much lost their significance as objects for military conquest, and India has preserved and even increased it – it would more proper to narrow that thought of the ancient geographers and make it more realistic and of practical value – i.e. to apply Afghanistan's significance exclusively to its relation to India.

Historically, that narrower idea crystallized long time ago. Without going into details and considering Alexander's phrase as a legend, I am going to point to the work of Abu-Fazl'[5] – the writer of the 16th century – who said that from time immemorial

---

4 Charles Simond, *L'Afghanistan. Les Russes aux portes de l'Inde*, Paris, 1885, p.323. (Author's note).

5 Abu-Fazl'-i-Allami (1551-1602) – was a minister, friend and historian for Akbar. He wrote many works and among those the most prominent is *Akbar-name.* It is a historical chronicle divided into three chapters. The first contains the history of Timur and his descendants and also the reign of Babur. The second chapter contains the history of the 46 years of the reign of Akbar; and the third (it has an original name *Ain-i-Akbari* – Akbar's mirror) has administrative directives and the statistics of the Great Mogul Empire of 1590. There are two English translations of the third – and most important – chapter of the work. The most recent translation is by H. Blochmann, Calcutta, 1873. (Author's note).

Afghanistan contained the doorway to India... Abu-Fazl' added (coming back to the old geographical idea) "And the European country, which captures Afghanistan, will establish its domination over all that part (i.e. Central Asia) of the world".[6]

Relations between Russia and England toward Afghanistan

Now I will move to the question – how have our relations with England in reference to Afghanistan been developing? To make the matter more understandable I will divide the issue into three periods. The first period starts from Napoleon's campaign in Egypt – from 1800 or from the 1801 "classic" expedition of Paul I to India – to beginning of our movements in Central Asia in the 1860s or up to the appearance of Henry Rawlinson's book.

The second period is defined as from our advance into Central Asia (or from the time of publishing the mentioned book) to the Pamir demarcation in 1896.

And the third period goes from the Pamir demarcation to the current time.

All these periods differ significantly from each other by length and importance, but I think it is possible to establish them because each of them has distinct aspects of the relations of Russia and England as it pertains to Afghanistan.

First period of Russian–English relations

The first period begins with the Egyptian campaign [by Napoleon]. Napoleon himself and the other key leaders of the French revolution clearly understood that they could deal a major blow to England's power through India. The same idea was shared by Catherine the Great – she had received a special proposal for an expedition into India by Saint-Genie through the Prince of Nassau.[7] True, if you analyze the Egyptian campaign, you will see that the idea flashes there as an extraneous thought – and only clearly comes to the surface in Napoleon's conversations and letters.[8] Though the Egyptian campaign

6 As an interesting sample of the same idea I would point to a phrase from an article "Afghanistan" in *Asiatisches Jahrbuch* – namely "Afghanistan Durchzugsland d. vorderasiat., tatar. u mongol. Volker nach Indien." *Asiatisches Jahrbuch*, 1913, p.89. The article is full of errors in the details. (Author's note).

7 In 1791, Captain A. M. de Saint Genie proposed a plan for the conquest of Hindustan to Catherine the Great. (Translator's note).

8 Napoleon's Egyptian expedition is quite often seen as a complete fancy of the great conqueror, but the newest research supports the supposition that the objective of it (if remote) was indeed India – where French officers and agents would incite an upspring of the local leaders against the Englishmen (W.M. Sloane *The Life of Napoleon Bonaparte*, volume 1, pp.487, 497; volume 2, pp.222-226). Also, there are fairly persuasive indications that India was a [French] objective even before this. For example, Langfrey who works with archives cited a secret decree of the French Directory (April 12, 1798) which assigned to Napoleon responsibility for "Capturing Malta and Egypt and *driving Englishmen out of all their possessions in the East*." (Langfrey, *Histoire de Napoleon I*, volume 1, p.360). As to the English, they quickly realized the real goal of the Egyptian expedition. Lord Wellesley, then Governor-General of India wrote: "In some letters I've received from England are mentions of a supposition – which I consider as fairly probable – that a part of the fleet concentrated in Toulon is intended for an expedition into India by the usual way past the

was aborted, it produced a strong impression on public opinion in England and maintained their attitude about Napoleon and everything related to India. In the course of 10 years (1798-1808), Napoleon retained the idea of destroying British dominion over India. He developed two detailed plans for expeditions into India (in 1800 and 1807).[9] The first was based on joint action with Russia and the second with assistance from Persia. Officers who were sent to Persia presented the Emperor with 124 routes crossing Persia in different directions – eight of them were direct routes into India. Both of these plans deserve more detailed discussion.

The end of the year of 1800 was marked by our split with England. On January 12, 1801, the Chieftain of the Don Cossack Host, General Orlov, received a handwritten letter from Paul I.[10] The Emperor ordered the Host to move to Orenburg and from there to follow three routes through Bukharia and Khiva to the Indus River. The Emperor suggested that the Chieftain *ruin all* English trading posts and institutions, free all oppressed landowners and "lead the land into Russia with the same dependence as it has to England and to turn all trade to us". As it is known, the Cossacks had moved out in strength with 22,500 men and 24 cannon. But they had not reached Orenburg when they received news of the Emperor's death and the new Emperor ordered them back to their permanent billets.

During the reign of Alexander I, we were supposed to participate in a joint expedition into India with the French Republic with the passive participation of Austrian Emperor who agreed to let the French troops pass through. An army of 70,000 was supposed to move to India. The Russian part consisted of 35,000 men: 25,000 regular troops and 10,000 Cossacks.

Astrabad was selected as the main headquarters of the allied forces and the center of communication between France and Russia. From Astrabad, the joint army was supposed to move through Herat, Farah and Kandahar to the Indus River. It was determined that it would take 45 days to reach the Indus River from Astrabad. The journey from France to the Indus River would take 120-150 days, i.e. forces leaving France in May would be on the Indus River in October. Special emissaries were supposed to be sent from Astrabad to all khans and rulers to create conditions for the success of the allied forces. Their mission was to win over the people and get them on the allies' side.

The 1801 expedition fell through mainly because of the unwillingness of Alexander I. Napoleon, after becoming the Emperor, still thought about the expedition, developed

---

Cape of Good Hope" (Letter to Admiral Rainer – See Bar Bartu de-Ponouen, *India Under British Rule*, Volume 1, p.226). The president of the Control Commission agreed with Wellesley, but he envisioned another, more natural way for the expedition: "...to Aleppo and after crossing the Euphrates – by the way of Alexander the Great – continue moving along the bank of that river into the Persian Gulf and further into India along the Gulf shore". The latter way, in reality, was outlined by the Emperor in the instruction given to General Gardane. (Author's note).

9 I direct those who want more detailed information to Batorski's (Vice-Director of the Asian Department in the Russian Foreign Ministry in 1837) article in *Anthology of Materials on Asia*, XXIII edition. (Author's note).

10 See V. A. Zakharov, *The Indian Expedition of Paul I.* (Author's note).

relations with Persia and in 1808 sent Caulaincourt to create conditions for success of the allied forces.[11]

As it is known, Caulaincourt could not get positive results and the mission was unsuccessful. Quite the opposite, several years later we were in alliance with England and fought the Patriotic War with British money.

The plan of the former expedition is of some interest to us as an example of strategic and political quixotism. Obviously, geographical knowledge of Central Asia during the reign of Paul I was well below elementary. The chosen route speaks on that very eloquently: Bukhara – Khiva – the Indus River; or the detachment assigned to tame the Englishmen – *20,000 troops with 24 cannons*. There are many quirks in the latter project as well, even though it was created by Napoleon's thoughts. Evidently, ignorance overpowers genius. You remember that the distance from Herat to Indus River is about 1,200 versts and almost 60 day-marches. But in Napoleon's project the march from *Astrabad through Herat to the Indus River* was planned for 45 days. The meagerness of the planned forces tells a lot about the flightiness of the authors of the project. Of course, 200 years ago, information about Central Asia was very murky – and that could be an excuse for the flighty approach.

In the history of the multitude of such expeditions and even greater number of expeditionary projects these two – by their military value –probably do not deserve to be mentioned. But their political significance was great and they shall take a higher place in our political observation. Though, at the beginning of the 19th Century, Russia and especially France were far away from India, England, at that time, was not the master of the situation in India. Punjab and Kashmir were not under its rule. At the time, the Englishmen were locked in Bengal Province, part of Calcutta and some of Bombay – i.e. they were huddled up on the coastline and the very valley of the Indus was far away from them.[12] But at any rate, the presence of England in India was already widely known and the advanced thinkers were aware that England was not too far from the complete capture of India. That realization explains the development of the two proposed expeditions as they highlighted the dangerous approaches to India – and that turned the Englishmen's eyes *toward Afghanistan* for the first time.

When Napoleon sent General Gardane to Persia in 1807, the English countered this move by sending their first embassy, headed by Elphinstone to Afghanistan in 1808.[13] The main mission of the embassy was to prevent the active participation of Persia in the Franco-Russian invasion of India. That spirit was behind the agreement with Shah-Shuja – than the ruler of Afghanistan. Generally speaking, the first quarter of the past century was the time when Englishmen were all under a psychosis from the Napoleon's projects and their eyes were turned toward Persia – as the first bridgehead leading to advancing

11 Armand-Augustin-Louis, Marquis de Caulaincourt, 1st Duc de Vicence (9 December 1773-19 February 1827) was a French general and diplomat. (Translator's note).

12 The small, but very well-written, work of Arthur D. Innes presents a graphic picture of the gradual subjugation of India by England related to the key events of 1783, 1808, 1833 and 1858. The second period is related to the first English contact with Afghanistan. *A Short History of the British in India*, by Arthur D. Innes, London, 1902, p.328. (Author's note).

13 Claude-Mathieu de Gardane was a French general and diplomat, and served as the Ambassador to Persia (December 1807-February 1809). (Translator's note).

columns into India. That explains the importance attached at the time to Khorosan – the eastern province of Persia and especially to Herat – the main city of Khorosan. At that time, everyone kept repeating the words of Nadir-Shah – the last conqueror of India: "Khorosan is the saber of Persia; the one who rules Herat holds it in his hands and could rule the whole world".

Elphinstone's mission did not achieve its political goal but it was a great boon to science. Elphinstone created a classic of his time with his work on Afghanistan. Together with his young traveling companions, who built their reputations with their own works – Cunningham, McCartney, Strachey, Irvin – they personally uncovered a huge geographical topic that previously had been discussed only on the basis of Greek, Arabic or Chinese geographers' information. They gave the world a large quantity of scientific material.

In any case, 1808 was the year that ties were established between England and Afghanistan. At that time, we were involved with the Napoleonic Wars and naturally did not care much about Central Asia and in particular about Afghanistan. But what was going on there? There were major troubles in Afghanistan. The country had split into three parts with the power seats in Kabul, Kandahar and Herat. Only in 1823, Dost-Mahomet – the founder of the current Barakzai dynasty – was able to unite most of the Kabul-Ghazni lands. As a strong monarch, Dost-Mahomet wanted to take over the rule of Afghan lands but he met strong resistance from the British government and he began to flirt with Russia. Poruchik Vitkevich did a lot of harm to the British.[14]

What were the goals of Dost-Mahomet, the first reformer of Afghanistan? His political agenda boiled down to the following: to unite Afghanistan bringing together all the Afghan tribes; then, to protect the country from Persia which had made some attempts to subjugate his country. In the question of relations with England and Russia, he, for unclear reasons turned toward Russia and spurned Great Britain. As Englishmen said – Dost-Mahomet began flirting with Russia and Poruchik Vitkevich was sent to Kabul. He was a man of exceptional energy and talent who did a lot of good. He could have done much more if he was not alone. Only two-three bureaucrats in the Foreign Ministry stood behind him – and that was it.[15] This was a time when we worked to influence Persia and paid much more attention to it. Afghanistan was then a political caprice, nothing more.

In 1823, Afghanistan was unified. Afghanistan's "flirting" with Russia worried England and these circumstances required them to build a definitive political course. And this period – from beginning of the Egyptian campaign to the 1860s– is saturated

14 Poruchik – in the old Russian army, a rank equal to First Lieutenant. (Translator's note).

15 The story of Vitkevich is still unclear today. His untimely death – as murky as his career's beginning – sharply tore down the political course he applied (could be it was too early for that course). As it is known, Vitkevich committed suicide after returning to Petrograd and finding a cold reception there. Englishmen gloated that Count Nesselrode apparently refused Vitkevich an audience when he came to present himself and ordered [his servant] to tell the Poruchik that "He does not know a Poruchik Vitkevich and only has heard about some adventurist Vitkevich, who has been busy with various intrigues in Kabul and Kandahar – without having any authority to do so." Kaye, *History of the War in Afghanistan*, Volume 1, p.209. (Author's note).

with the British idea of drawing Afghanistan into its sphere of political influence. Their idea boiled down to two major goals: having a British representative at the Emir's court and depriving Afghanistan of the ability to deal with foreign countries. The idea of drawing Afghanistan under their political control dominated that period. As to Russia, I repeat that we did not develop any political goals toward Afghanistan during that period – as we did not develop any in the following periods.

At first, England failed miserably. They tried to wrestle control of Dost-Mahomet with diplomacy and money. But Dost-Mahomet was a strong and persistent man and the British attempts came to naught. The English then decided to finish Afghanistan by force, put their own man on the throne instead of the recalcitrant Dost-Mahomet, split Afghanistan and get it under their control.

The First Anglo–Afghan War, 1838-1842

In the fall of 1838, the English declared war on Afghanistan and formed an invasion army. The invasion force included the Bengal column of 9,500 men with 38,000 auxiliaries and carriers and 30,000 camels. It was to assemble in Firoznur [Ferozepur] and after joining 6,000 local Afghans – supporters of Shah-Shuja (Dost Muhammad's enemy) move to Shikarpur. There, the Bombay column of 5,600 people was supposed to join it. The objective for both columns was Kandahar. The third column was supposed to move on Kabul. On March 6, 1839, the Bengal and Bombay columns arrived at the Bolan mountain pass. They did not meet any resistance and after passing through it, they declared Shah-Shuja the Emir. Then the English sent a 5,000-strong detachment to Ghazni and captured it by an assault. Dost Muhammad left Kabul and went to the north into Afghan Turkestan. On August 7, 1839, the English entered Kabul.

Our goal at the time was to strengthen and expand Persia, which was under our influence – and with that goal we had been helping it on the matter of Herat, which came to naught due to the Englishmen's intrigues. We also tried to reinforce Dost Mahammmad in Afghanistan, but we did it in a purely platonic way. In November 1839, we decided to finish our problem with Khiva and sent Perovsky's expedition.[16]

At that time, the Afghan population found out about our move and became aroused and went to Dost Muhammad's side. The movement against the Englishmen started. Dost Muhammad mustered a sizable force, crossed the Hindu Kush and inflicted a serious defeat on Englishmen near Pervandarra mountain pass. His success seriously frightened the Englishmen and they did not know what to do. But Dost Muhammad himself had helped them. He voluntarily came to the English camp. What prompted that prominent man to make that step is unclear. It could be a far reaching political

16 Count Vasily Alekseevich Perovsky (1794-1857) was a Russian general and statesman who was appointed military governor of Orenburg in 1833. In 1839, he led an expedition against the Khanate of Kiva to free Russian slaves and extend Russian borders while Britain was involved in the First Anglo-Afghan War. His force of 5,000 infantry and 10,000 camels set off in November 1839 but turned back on 1 February 1840 due to the severe winter weather. They arrived back at Orenburg in May, after losing 1,000 men without a single skirmish. (Translator's note).

calculation or hope for British clemency or something else. The English arrested him and exiled him into India.

The Afghan population got agitated and discontented. A year later, on the anniversary of the battle of Pervandarra Pass (November 2, 1841), the fearsome upspring began. Many English members of the mission were killed. The commander of the English detachment near Kabul was indecisive and let the Afghans encircle and defeat his forces in a battle. The English the Chief of Staff was invited to negotiations and insidiously killed. The detachment of 4,500 men withdrew to Jalalabad. During the withdrawal, the English were systematically killed at the mountain passes by the Afghans. The English later took revenge by sending a 15,000-man detachment which defeated the Afghans near the Khurd-Kabul [Pass], and then captured and plundered Kabul. But in the end they were forced to leave Afghanistan completely.

During the campaign of 1838-1842, the Englishmen lost more than 30,000 men and over 50,000 camels. They spent more than 100 million rubles. In the end, the Englishmen were forced to release Dost Muhammad who reigned happily until 1863.

In the works of Sobolev, Grigor'ev and some Englishmen, you can find a detailed analysis of that war from political and military standpoints. One can hardly find another example of a war which began so insolently and ended so humbly.

But what marks did the war leave on the Afghan people's memory? It was the least favorable to the Englishmen. The war lifted the self-assurance and pride of the people, illustrated the military weakness of Albion and its unpopularity in Central Asia. In the collection of Afghan songs from 1830s-40s, you can find clear marks of that unfortunate English period. One cannot avoid war in Asia – it is a necessary proof and support of your might – but it must be decisive and victorious. The first Anglo-Afghan war severely hurt Englishmen, lowered their prestige,[17] and only our negligence and absence of timely political instincts gave Britain a chance to repair its shaken imperial image – not by war but by other means.

But what did we do at the time? We gave Herat to Persia – though not for long – and later went after Khiva. Neither of those actions was well-planned or serious. But after all we understood that the Englishmen – if not us – attached a serious importance to Afghanistan and that the country contained coiled springs of great political possibilities. England also understood that if Russia currently could not operate actively then in the nearest future it would be able: first – to undertake more serious steps in that (Afghanistan's) direction; second – the very fact of Russia's drawing closer to Afghanistan could produce very serious consequences.

Their setbacks in Afghanistan and our advances into Central Asia lead to England's participation in the war of 1854-1855. For us though, there were more immediate reasons apparent. We must remember that at that time our aspirations toward the Mediterranean

17 About the same conclusion has been made by Kaye – the best historian of the first Anglo-Afghan war. He said in the conclusion: "After an enormous waste of blood and treasure, we left every town and village of Afghanistan bristling with our enemies"; or "In their place (instead of our former honor in Afghanistan – we left galling memories of the progress of a desolating army"; or "There was scarcely a family in the country which had not the blood of kindred to revenge upon the accursed Feringhees. The door of reconciliation seemed to be closed against us...", etc. William Kaye, *History of the War in Afghanistan*, London, 1890, Volume 3, p.399. (Author's note).

Sea were in high gear and the ideology of Orthodox Cross in Sophia had reached fever pitch. Liberation of our Slavic brothers from the Turkish yoke was in full swing. All of that presented a great danger to the main communications line connecting England with India. This same line grew in importance with every cubic meter of soil removed from the future Suez Canal that was under construction at the time.

Significance of the Crimean War

The Crimea campaign played a large role in Central Asian issues as it defined the political orientation of Russia and England for long time. The destruction of our Mediterranean [Black Sea] Fleet nipped in the bud all our aspirations of conquering Tsargrad and the straits.[18] But the same destruction which humiliated us before England, forced us to look for other ways to restore our influence over it – or more precisely – its dependence on us. The Crimean War mainly defined the essence of our future approaches to India as it uncovered the essence of the Central Asian issue. Although it was clear that we were fairly weak in Central Asia and could not conduct any offensive operations against India, the theoretical and later "official" understanding of the fact that the road to recovery of our world balance with England runs through Central Asia – not through the Mediterranean as it was before. And the remote lantern which lighted that grand road was India.

This realization came at the beginning of the Crimean War and it was completely formed by its end and at that time influenced plans for expeditions into India in an interesting way. For example, Chikhachyov's proposal was to send an expeditionary corps to Astrabad, occupy Herat and from there send 30,000 troops to Kandahar and Dera-Ismail-Khan and further to Lahore.[19] Thus the plan envisioned cooperation with Persia and Afghanistan.

There also was Khrulyov's plan with approximately the same plot.[20]

In these plans we can see the overlap of bases and operational sectors. As I've already mentioned, there were numerous military expeditions into India, but there were only 20 great ones in history. These expeditions or the plans which expeditions were based on can be divided into the two groups of *European* and *Asian*. The first group, less numerous and usually less successful, were based out of Europe and the advance went in the eastern or south-eastern direction. The second group was based out of Asia (Turkestan {*Turan* in antiquity} in particular) and the advance had been conducted in a southwestern or southern direction. The first group includes expeditions by Alexander the Great, Nadir-Shah (in 1735 – the last of the great expeditions) or plans by Napoleon, Chikhachyov and Khrulyov. The second group were all implemented (and there probably were plenty of different plans – judging by Babur's memoires), by Demetrius of Bactria, Scythians or Saks, Genghis-Khan, Timur and many others.

18 Tsargrad "The City of the Tsar" was the ancient Russian name for Constantinople, currently Istanbul in Turkey. The straits are the Straits of the Dardanelles, connecting the Black Sea and the Mediterranean Sea. (Translator's note).

19 P.A. Chikhachyov (1808-1890) – famous Russian geographer and geologist. (Translator's note).

20 S.A. Khrulyov (1807-1870) – Russian Lt. General who participated in the Kokand campaign and Crimea War. (Translator's note).

The proposed plans of Chikhachyov or Khrulyov do not represent interest in their essence or content. They, if you wish, are as superficial as those of Napoleon and not much above the fancy project of Paul I. But they show the really distinctive direction of the Russian political thought toward Central Asia. They show that, from the time of the Crimean War, a more real and concrete problem arose for Russia. The reality of the problem was supported by our conquests in Turkestan during the 1860s and 1870s. Tashkent, Khiva, Kokand, Samarkand and Bukhara fell like grass under a scythe. We had never achieved such quick and brilliant results before. And, as expected, our success had thrown the English into a panic and that lead them conclude that the old policy toward Afghanistan, whose essence was to use passive measures (presence of their resident in Kabul and their prohibition of Afghanistan's foreign contacts) was a mistake and did not bring any results in securing India. It became clear that the point of gravity was not in Afghanistan itself but in Russia and to wit – in the activity of Russia's Central Asian policy and the distance of Russia from Afghanistan. So the British goal became to stop the Russian advance and reduce the activity of Russian policy by all measures. That goal defined the tone of British actions in the second period we are studying (from the 1860s until the Pamir demarcation).

Second Period of Russian–English Relations

The second period begins with the famous memorandum of Sir Rawlinson[21] who presented it to the conservative State-Secretary on Indian issues. The author insisted on capturing Quetta, establishing the British residency in Kandahar, etc. – due to the Russian successes which threatened India. In the same memorandum, the author insists on interfering with the internal affairs of Afghanistan "in the name of the peace, trade, moral and industrial development" of India as much as Afghanistan. Of course, these verbal niceties were far from the essence of the Rawlinson book. A singular idea ran through the entire work and gives it historic value. Russia is implacably advancing on India. And this idea was presented very vividly and expressively by Rawlinson.

He wrote "If we draw the track of the Russian moves on a map of Asia over different periods of time, everyone will be astonished by the similarities of these with the movements of an army conducting parallel operations against a besieged fortress. The first parallel can be dated from the late 1840s and run from the northern shore of the Caspian Sea by the Orenburg and Siberian lines north of the steppe zone, toward the Irtush River. Strategically, that line can be considered an observation line".

"The second parallel, which represents a demonstration line, is the future Russian frontier which is prepared now.[22] It will go from Krasnovodski Bay to the Amu-Darya River to a point in southern Khiva and from there along the Amu-Darya to the Pamirs. That parallel will be 1,500 versts in the front of the first one."

"The third parallel – as a natural result of the preceding operations—shall go from Astrabad [Jurjan] to the south-eastern corner of Caspian Sea, along the Persian border to Herat and from there by the Hazara Upland to the Panj (Oxus) [Amu-Darya] River and

21 This memorandum, along with other articles by this author, are published in a classic book which I've already mentioned, *England and Russia in the East.* (Author's note).

22 i.e. at the end of the 1860s. (Author's note).

possibly through Kandahar to Kabul. After consolidating that line, Russia would have the river as an impregnable position".

Probably only the late author himself could sort out all that vinaigrette hodge-podge cooked up out of military, political, geographical and other ingredients. But that balderdash produced quite an impression on British public opinion. Manipulation of the military terminology and the haphazard use of it could confuse even a person who carefully studied Rawlinson's "parallels". Isn't it funny to watch India from our old "lines" or demonstrate from the line Krasnovodsk [Turkmenbashi] – Amu-Darya? And how are those accidental (and purely external, geographical) similarities to parallels related to reality when it is impossible to compare the content of the real one to those of Rawlinson? Would China be a thousand-fold more correct if it started to misuse fortifications in response to the Cossacks' moves – as the English scientist proposed? But the goal – to attract the attention of England to those remote corners of Central Asia – was achieved. Public opinion was so disturbed that the English government engaged Russia in negotiations about the objectives and limits of Russian conquests. The negotiations led to establishing the northern border of Afghanistan and in so doing Duke Gorchakov declared that "his Majesty considers Afghanistan out of the Russian sphere of influence." One would think that the English would calm down, but our success in Khiva and Kokand became the last straw. The Englishmen did everything they could to push Turkey toward war with Russia to stop our future expansion because after the Sevastopol campaign, England itself did not have enough determination to move actively against us.

For those who are interested in Central Asian political issues, Rawlinson's book is a must read– even if it is extravagant and nervous – and very interesting.

In direct connection with Rawlinson's book is McGregor's memorandum about the defense of India, written in 1889 when he was the Quartermaster-General of the Anglo-Indian army.[23] It contains a detailed and thorough plan – even sometimes deeply cynical and arrogant in the details – which boils down to a whole row of preventive measures against Russia with the goal not only to stop its expansion into Asia but to oust it completely beyond the bounds of Asia. "The Defense of India"[24] represents an unattainable example of cruelty and misanthropy, suggested to the author by sick patriotism and exorbitant ambitions.

By their content and tone, the two named works reflect the whole idea of the second period of relations between England and Russia. Through it, England defined its main political goal in Central Asia as *to stop Russia at a sizable distance from Afghanistan (and that meant from India) by all resources and to weaken the scope of Russian actions in Central Asia*...It is true that the first period's idea of taking control over Afghanistan was still alive among Englishmen and the Second Anglo-Afghan War was run under that banner. But this idea was dying because it had been fulfilled in part; besides, it became clear to Englishmen that the center of gravity since the 1860s had moved to the actions and moves of Russia...these must be stopped by any means.

---

23 The memorandum, which at the time was a top secret document, was masterfully stolen by us and immediately translated. See the *Anthology of Materials on Asia*, releases XII and XIV. (Author's note).

24 Appendix XXIII. (Author's note). Not published. (Translator's note).

But we also see Russia's significant achievement in Central Asia. There was a growing understanding in Russia that India's proximity to us is a huge political trump card and thanks to this geographic blessing of fate, we can exercise a huge influence over England by threatening its precious colony. In Russian political circles, there was a fruitful idea that we can answer all the demands and intrigues of England with great success by applying a corresponding pressure in Central Asia.

Skobelev's proposal before the Russo-Turkish War and our [military] demonstrations after the war are a characteristic reflection of that idea. It is interesting to look into it. The essence of Skobelev's proposal boiled down to three points: 1) To open negotiations with Kabul's Emir and support him by sending a corps to Kabul; 2) After taking over Kabul, establish contacts with all the discontented people in India and organize them by creating a unified command and control system; 3) Gather a mass of irregular cavalry and launch it into India – as Timur had done. Even a superficial look will show you that there is a huge distance between this project and those of Napoleon, Chikhachov or Khrulyov. In [Skobelev's] proposal, there are three successive phases, obviously developed based on the best examples of Asian conquests of India. The operational sector was selected sensibly with history lessons taken into account. Even small details seem to have been worked out as vital and purposeful – even though the proposal was developed in haste.

As to the [military] demonstrations after the war of 1877-1878 – they are characterized not by their factual side but mainly by the interesting idea behind them. Because of hostile position taken by Britain before the Congress of Berlin,[25] Alexander II ordered General Grottinghelm to move a detachment from Petro-Alexandrovsk [Turtkul'] to the Amu-Darya River to Chardjui [Turkmenabat] where troops of the Trans-Caspian Region were supposed to join him. General Kauffman was ordered to move from Samarkand through Bukhara to Balkh, Bamian and Kabul. General Abramov was supposed to move from Samarkand through the Alai Mountain Ridge to Chitral and Kashmir. Generally, it was a typical [military] demonstration, with each of the three columns having some 20,000 men.

All three columns stayed in their forming-up areas, except for Abramov's detachment which went fairly far into unknown Pamir. The demonstration did not produce any political pressure on India, but formidable scientific personnel such as Severtsov[26]

25 The Congress of Berlin (13 June – 13 July 1878) was a meeting of the European Great Powers' and the Ottoman Empire's leading statesmen in Berlin in 1878. In the wake of the Russo-Turkish War (1877-1878), the congress' purpose was to reorganize the countries of the Balkans. Otto von Bismark, who led the Congress, attempted to balance the interests of Great Britain, Russia and Austria-Hungary. The congress wanted to keep Constantinople in Ottoman hands. It effectively disavowed Russia's victory over the Ottoman Empire in the Russo-Turkish War. The Congress of Berlin returned Macedonia from Bulgaria to the Ottoman. The congress formally recognized the independence of Montenegro, Serbia and Rumania. (Translator's note).

26 Nikolai Alekseevich Severtsov (1827-1885) was a Russian explorer and naturalist. On an expedition to the Syr Dara River, he was captured by bandits and freed after a month. In 1865-1868, he explored the Tien Shan Mountains and Lake Issyk Kul in present-day Kirghizia. In 1877-1878, he explored the Pamir Mountains as far as Lake Yashil Kul on the Gunt River in present-day Tajikistan. (Translator's note).

accompanied them so the demonstration was a great boon for science. The organizational and technical development of the demonstration, as you can see, was very rough, I would even say – naïve. One general said frankly "We did not know the terrain we had to move on or the population we were to meet". But what do those technical imperfections tell us? Only – or primarily – that the Central Asian question had not been fully developed even after the war of 1877-1878. It was understood in its essence but had not been developed practically, remaining abstract and far removed from an expedient and practical implementation.

Significance of the Russo–Turkish War, 1877-1878

The War of 1877-1878, as well as the Crimea War, were significant steps for helping Russia see things clearly and clarify the Central Asian question. From that moment, we deepened our understanding of the issue and even came to some practical realizations – though very imperfect even now. Generally speaking, we learned our lessons in Asia by wars – i.e. through the moments of severe trials, when political centers and shifts became more distinct and when England in particular opened secret vaults containing its intrigues, worries and fears.

So, the Russo-Turkish War completed our understanding of Britain's "Achilles' heel" and after the war we entered the field using practical deeds to create pressure. On top of the previously-mentioned demonstrations, we started relations with the Emir of Afghanistan, Shir Ali Khan, who had a favorable attitude toward us. And these relations were different from our previous attempts. They were not limited to sending some young boy 'with his own means and at his own risk"[27] or to a "very-secret" letter of Turkestan's Governor-General to such and such". This time the actions were decisive and direct, which are greatly appreciated in the East. Russia dispatched a large embassy to the Emir from Tashkent headed by General Stoletov.[28] True, the choice of the embassy's head was not very appropriate and as usual the consequences of our strong move had not been taken into account, but our tone toward Afghanistan and England was real for the first time. England just had to pick up the gauntlet we had thrown down – and Central Asia had to live through one more war – the so-called Second Anglo-Afghan war of 1878-1882.

27 Characteristically, at the same time, England also went through the same method of military-political reconnaissance and building political influence by dispatching a single person, such as the famous Burns, and Stoddart and Connolly who were executed in Bukhara In 1842. (Author's note).

28 Lieutenant General Nikolai Grigorevich Stoletov (1834-1912) fought in the Crimean War, the Russian conquest of Turkestan and the Russo-Turkish War of 1877-1878. During this conflict, he commanded the Russian and Bulgarian forces at the Second Battle of the Shipka Pass. At the time of this embassy, Stoletov was Commander of the Turkestan Military District. (Translator's note).

Second Anglo–Afghan War of 1878-1882

This war stands at the crossroads between the first and the second periods of Anglo-Russian relations, though by its timing, it is in the second period. The prime goals of the war were obtaining control over Afghanistan to the largest degree possible and stopping the Russian active surge in the area. The following are the most prominent facts of the war. The Anglo-Indian army of 35,000 men invaded Afghanistan with three columns. The Peshawar column, headed by Lt. General Brown (16,000) moved through the Khyber Pass to Fort Dakka [located at the Afghanistan end of the Khyber Pass] and Jalalabad. The Afghans withdrew from the Khyber Pass undefeated. The Kurram column, headed by General Roberts) moved along the Kurram River Valley and on November 18, 1878 attacked the Peiwar-Kotal mountain pass. The assault was unsuccessful. Two days later, Roberts launched a new assault that captured the pass. The southern column (Stewart) was 11,000 strong moved through the [southern] Bolan mountain pass. The column won a skirmish on December 26 near Takht-i Pul and captured Kandahar the next day.

The Afghan army suddenly disappeared. The Emir Shir Ali Khan (our supporter) left Kabul and moved to Mazar-i Sharif. He transferred command and control of the country to his son Yakub Khan.[29] Total chaos spread across Afghanistan and Afghans were in constant quarrels among themselves. But they soon came to their senses and attacked British communications. The British rear area became a total mess. This setback forced the Englishmen to forget their dreams of conquering Afghanistan and they spent all their time protecting their communications lines.

Fortunately for them, Shir Ali Khan died in February 1879 and Yakub became the monarch. The new Emir did not understand Britain's difficult situation and hurried to conclude the Gandamak Peace Treaty with the English on May 15, 1879. According to the treaty: 1) Afghanistan ceded all mountain passes leading to India to the English; 2) all Afghanistan's foreign contacts must be done through the British government; 3) a British Resident must be present in Kabul; and 4) a pension of 60,000 pounds per year would be paid to the Emir. Cavagnari was appointed as the British resident in Kabul.[30] The Gandamak Peace Treaty – though incidental – marked the highest level of British achievements in Afghanistan; later they were forced to accept fewer concessions.[31]

29 The disappearance of the Army and the withdrawal of the Emir to Afghan Turkistan are very characteristic of the Afghan way of conducting war. They have a penchant for and are accustomed to conducting partisan actions. (Author's note).

30 Sir Pierre Louis Napoleon Cavagnari (1841-1879) was a British officer and Political Officer in the Northwest Frontier Province. He negotiated and signed the Treaty of Gandamak with Shir Ali Khan's son and successor Mohammad Yakub Khan and became the Resident in Kabul under the terms of the treaty. He took up residence in Kabul in July 1879 and was killed by mutinous Afghan troops on 3 September 1879. This act restarted the Second Anglo-Afghan War. (Translator's note).

31 One can find the text of the Gandamak Peace Treaty in the First Edition of L.N. Sobolev's *Anglo-Afghan Quarrels*, p.p.37-141. It is interesting that some fanatics in England were not even satisfied with that treaty. See, for example, Rawlinson's 1879 article "The Nineteen Century"; in the article, the author scolds the authors of the treaty for returning Kandahar to Afghanistan according to the treaty. He considered the treaty "incomplete and spotted". (Author's note).

The people were outraged by the treaty and on September 3rd of the same year Major Cavagnari and his convoy were killed.

It became necessary to start a new war and move on Kabul. Roberts hastily gathered an army and moved on Afghanistan's capital. Yakub-Khan came to Roberts in Kush asking for peace and protection. Roberts met him rudely and superciliously snubbed the Emir and sent him to exile in India. Lately he was deposed from the throne.

Fifteen versts from Kabul, Roberts met a 7,000-strong poorly-armed Afghan militia. In a battle near Charasia (on the Kurram road), the British 5,000-man force defeated the militia. On October 12, Roberts captured Kabul where he conducted such a savage reprisal against Afghans that even the English parliament shuddered.[32] Deep patriotism seized the Afghans and soon Roberts ran into a fortified camp at Sherpur near Kabul to save himself. Roberts had 10,000 men and there were reinforcements coming from Peshawar (12,000), by Kurram (9,000) and from Kandahar (9,000). The English success in the battle near Ghazni failed to pacify the population and Englishmen did not know how to end this sordid story. Fortunately, Russia released Abdur Rahman Khan– Dost-Mahomet's grandson.

He appeared in Badakshan where people proclaimed him the Emir. England happily recognized him and on July 24, 1880 he was enthroned as the Emir in Kabul. Roberts helped him to become firmly established by defeating his adversary Ayub-Khan – the ruler of Herat.

After a new Rawalpindi peace treaty was concluded in 1880, England gave a subsidy to Afghanistan and preserved the right of [controlling foreign] political contacts for Afghanistan, but denounced the former Gandamak treaty and recalled its garrisons.

The results of the Second Anglo-Afghan war had been very unpleasant. England did not achieve any significant results in Afghanistan despite significant human loss and millions of rupees spent.

And I repeat – the second war by its goals belongs more to the *first* period. But the characteristic feature of the *second* period was systematic attempts by England to stop our advance in Asia. All means to achieve that goal were fair. I'll name some typical ploys: quibbles about any of our combat success; attempts to catch us cheating in diplomacy and promises; building defensive lines to block future moves; creation of a multitude of demarcation committees with a mandatory British presence (even when there is business only between us and Afghanistan); a systematic smear campaign in the press (and not only in the British press); and intensive reconnaissance and spying.[33] The second period stretched for 30 years and its outward appearance was such: Russia

32 British newspapers were full of astonishing details describing the brutality of Roberts – i.e. British officers and soldiers. Especially alarming was an article in *The Fortnightly Review* of 1879 entitled "Military Law in Kabul" by Harrison, a famous jurist. He wrote: "the British army, more frequently than any other army in the world, put prisoners of war to death by hanging, firing squad or torture". (Author's note).

33 M.A. Terent'yev cites some very interesting examples of the cases of reconnaissance and spying and also the types of agents. See M.A. Terent'yev, *History of the Conquest of Central Asia*, St. Petersburg, 1906, Volume 1, pp.118-120, 382; Volume 3, pp.139-142, 249. (Author's note). Major General Mikhail Africanovich Terent'yev (1837-?) was a famous Russian linguist, Orientalist, publisher and inventor. (Translator's note).

advanced victoriously, expanded and solidified its positions by armed might having many real and expedient reasons for such and external policy. England, seeing in every Russian advance an attempt to take India, became nervous and fought Russia with the diplomacy, money and intrigue. Details of the fight are in any English book dedicated to Anglo-Russian relations in Central Asia.[34] It will be enough to point out the most prominent facts of that period. Our first steps in Central Asia, after crossing the Syr-Darya River (the capture of Chimkent for example) evoked alarm in England and an inquiry of the British government. The Russian government, in the person of Duke Gorchakov, the foreign minister, from the beginning adopted in the replies an evasive and clearly diplomatic tone to justify its actions (and such replies filled the whole period). This was beneath Russia, useless and unnecessary in its essence and, by Asian standards, stupid.

What should we have feared at the time from England? Not much, really. India had only recently taken over the Punjab and so it advanced to the middle of the Indus River; in the north it had not yet reached the Hindu Kush. So, at the time, Russia was invulnerable in Asia from England's efforts. We were completely guaranteed protection from direct English strikes. Who else could they raise against us? No one. Persia was too weak an adversary against us. In Afghanistan, Shir Ali Khan tried in vain to stabilize his reign and create at least a semblance of order. And there were no mercenaries available for military attacks. Of course, England could create some troubles in Europe – something akin to a second Crimea War, but our side would not give cause in Europe and it was not that difficult. As to our Central Asian advance – it did not bother Europe and it was the subject of envy and worry only in Asia. Our Foreign Ministry obviously missed that important and real factor and had chosen a road of self-justification, explanations and juggling of facts. I will name the most notable facts in the struggle of the second period.

In relation to capturing Chimkent and [the city of-Author's note] Turkestan, Gorchakov gave an explanation that it was necessary due to the treacherous and predatory character of nomads living along the Russian border and that Russia has now reached the necessary boundaries coming to contact with larger and more solid states; "the latter define, with sufficient geographical reliability, the limit of necessary movement we had to do and where we shall stop."

Naturally, life proved our diplomatic tricks false and as Rawlinson remarked at the time– the ink was still fresh on the manifest (meaning Gorchakov's statement of November 1864) when Russia moved further into Central Asia. Tashkent was captured and then Khodjent. The Kokand Khanate was encircled and Russian forces moved to Bukhara's borders. Soon, after the capture of Samarkand, Bukhara was deprived of water and capitulated unconditionally. As a result, a new series of English inquiries followed. Among those, one deserves attention—Clarendon's proposal in 1869 to make Afghanistan a neutral zone.[35] This funny idea created plenty of trouble at the time

---

34 These are the most recent and through: Bruce, *The Forward policy and its Results*; Chirole *The Middle Eastern Question*; The Works of Curzon; Holdich *The Indian Borderland*; Lansdell *Russia in Central Asia*. Also an old work of Roberts *Forty One Years in India*; Skrine and Ross, *The Heart of Asia*; A.C. Yate *England and Russia Face to Face*. (Author's note).

35 George William Frederick Villiers Clarendon (1800-1870) was a British statesman. (Translator's note).

and England managed to utilize it as Anglo-Russian relations became more and more complicated. Duke Gorchakov was more than glad to accept Clarendon's proposal and he used the incautious phrase that "His Majesty considers Afghanistan completely outside of the Russian sphere of influence." That historical phrase brought us a lot of trouble and Englishmen were able to use it every which way. Gorchakov was forced to repeat it again in 1875, than it was said by Giers[36] to Mr. Kennedy on October 02, 1883, etc.

As to Clarendon's proposal, the Anglo-Indian government realized that the central government went too far on the issue and that it was impossible for England to give up influence over Afghanistan. The proposal melted away during two years of diplomatic correspondence and England returned to their tactics of inquiries and requests for replies. We had enough cowardice and stupidity to reply with such wording as "Russia has no intentions to move deeper into the South and it considers expansion of its territory as an element leading to increasing weakness."

That lengthy and essentially-empty dialog between the two countries ended up with the signing of the 1873 Agreement whereby Russia agreed to accept the Amu-Darya River from Zorkul Lake to the confluence with the Kokcha River as the northern border of Afghanistan. The Agreement was the most important act of the second period of our relations with England. It represented the first completed attempt of England to establish a definitive line that Russia must not cross.

But even if the Amu-Darya River is a first-rate barrier, it does not extend along our entire border with Afghanistan. Naturally, soon a gap was found through which went the offensive energy of Russia. The gap was the space between the Amu-Darya River and the Zulfikar Pass. The first half of the 1880s was full of squabbles between Russia and England on the matter. England resuscitated its old tricks – inquiries, spying, newspaper hounding and political pamphlets. They made Merv [Mary] the "key" to Herat and to the entire Afghanistan and almost to India....But all that did not stop Russia, and in February 1884, Merv was captured. After continued British insistence, the governments decided in October to create an Anglo-Russian demarcation commission. The commission was to work in Sarakhs – which was also captured by Russia. But instead their "rendezvous" followed the capture of Puli-Khatum – the point to which the Englishmen attached a nervously-exaggerated significance. The discussions about the "legality" of our action began through correspondence between London and Petrograd, Kabul and Calcutta. Our diplomacy had tried to justify itself and Russian forces continued to do their business and in 1885 captured the Zulfikar Pass and Ak-Rabat; after that they made a move toward the Panjdeh Oasis – a really valuable point.

---

36 Nicholas de Giers (*Nikolay Karlovich Girs*) (1820-1895) was a Russian Foreign Minister during the reign of Alexander III. He was one of the architects of the Franco-Russian Alliance, which was later transformed into the Triple Entente. (Translator's note).

England went through a period of serious indecision.[37] They had already issued an order to "mobilize two army corps,"[38] Lumsden,[39] the British co-chair of the demarcation commission was recalled; everything was pointing to war. The English were not satisfied with diplomatic threats. They incited Afghan border troops to action using all means possible, promising them full cooperation. In one case, near Tash-Kepri, Afghanistan's insolent behavior provoked a skirmish on March 30, 1885. The encounter resulted in the complete defeat of the Afghan detachment and a group of British provocateurs shamefully ran away from the battlefield leaving behind their boots which they did not have time to put on. The Kushka episode (as we called it) achieved the desirable effect: the commission gathered again and on November 12, 1885, the first border signpost was erected. In September 1886, the commission finished its task. True, not everything was completed in the commission's work and, following discussions, the commission moved to Petrograd where, in the winter of 1887, it finally established the north-western border between Russia and Afghanistan, which I've mentioned before.[40]

Through those agreements, England was able to stop our advance and our "threat" to India. But soon it came to realize that there was one more approach without a barrier. It was the Pamir approach. The English attempted two methods to stop us: first they incited Abdur Rahman to take over the right-bank of the Wakhan River and, Shughan and Rushan which allegedly were earlier a part of Badakhshan. Small detachments of Afghan troops crossed the Pandj River and advanced east up to the limits of Kirgiz Pamir but the brutal destruction of the Afghan detachment near Somatash on the Alichur River on 22 June 1892 and one more defeat near the Badakhshan border fixed the problem and, along with it, proper civility returned to the Englishmen. The second method was a "scientific" attempt to play on the "true source of the Amu-Darya" and keep us much to the north of the line which was established by the agreement of 1873. This scientific casuistry accomplished little and the two good combat lessons pushed the Englishmen to resort to a demarcation commission that established the present border in 1896.

The Pamir demarcation concludes the second period. During that period, England tried by all means to stop our advance and limit it. Russia tried to justify its actions and defended itself with diplomacy while moving forward unstoppably while applying military force.

37 England was having serious problems elsewhere at this time. The Khartoum Relief Expedition arrived too late to save General Charles George Gordon—"Chinese Gordon". The Liberal Government barely survived a vote of censure in the House of Commons and its majority fell to 12. Germany was increasingly hostile toward England and Prince Bismark concluded a secret treaty of neutrality with Russia in 1884 behind the backs of England and France, Russia's putative allies in the Triple Entente. (Translator's note).

38 Abdur-Rahman was told about this at a durbar [formal reception] in Rawalpindi. The wise ruler was hardly impressed by the fancy word "corps". (Author's note).

39 General Sir Peter Lumsden. (Translator's note).

40 Appendix XXV [not published – Translator]. More detailed information about the events and negotiations between Russia and England could be found in materials published by the Foreign Ministry *Afghan Demarcation* (Delemination Afghane). St. Petersburg, 1886, 379. (Author's note).

Third period of Russian-English relations in Central Asia

I consider the last twenty years as the third period of Russian-English relations in Central Asia. The dominant theme during this period was the idea that the clash between Russia and England was unavoidable and, at same time, it was necessary to foresee the consequences of that collision. The old idea of gaining control over Afghanistan was thrown away as it became clear that Afghanistan itself is poor, weak and feeble and influence over it results in nothing serious. The second theme that dominated the second period was to stop Russia by diplomatic means and treaties. England could not do this. England had to think about how to win the Central Asian War it now considered unavoidable – not merely about preventing Russia from approaching India. And what caused England to lose confidence in the power of treaties and peaceful methods to stop Russia? There were many reasons. I will mention just some of them.

1) The gradual and unstoppable realization of commercial ties between Russia and Afghanistan. These ties had enormous potential consequences that England might not be able to overcome.
2) The personal policy of the late Emir Habibullah Khan, who despite his laziness and negligence in internal affairs conducted a fairly strong and independent foreign policy. The shameful Dan mission, in March 1905, did not acquire any new concessions and only added more power to the throne. The mission brilliantly showed England's impotence and the Emir's independence.[41]
3) The undoubted increase of the military might of Afghanistan and its improved logistics. England proved powerless in stopping the accumulation of military supplies despite Lord Curzon's actions to stop the flow of military material.
4) The growing understanding within Russian society of the necessity of having direct relations with Afghanistan – and even more – the shame of not having such relations. In the first years of the 20th Century, the Russian press (St. Peterbugskie Vedomosti, Novoe Vremya, etc.) raised the issue of establishing our permanent diplomatic representation in Kabul. The Governor-General of Turkestan returned several deserters to Afghanistan along with a special note. He also sent a Muslim delegation to Kabul to congratulate Habibullah. Before that, General Kuropatkin, when he was War Minister and visiting Turkestan in 1901, released six Afghan spies from Merv's jail and sent them to Afghanistan with good wishes to the new Emir... In a word, the long-standing dam that blocked Afghanistan's door to Russia was finally ready to burst.

These and other reasons forced England to examine the Central Asian issue with a fresh, sober look. That new understanding, which permeated the last period, boils down to the point that the war with Russia is imminent and the only question is *how to prepare for it and how to conduct it*? Afghanistan, in that struggle, is considered only an accidental bridgehead. There could be combat in that country or Russian forces might

41 Lewis Dan headed a British embassy to Kabul in 1904-1905. The goal was to get new concessions from Afghanistan but Habibullah Khan agreed only to confirm the previous agreements. A. Hamilton, "Mission to Kabul", *Fortnight Review*, 1905, p.390. (Translator's note).

cross it unimpeded. The practical question for the new political credo of England was *how to defend India?*

Any defense can be active or passive. Accordingly, there is an ongoing struggle in England during the past 30 years between the proponents of these methods.

On the side of passive defense, we can count such experts on Afghanistan as Lord Roberts, Lord Lawrence, Lord Napier of Magdala, [1st Viscount Sandhurst] Mansfield and Lord Chelmsford. They argue that Afghanistan is a wild and hostile country and one could not rely on it. Occupation of Afghanistan would lengthen communications lines and the supplies and reserves would be further away.[42]

Also, by their reasoning, the north-western border, i.e. the terrain between the Indus River and the Kabul-Ghazni-Kandahar line is good for a strong defense and the terrain near Kabul is unsuited for that purpose. If the line of defense is moved forward, the Anglo-Indian army will have its positions in front of difficult defiles which, in the case of setback, could contribute to defeat, while with success, would interfere with logistics.

The Russian army will have to go a long way to the Indus River and that would require huge number of troops for the lines of communications, making logistics difficult and the [Russian] rear vulnerable to Afghan attacks. Consequently, the army that reaches the Indus River would be weak and poorly equipped.

The party [of passive defense] insists on the development of communications along the north-western border to improve conditions for the quick concentration of forces where required in the vulnerable sector. Besides building the strongest fortified regions near Quetta and Peshawar, the group recommends maintaining an accessible sector of the Indus River between Kalabagh and Dera Ismail Khan while blocking exits from the valleys of the rivers Kurama, Touchi and Gomula using fortified areas.

As to the defense of the northern border, the group recommends meeting the Russians as they debouch from the mountains and for that purpose they recommend not occupying forward positions in Chitral and Gilgit or building roads to them but to let the terrain stop the attackers. The main defense should be located in the Lahore – Rawalpindi area.

Critics of the passive defense (inside of the India's borders) favor an active defense and argue that defending positions behind the Suleiman Mountain Range on the line Peshawar – Bannu – Dera Ghazi Khan –Jacobabad would permit Russia to occupy all Afghanistan, firmly establish itself there and extend the railroad from Kushka to Herat and Kandahar and also to Kabul – thus removing all problem of concentrating troops and supplying them with food. The [English] defense line would be too extended and Russian would be able to break through it considering that all the mountain gaps and passes will be in their hands and provide cover to their actions.

Thus the uncertainty and separation of forces would be on the defensive side and the initiative, force concentration and ability to demonstrate action – would be on the Russian side.

42 The proponents of the passive defense are mostly people who were in Afghanistan during the Second Anglo-Afghan War and are embittered by failures there. Because of that, they cannot sincerely believe in an alliance with the Afghans – they are not sick with optimism – that is why they insist on the passive defense – i.e. on the territory of India. (Author's note).

The critics of the passive defense of India behind the Suleiman Mountain range also criticize a defense moved forward to the Haji-Amran Mountain Range (a variant of the passive defense) and consider that plan unsuitable due to: 1) the defense of fortifications near Peshawar, Bannu, Dera Ismail Khan, Sukker and Quetta would lead to the passive-cordon system. Troops would be spread out, tied to particular points and idoomed to weakness and inactivity that will undermine the defense; 2) If Russian forces would occupy most of Afghanistan, the situation of the troops defending the Pishin position becomes precarious – Russia could break through the British lines of communications and enter their rear defense area.

In general, according to them, the plan gives relinquishes Afghanistan into Russian hands, pushes it over to the more powerful side and also allows Russia to raise the warlike tribes of north-western India against England.

The late Lord Kitchener[43] was a strong proponent of the active defense using the plan developed by McGregor[44], Bell[45] and others. They insist on building a strong British rule over Afghanistan or, at least of spreading British "civilizing" influence among the Afghan population, and push for the immediate construction of a dense network of highways and railways.

At the same time they propose moving the defensive line forward to Herat and operating against the Russian rear defense area from Khorosan [in eastern Persia]. The defense of Kabul and Kandahar should be conducted ahead of those points. In the words of Bell – Afghanistan's relation to India is to play the role of the forward fortified position or glacis – using the favorite word of the British political tomes. Obviously, these plans triumphed over the others because Dan's mission to Kabul was guided by its principles. Among other proposals, they planned to build a serious defensive line on the Helmand River. At any rate, we can assume that in a case of war with us, Britain would try to capture the line Kabul – Kandahar (450 versts) before we do, significantly shortening the existing communications line Peshawar – Kandahar or Sukkur—Kandahar (725 versts).[46] Would the Englishmen stop at that middle solution or would they move to the line of Herat? This would depend on many combinations, but mainly – on the energy and success of our forces, and also on the Anglo-Indian Commander-in-Chief's personality – who would need to believe if not in his Anglo-Indian troops, then in himself as a prominent military leader.

Despite these new currents in Central Asian issues, the old major question about the possibility (or probability) of a Russian expedition into India remains. Without its absolute clarification, these two trends of British thought cannot be understood completely.

---

43 Lord Horatio Herbert Kitchener (24 June 1850-5 June 1916) was a British Field Marshal, diplomat, and statesman. (Translator's note).

44 The exposition of McGregor's ideas can be found in "The Anthology of Materials on Asia". Release XIII and XIV. (Author's note).

45 The translation of this article can be found in Volume XIV "The Anthology of Materials on Asia". Two suppositions form the basis of the major idea of the article: 1) The defense of India is based on the defense of Afghanistan; 2) The Hindu Kush Mountain Ridge with all its western spurs, northern and western slopes must be the *border*. (Author's note).

46 With due respect to Snesarev, it is probably more about shortening the frontline, not the lines of communication. (Translator's note).

But I absolutely cannot touch that major issue because of lack of time. The issue belongs to the category of deep and complex topics and to merely skim its surface would be a crime.

The last political act establishing mutual Anglo-Russian relations toward Afghanistan is the Convention of August 18 (31), 1907.[47]

CONVENTION CONCERNING AFGHANISTAN.

The High Contracting parties, in order to ensure perfect security on their respective frontiers in Central Asia and to maintain in these regions a solid and lasting peace, have concluded the following Convention: -

ARTICLE I.

His Britannic Majesty's Government declare that they have no intention of changing the political status of Afghanistan.

His Britannic Majesty's Government further engage to exercise their influence in Afghanistan only in a pacific sense, and they will not themselves take, nor encourage Afghanistan to take, any measures threatening Russia.

The Russian Government, on their part, declare that they recognize Afghanistan as outside of the sphere of Russian influence, and they engage that all their political relations with Afghanistan shall be conducted through the intermediary of His Britannic Majesty's Government; they further engage not to send any Agent into Afghanistan.

ARTICLE II

*The Government of His Britannic Majesty having declared in the treaty signed at Kabul on the 21*st *March, 1905, that they recognize the Agreement and the engagements concluded with the late Ameer Abdur Rahman, and that they have no intentions of interfering in the internal government of Afghan territory, Great Britain engages neither to annex nor occupy in contravention of that Treaty any portion of Afghanistan or to interfere in the internal administration of the country, provided that the Ameer fulfils the engagements already contracted by him toward His Britannic Majesty's Government under the above-mentioned Treaty.*

ARTICLE III

The Russian and Afghan authorities, specially designated for the purpose on the frontier or in the frontier provinces, may establish direct relations with each other for the settlement of local questions of a non-political character.

ARTICLE IV

His Britannic Majesty's Government and the Russian Government affirm their

47 The entire convention covers British-Russian relations with Persia, Afghanistan and Tibet. The full text of the convention is at Appendix 1 since it shows how the entire region was part of the "great game". (Translator's note).

adherence to the principle of equality of commercial opportunity in Afghanistan, and they agree that any facilities which may been, or shall be hereafter obtained for British and British-Indian trade and traders, shall be equally enjoyed by Russian trade and traders. Should the progress of trade establish the necessity for Commercial Agents, the two Governments will agree as to what measures shall be taken, due regard, of course, being had to the Ameer's sovereign rights.

ARTICLE V

The present Arrangements will only come into force when His Britannic Majesty's Government shall have notified to the Russian Government the consent of the Ameer to the terms stipulated above.

According to the Convention, Russia completely recognized Afghanistan as outside of its sphere of influence and pledged to use the British government as an intermediary for all its political contacts with Afghanistan. Russia also pledged not to send agents to Afghanistan.

In my public lecture in Petrograd, I discussed the convention in detail and you can find it in my brochure *Anglo-Russian Agreement of 1907*. By its essence I place the convention in the second period of our Central Asian relations with Britain. I do not attach any weight to the convention and I can admit its rationality (for England) only from the point of view of some obscure European developments – understandable only now – after the World War. At a first glance, there is a new item, the admission of immediate cross-border contacts on non-political matters. But there is practically nothing else new. These contacts have always been and they are so unavoidable, that it is impossible to eliminate them by any means. How one could to isolate parts of the near-border population, say across the Panj River, where brothers live on different banks; where a Bukhara Tajik marries a woman from the "Afghan side" and where an ishan rules in a spiritual sense over a number of kishlaks without regard to whether they are located on the "right" or "left" side of the Panj. Then, as a quirk, there is a point of putting all articles of the agreement in relation to the Afghan Emir's consent. And, so far, I've not heard that he notified the world about his consent.

As a conclusion of my political essay on Afghanistan, I have to tell about our latest contacts with it. I would emphasize two sides of the issue. First, Soviet Russia established direct relations unimpeded and apparently easily with Afghanistan that before could not be done; the old government saw such an act as a *casus belli*. It proved to be a political mirage. Today Russia has its representative in Kabul; it has sent an embassy to Afghanistan and received an Afghan mission in Moscow. Russia established systematic communications with Afghanistan. True, England conducted war against Afghanistan, but after its quick victory it has not achieved anything with it. Now, it is forced to turn a blind eye to the Russian contacts with Afghanistan… Specialists long ago predicted such an outcome and they said many times that if one uses strong and decisive language, England – essentially a weak entity in Central Asia – always will have to give up.

The second – and more important – moment is the absolutely correct look of the Soviet Russia at the Central Asian problem. It sees it as the only or – at least – main loudspeaker through which it is possible to talk to Britain and count on its sincere attention. In India it sees not just the theoretical "Achilles Heel" of the British might, but the really vulnerable spot of British imperialism. I do not know objectives and details, but undoubtedly Soviet Russia is definitely working in the spirit of that understanding. I, who have been pushing through those ideas for a long time, could not agree more. As a specialist, I may disagree on some technical methods and calculations – and, for example, I would not approve the planned dispatch of a cavalry detachment through the Pamir approach. But these are details and even trifles. The main idea is still correct and it will yield desirable political fruits. Many times in my life, I've said that India is the most precious but also the most vulnerable treasure of England. If you want to overthrow a world ruler or – as is sometimes said – world aristocrat – strike him at India. If you want to undermine world capitalism and the tyranny of Britain – strike it at India.

But you may ask a question – how would India react to the beating? How will it affect it? The question naturally stems from all I have told you about Afghanistan and this would be my reply. In one of the Japanese temples, the visitors are shown a statuette of three monkeys: one with closed eyes and ears, another – with open ears but closed eyes and the third – with open eyes and ears but with a hand over its mouth. By Japanese interpretation, the first monkey represents India – which does not see or hear anything; the second monkey represents China – which hears but is not seeing yet. And the third monkey – it is Japan which sees and hears everything but is silent until the right time.

And like a poor monkey which does not see or hear anything – i.e. does not understand anything – so India appears to the Orient and its rulers – the British. But in time, I will paint the image of an India which is far different from that sad and distorted picture. But that is going to be later. Now I am finishing my brief essay on Afghanistan – brief due to lack of time and material. But if you have got the picture of that country – poor and discordant – yet the main gate to India, I may hope that my major idea has been expressed successfully.

Appendix

Convention signed on August 31, 1907 between Great Britain and Russia, containing arrangements on the subject of Persia, Afghanistan, and Tibet

No. 1.
Sir Edward Grey to Sir A. Nicolson

Foreign Office, *August 29, 1907*

Sir,
I have to-day authorized your Excellency by telegraph to sign a Convention with the Russian Government containing Arrangements on the subject of Persia, Afghanistan, and Tibet.

The Arrangement respecting Persia is limited to the regions of that country touching the respective frontiers of Great Britain and Russia in Asia, and the Persian Gulf is not of those regions, and is only partly in Persian territory. It has not been considered appropriate to introduce into the Convention a positive declaration respecting special interests possessed by Great Britain in the Gulf, the result of British actions in those waters for more than a hundred years.

His Majesty's Government have reasons to believe that this question will not give rise to difficulties between two Governments should developments arise which make further discussions affecting British interests in the Gulf necessary. For the Russian Government have in the course of the negotiations leading up to conclusion of this Arrangement explicitly stated that they do not deny the special interests of Great Britain in the Persian Gulf – a statement of which His Majesty's Government have formally taken note.

In order to make it quite clear that the present Arrangement is not intended to affect the position in the Gulf, and does not imply any changes of policy respecting it on the part of Great Britain, His Majesty's Government think it desirable to draw attention to previous declarations of British policy, and reaffirm generally previous statements as to British interests in the Persian Gulf and the importance of maintaining them.

His Majesty's Government will continue to direct all their efforts to the preservation of the status quo in the Gulf and the maintenance of British trade; in doing so, they have no desire to exclude the legitimate trade of any other Power.

I am,&c.
(Signed) E. Grey.

No. 2.
Sir A. Nicolson to Sir Edward Grey

St. Petersburgh, *August 31, 1907*

Sir,
I have the honour to transmit herewith the Convention which was signed to-day by M. Iswolsky and myself for the settlement of certain questions affecting the interests of Great Britain and Russia in Asia.

I also beg leave to forward a note which I received from M. Iswolsky in response to a communication from me, of which a copy is herewith inclosed, on the subject of the entry of scientific missions into Tibet.

I have, &c.
(Signed) A. Nocolson.

Convention

His Majesty the King of the Great Briton and Ireland and of the British Dominions beyond the Seas, Emperor of India, and His Majesty the Emperor of the Russias, animated by the sincere desire to settle by mutual agreement different questions concerning the interests of their States on the Continents of Asia, have determined to conclude Agreements destined to prevent all cause of misunderstanding between Great Britain and Russia in regard to the questions referred to, and have nominated for this purpose their respective Plenipotentiaries, to wit:

His Majesty the King of the United Kingdom of Great Britain and Ireland and of the British Dominions beyond the Seas, Emperor of India, the Right Honorable Sir Arthur Nicolson, His Majesty's Ambassador Extraordinary and Plenipotentiary to His Majesty the Emperor of All the Russias;

His Majesty the Emperor of the Russias, the Master of his Court Alexander Iswolsky, Minister for Foreign Affairs;

Who, having communicated to each other their full powers, found in good and due form, have agreed on the following: -

ARRANGEMENTS CONCERNING PERSIA

The Governments of Great Britain and Russia having mutually engaged to respect the integrity and independence of Persia, and sincerely desiring the preservation of order throughout that country and its peaceful development, as well as the permanent establishment of equal advantages for the trade and industry of all the nations;

Considering that each of them has, for geographical and economic, a special interest in maintenance of peace and order in certain provinces of Persia adjoining, or in the neighbourhood of, the Russian frontier on the one hand, and the frontiers of Afghanistan and Baluchistan on other hand; and being desirous of avoiding all cause of conflict between their respective interests in the above-mentioned Provinces of Persia;

Have agreed on the following terms: -

I

Great Britain engages not to seek for herself, and not to support in favour of British subjects, or in favour of the subjects of third Powers, any Concessions of a political or commercial nature – such as Concessions for railways, banks, telegraphs, roads, transport, insurance, &c. – beyond a line starting from Kasr-i-Shirin, passing through Isfahan, Yezd, Kakhk, and ending at a point on the Persian frontier at the intersection of the Russian and Afghan frontier, and not to oppose, directly or indirectly, demands for similar Concessions to this region which are supported by the Russian Government. It is understood that the above-mentioned places are included in the region in which Great Britain engages not to seek the Concessions referred to.

II

Russia, on her part, engages not to seek for herself and not to support, in favour of Russian subjects, or in favour of the subjects of third Powers, any Concessions of a political or commercial nature – such as Concessions for railways, banks, telegraphs, roads, transport, insurance, &c. – beyond a line going from the Afghan frontier by way of Gazik, Birjand, Kerman, and ending at Bunder Abbas, and not to oppose, directly or indirectly, demands for similar Concessions in this region which are supported by the British Government. It is understood that the above-mentioned places are included in the region in which Russia engages not to seek the Concessions referred to.

III

Russia, on her part, engages not to oppose, without previous arrangements with Great Britain, the grant of any Concessions whatever to British subjects in the regions of Persia situated between the lines mentioned in Articles I and II.

Great Britain undertakes a similar engagement as regards the grant of Concessions to Russian subjects in the same region of Persia.

All Concessions exiting at present in the regions indicated in Articles I and II are maintained.

IV

It is understood that the revenue of all Persian customs, with the exception of those of Farsistan and the Persian Gulf, revenue guaranteeing the amortization and the interest of the loans concluded by the Government of the Shah with the "Banque d'Escompte et des Prets de Perse" up to the date of the signature of the present Arrangement, shall be devoted to the same purpose as in the past.

It is equally understood that the revenue of the Persian customs of Farsistan and of the Persian Gulf, as well as those of the fisheries on the Persian shore of the Caspian Sea and those of the Post and Telegraphs, shall be devoted, as in the past, to the service of the loans concluded by the Government of the Shah with the Imperial Bank of Persia up to the date of the signature of the present Arrangement.

V

In the event of irregularities occurring in the amortization of the payment of the interest of the Persian loans concluded with the "Bank d'Escompte et des Prets de Perse" and with the Imperial Bank of Persia up to date of the signature of the present Arrangement, and in the event of the necessity arising for Russia to establish control over the sources of revenue guaranteeing the regular service of the loans concluded with the first-named bank, and situated in the region mentioned in Article II of the present Arrangement, or for Great Britain to establish control over the sources of revenue guaranteeing the regular service of the loans concluded with the second-named bank, and situated in the region mentioned in Article I of the present Arrangement, the British and Russian Governments undertake to enter beforehand into a friendly exchange of ideas with a view to determine, in agreement with each other, the measures of control in question and to avoid all interference which would not be in conformity with the principles governing the present Arrangement.

CONVENTION CONCERNING AFGHANISTAN

The High Contracting parties, in order to ensure perfect security on their respective frontiers in Central Asia and to maintain in these regions a solid and lasting peace, have concluded the following Convention: -

ARTICLE I

His Britannic Majesty's Government declare that they have no intention of changing the political status of Afghanistan.

His Britannic Majesty's Government further engage to exercise their influence in Afghanistan only in a pacific sense, and they will not themselves take, nor encourage Afghanistan to take, any measures threatening Russia.

The Russian Government, on their part, declare that they recognize Afghanistan as outside of the sphere of Russian influence, and they engage that all their political relations with Afghanistan shall be conducted through the intermediary of His Britannic Majesty's Government; they further engage not to send any Agent into Afghanistan.

ARTICLE II

The Government of His Britannic Majesty having declared in the treaty signed at Kabul on the 21st March, 1905, that they recognize the Agreement and the engagements concluded with the late Ameer Abdur Rahman, and that they have no intentions of interfering in the internal government of Afghan territory, Great Britain engages neither to annex nor occupy in contravention of that Treaty any portion of Afghanistan or to interfere in the internal administration of the country, provided that the Ameer fulfils the engagements already contracted by him toward His Britannic Majesty's Government under the above-mentioned Treaty.

ARTICLE III

The Russian and Afghan authorities, specially designated for the purpose on the frontier or in the frontier provinces, may establish direct relations with each other for the settlement of local questions of a non-political character.

ARTICLE IV

His Britannic Majesty's Government and the Russian Government affirm their adherence to the principle of equality of commercial opportunity in Afghanistan, and they agree that any facilities which may been, or shall be hereafter obtained for British and British-Indian trade and traders, shall be equally enjoyed by Russian trade and traders. Should the progress of trade establish the necessity for Commercial Agents, the two Governments will agree as to what measures shall be taken, due regard, of course, being had to the Ameer's sovereign rights.

ARTICLE V

The present Arrangements will only come into force when His Britannic Majesty's Government shall have notified to the Russian Government the consent of the Ameer to the terms stipulated above.

ARRANGEMENT CONCERNING TIBET

The Governments of Great Britain and Russia recognizing the suzerain rights of China in Tibet, and considering the fact that Great Britain, by reason of her geographical position, has a special interest in the maintenance of the status quo in the external relations of Tibet, have made the following Arrangement: -

ARTICLE I

The two High Contracting Parties engage to respect the territorial integrity of Tibet and to abstain from all interference in its internal administration.

ARTICLE II

In conformity with the admitted principle of the suzerainty of China over Tibet, Great Britain and Russia engage not to enter into negotiations with Tibet except through the intermediary of the Chinese Government. This engagement does not exclude the direct relations between British Commercial Agents and the Tibetan authorities provided for in Article V of the Convention between Great Britain and Tibet of the 7th September, 1904, and confirmed by the Convention between Great Britain and China in Article of the 27th April, 1906; nor does it modify the engagements entered into by Great Britain and China in Article I of the said Convention of 1906.

It is clearly understood that Buddhists, subjects of Great Britain or of Russia, may enter into direct relations on strictly religious matters with the Dalai Lama and other representatives of Buddhism in Tibet; the Governments of Great Britain and Russia engage, as far as they are concerned, not to allow those relations to infringe the stipulations of the present Arrangement.

ARTICLE III

The British and Russian Governments respectively engage not to send representatives to Lhassa.

ARTICLE IV

The two High Contracting Parties engage neither to seek nor to obtain, whether for themselves or their subjects, any Concessions for railways, roads, telegraphs, and mines, or other right in Tibet.

ARTICLE V

The two Governments agree that no part of the revenue of Tibet, whether in kind or in cash, shall be pledged or assigned to Great Britain or Russia or to any of their subjects.

ANNEX TO THE ARRANGEMENT BETWEEN GREAT BRITAIN AND RUSSIA CONCERNING TIBET.

Great Britain reaffirms the Declaration, signed by his Excellency the Viceroy and Governor-general of India and appended to the ratification of the Convention of the 7th September, 1904, to the effect that occupation of the Chumbi Valley by British forces shall cease after payment of three annual installments of the indemnity of 25,000,000 rupees, provided that the trade marts mentioned in Article II of that Convention have been effectively opened for three years, and that in meantime the Tibetan authorities have faithfully complied in all respects with the terms of the said Convention of 1904. It is clearly understood that if the occupation of the Chumbi Valley by British forces, for any reason, not been terminated at the time anticipated in the above Declaration, the British and Russian Governments will enter upon a friendly exchange of views on this subject.

The present Convention shall be ratified, and the ratifications exchanged at St. Petersburgh as soon as possible.

In witness whereof the respective Plenipotentiaries have signed the present Convention and affixed thereto their seals.

Done in duplicate at St. Petersburgh, the 18th (31st) August, 1907.

(L.S.) A. Nicolson
(L.S.) Iswolsky.

Inclosure 2 in No. 2

Sir A. Nicolson to M. Iswolsky

St. Petersburgh, *August 18 (31), 1907*

M. le Ministre,

With reference to the Arrangement regarding Tibet, signed today, I have the honour to make the following Declaration to your Excellency: -

"His Britannic Majesty's Government think it desirable, as far as they are concerned, not to allow, unless by a previous agreement with the Russian Government, for a period of three years from the date of the present communication, the entry into Tibet of any scientific mission whatever, on condition that a like assurance is given on the part of the Imperial Russian Government.

"His Britannic Majesty's Government propose moreover, to approach the Chinese Government with a view to Induce them to accept a similar obligation for a corresponding period; the Russian Government will, as a matter of course, take similar action.

"At the expiration of the term of three years above mentioned His Britannic Majesty's government will, if necessary, consult with the Russian Government as to the desirability of any ulterior measures with regard to scientific expeditions to Tibet."

I avail, &c.
(Signed) A. Nicolson.

Inclosure 3 in No.2
M. Iswolsky to Sir A. Nocolson

St. Petersburgh, *August 18 (31), 1907*

M. l'Ambassadeur,
In reply to your Excellency's note of even date, I have the honour to declare that the Imperial Russian Government think it desirable, so far as they are concerned, not to allow, unless by a previous agreement with the British Government, for a period of three years from the date of the present communication, the entry into Tibet of any scientific mission whatever.

Like the British Government, the Imperial Government propose to approach the Chinese Government with a view to induce them to accept a similar obligation for a corresponding period.

It is understood that at the expiration of the term of three years the two Governments will, if necessary, consult with the each other as to the desirability of any ulterior measures with regard to scientific expeditions to Tibet.

I have, &c.
(Signed) Iswolsky.

INDEX